The Big Muddy

Adventures up the Missouri

By the same author

In Clive's Footsteps

The Big Muddy

Adventures up the Missouri

Peter Holt

HUTCHINSON
London Sydney Auckland Johannesburg

This edition first published in 1991 by
Hutchinson

Random Century Group Ltd
20 Vauxhall Bridge Road, London SW1V 2SA

Random Century Australia (Pty) Ltd
20 Alfred Street, Milsons Point, Sydney, NSW 2061, Australia

Random Century New Zealand Ltd
PO Box 40–086, Glenfield, Auckland 10, New Zealand

Random Century South Africa (Pty) Ltd
PO Box 337, Bergvlei, 2012, South Africa

British Library Cataloguing-in-Publication Data
Holt, Peter
  The big muddy: Adventures up the Missouri.
  I. Title
  917.8

  ISBN 0 09 174528 4

Set in Sabon 11/13pt by Input Typesetting Ltd, London
Printed and bound in Great Britain by Mackays of Chatham PLC

For my grandparents, John and Dolleen Sanger

'Of all the most variable things in creation, the most uncertain are the action of a jury, the state of a woman's mind, and the condition of the Missouri River.'

The Sioux City Register, 1868.

'The Indian women did all the cooking and cleaning while the men hunted and fished. Then these Europeans arrived and said they would make our lives better. Who were they kidding?'

Pat Falcon, Williston, 1990.

ACKNOWLEDGEMENTS

My thanks to everyone mentioned in this book for their time and cooperation. The following people also gave invaluable assistance at various stages of my journey: Mark and Pammie Borcher, Roger Blaske, and Jeff Covinsky for organizing my ride on the Dan C. Burnett; Catherine Harriet Cludde, my mother Elizabeth Holt, Patrick Humphries, Steve Karten, Dale Lewis of the South Dakota Hall of Fame, Jade McGuiggan, Janet Ogle, Greg Parker, Jan Pettigrew, Eddie and Jack Winthrop, and The Cody Road Band, the best hoedown merchants north of Kansas.

CONTENTS

PRELUDE

The Cherokee was going to scalp me. Barely three hours after arriving in America, I was about to be beaten up in a Chicago bar.

I was enjoying a quiet beer, having checked in at the Blackstone Hotel, an art deco palace in downtown Chicago. The Blackstone was on the faded side with gilt mirrors and a forest of dark wood panelling in the lobby. It was January and from my room I had a panoramic snow-swept view of the city's legendary skyline. The thermometer had dropped to minus five degrees outside and the aloof skyscrapers stood like stony-faced ice maidens guarding the frozen shores of Lake Michigan. Now I was in the bar trying to unwind after the flight from London.

Two men were seated on stools next to me. We drifted into conversation. They were among 100 representatives from Indian reservations around the United States who were attending a conference in the hotel on reservation housing.

'So you're from England,' the first Indian said. 'Never met anyone from England before.' His name was Jerry and he was from an Ojibwa reservation in Wisconsin. He was very fat, perhaps twenty stone, with a sallow face and the jovial, laugh-a-minute manner of a gameshow host.

His friend, the Cherokee, was a picture of gloom. He was slumped precariously over the bar with one hand firmly gripping a bottle of beer. He was in his fifties and looked more like a bank manager with thick, horn-rimmed spectacles and a dark suit that might have been immaculately pressed a few hours earlier but was now distinctly shagged out. The knot of his tie was well off-centre and he was

I

grunting a lot, apparently enjoying a conversation with a line of empty beer bottles on the bar in front of him.

Jerry asked me what I was doing in the States. I explained I was researching a book about the Missouri River. 'I'm spending a night here in Chicago before flying to St Louis tomorrow to start work.'

'D'you hear that?' Jerry said cheerfully. He nudged the other Indian. 'This English guy's going up the Big Muddy.'

The Cherokee looked up slowly from his beer. He rolled his eyes and let rip with an inebriated roar.

'Why?' he snarled. 'What gives you the right? Tell me, what gives you the right? That's our land up there. Indian land. What gives you the right to write about it?'

Jerry found it all hugely amusing. He put an arm around my shoulder and said I shouldn't take any notice. Then he began to poke fun at his friend. 'Go on. Show the Englishman your feathers.'

'Feathers?' I inquired.

'His feathers. You know, his war bonnet, or his head-dress as they call it in Hollywood. He's behaving like a Cherokee chief, so he must have his feathers.' Jerry nudged the Cherokee playfully in the ribs. The Cherokee did not find this at all funny and muttered something warlike. Jerry took a swig from a bottle of beer. 'Damned Cherokees. Never trust 'em.' Then he slapped his friend on the back and collapsed into more laughter. He choked on his beer and sprayed it over the bar.

Jerry turned back to me. 'So what are you going to do up the Missouri?' I said I didn't know. I sounded rather vague.

'You should shoot an elk. When you get to North Dakota you should shoot an elk.'

I said I didn't think I wanted to shoot an elk very much. 'When is the elk hunting season?' I asked. Jerry winked conspiratorially. 'Whenever you're hungry,' he said with a big smile.

Our conversation was interrupted. 'What gives you the right?' Having been mercifully silent for a few minutes the Cherokee was up and running again. His voice was slurred and he was turning into the bar-room bore. 'We don't want you white people writing about our river.'

I replied that since I came from England I had no preconceived ideas about the Missouri nor the Indians that lived alongside it.

I pointed out that there weren't an awful lot of Red Indians in England.

'You're prejudiced, boy. All white men are.' The Cherokee slammed his bottle on the bar and yelled again, 'What gives you the right?'

The flight from London was taking its toll. I was tired and short-tempered. I have never had much time for drunks in bars and this was turning into a stupid, unnecessary argument.

'Oh for God's sake,' I said, 'what gives anyone the right to write about anything? If everyone had the same attitude as you no books would ever get written.'

This was the wrong thing to say. My aggressive tone of voice didn't help either. The Cherokee glared at me ferociously. Jerry looked nervous. He sighed and looked at me as if to say, 'You've really gone and done it now.'

'I don't like you,' the Cherokee said. He kicked over his bar stool, pulled himself up to his full height and jabbed a finger in front of my face. 'I don't like you and I'm going to tear your head off.'

'Hang on a moment,' I said, thinking that 'tear your head off' was a twentieth-century euphemism for scalping.

'Whoa there!' Jerry said. He pulled his friend away and sat him back on the stool. The Cherokee stared drunkenly at the floor, all thoughts of a fight suddenly gone. I brushed some spilt beer from my shirt. Jerry laughed again. 'Damned Cherokees. Always causing trouble.'

Jerry bought me another drink and asked about my journey. I explained that I planned to follow the 2,500 miles of the Missouri from the confluence with the Mississippi near St Louis to the head-waters at Three Forks, Montana.

'So you know all about Lewis and Clark then,' Jerry said. I replied that I did. I was armed with a copy of their journals and I intended to follow their exploits closely. And while the Cherokee proceeded to fall asleep at the bar, Jerry and I began talking about one of the most exciting adventures of modern man . . .

The story of the Lewis and Clark Expedition of 1804–6 is an American epic of courage and endurance. Meriwether Lewis and William Clark were young men with little experience of exploration, who sacrificed more than two years of their lives for a journey that was to cover a distance equal to one third the circumference of the earth. They were wholesome and hard-working. They were prepared to put up with incredible hardship in the name of their country and they brimmed with the moral fortitude that is the stuff of New World legends. Indeed, it can be said that they were the original All-American Boys.

The expedition was the result of a lifelong ambition of that most eclectic of US presidents, Thomas Jefferson, linguist, philosopher, lawyer, gentleman farmer and author of the Declaration of Independence. A keen amateur scientist with a relentlessly inquiring mind, Jefferson had always dreamed of opening up the vast unexplored territory stretching from the upper Missouri River across the Rockies to the Pacific Ocean. Towards the end of the eighteenth century, Jefferson had made several attempts to send expeditions up the Missouri, but all had ended in failure, chiefly due to the low calibre of the men assigned to lead them. In early 1803 Jefferson decided to try again. He sent a secret message to Congress, requesting $2,500 to send an expedition up the river through the then French-owned Louisiana Territory. Congress agreed and Jefferson set about finding a leader.

He did not have to look far. Jefferson had long had his eye on Captain Meriwether Lewis, whose family were neighbours of Jefferson in Virginia. Two years earlier the Captain had received a letter from the newly-elected president asking him to abandon temporarily his military duties for the post of presidential secretary. Jefferson's choice of Lewis as secretary was mystifying, not least because his spelling was diabolical. It is obvious that the president was already thinking of him as leader of the expedition.

Lewis fitted the role well. He was the outdoor type having spent his childhood roaming the fields and forests of his native Virginia. 'Rambling,' as he put it, was his great love. He was a dedicated naturalist, trapper and woodsman, handy with a hunting rifle and possessing a good knowledge of Indians. He was also a loner and a thinker, moody and introverted with a taste for solitary adventure. As the historian Bernard DeVoto says, 'He pondered problems of politics and human fate while patrolling alone with his eye cocked for grizzly bears, new species of plants, and hostile Indians.'

At 20, Lewis had left the 1,000-acre wheat farm he inherited from his father and enlisted in the Virginia militia. He earned rapid promotion and transferred to the regular army where he served for a time in an élite rifle company. Here he met the fellow officer who was to become his partner on the expedition.

Unlike the sombre Lewis, Captain William Clark was outgoing and personable. Red-haired William enjoyed the company of people and this was to prove an invaluable asset when it came to handling Indians. He was also a skilled topographer, whose job it would be to draw the expedition maps. Through his military training he was expert at designing and constructing forts. Although there is no evidence that he knew Lewis as a boy, Clark was from a similar, middle-class Virginian rural background. He too lived for the countryside and was an avid reader of natural history.

The pair were ideally suited. Whereas Lewis was the slightly humourless, methodical leader, Clark would jolly things along with the gritty, pioneering spirit of a born frontiersman. Upon receiving Lewis's letter inviting him to join the expedition, Clark (also not exactly top of the class in spelling) wrote back with the words, 'No man lives with whome I would perfur to undertake Such A Trip as your self.' Towards the middle of 1803 the two men began assembling the men and equipment needed for what was now known as the 'Corps of Discovery'.

Jerry was misty-eyed. I was to discover that Lewis and Clark aroused feelings of deep emotion in Americans.

'Yeah, those guys certainly had something going for them,' he said. 'I sure wouldn't have liked to have gone up the Missouri in those days not knowing what to expect. Especially with all us damned Indians to give 'em hell.' And he gave another throaty laugh.

I changed the subject. 'Well, if you think of what Lewis and Clark got up to, then the story of Prince Madoc is even more amazing.'

'Madoc?' Jerry said. 'And who was he?'

It was nearly midnight and the combination of creeping jet-lag and several beers was making me drowsy. But Jerry was a good listener and I was enjoying the company. I launched into the famous myth of Madoc, the twelfth-century Welsh prince, to whom is given the distinction of being one of the first Europeans to discover America.

This highly dubious story first appeared in print in the sixteenth century. Briefly, it goes something like this: Upon the death of Owen

Gwyneth, King of North Wales, civil war broke out. The king's son, Madoc, was a peaceful cove who didn't want the hassle of sorting out his warring nation. Instead, he set out to find a new land where he and his loyal followers could make a new start. He and a party of 120 would-be colonists sailed west in 1170 and found a suitable place that turned out to be Virginia. Then Madoc returned to Wales where he filled another ten flimsy little wooden ships with more men and women, before sailing the 3,000-odd miles back to America. And that is the last we hear of him and his merry band. Or, at least, that is the last direct contact we have with Madoc. For over the next five or six centuries we hear rumours that the Welsh moved north-west through America up the Missouri and settled in what is now North Dakota. There they integrated with the Mandan tribe of Indians. And, so the story goes, the Mandan language bears a close resemblance to Welsh.

It must be said that only the Welsh themselves have ever taken this tale seriously. Historians have spent many hours pooh-poohing it. 'The pretensions of the Welsh to the discovery of America seem not to rest on a foundation much solid,' noted William Robertson, principal of Edinburgh University, in 1792. 'The naval skill of the Welsh in the twelfth century was hardly equal to such a voyage. If Madoc made any discovery at all, it is more probably that it was Madeira, or some other of the Western isles.' And with a nice line in insults, Mr Robertson added: 'Among a people as rude and as illiterate as the Welsh at that period, the memory of a transaction so remote must have been very imperfectly preserved.'

But to this day the Welsh stubbornly maintain that it's all true. After all, Wales is not exactly overburdened with great explorers. Presumably the fable of Madoc is better than nothing. Shortly before I left for America I visited the Welsh gift shop in London's Piccadilly to see what literature I could find about our intrepid prince. The Welsh lady at the cash desk knew all about Madoc. 'Of course he discovered America,' she said with no trace of humour in her voice. 'It's common knowledge in Wales.'

But the legend of Madoc was not common knowledge in the bar of the Blackstone Hotel. Jerry had certainly never heard of it. Nor had the Cherokee, who by this stage was listening to me with renewed interest. They both looked at this crazy Englishman with expressions of disbelief.

'Jesus!' said the Cherokee, who had forgotten his 'who gives you the right' theme.

'Christ!' Jerry said. 'Are you trying to tell us that the Welsh discovered America?'

'Well, that's what the Welsh like to think,' I said. 'And one of the things I'm going to do on this trip is visit the Mandans and sort out this thing once and for all.'

Jerry was lost for words. 'But it's garbage.'

'Propaganda!' There was a vicious war-cry from the Cherokee. He was back on old form again. 'Do you mean to say that the Welsh came here first? That's white man's propaganda. That's a story made up by white people to discredit the Indians.'

It was late and I had no intention of suggesting that perhaps the Cherokee was being a trifle paranoid. The bartender had cleared away our beer bottles and was adding up the till. The evening was over. I said goodnight and went up to my room where I mulled over the Cherokee's final outburst.

He certainly had a point. Almost every major civilization in history has at one stage or another been given credit for being the first inhabitants of America. As the author William Brandon notes in his book *Indians*, the native Americans have been suspected of being everything from Egyptian, Phoenician and Japanese to having arrived by way of the lost continent of Atlantis. However, there is evidence to suggest that they are the oldest known race on earth with an ancestry going back between 15,000 and 20,000 years. The most popular theory is that the original settlers were nomads from Mongolia who crossed from the Old World into Alaska via the frozen wastes of the Bering Strait.

Maybe it was the romantic in me – and the fact that I was brought up in Shropshire twenty miles from the Welsh border with Welsh family connections – but I still liked the idea that Madoc had got there first. And anyway, it was a good excuse for me to explore a part of America that I had wanted to see ever since watching cowboy television shows as a child when I would spur on the Lone Ranger with a volley of shots from my scaled-down plastic-handled Colt 45 cap gun.

Before leaving England I had spent much time studying maps of the Mid- and Great North West and wondering what I could expect along the way in little rivertowns like Pierre and Williston, tiny cartographical pinpricks apparently stuck in the middle of nowhere. But it was Lewis and Clark that had really grabbed my imagination. The pair are virtually unknown in Britain and I had first heard of them only six months earlier after chatting with a London-based American friend. The next day I pottered along to the Royal Geographical Society where I looked them up in the library. Four hours later I was thoroughly immersed in Meriwether and William's extraordinary adventures. I decided immediately that I would follow their trail up the Missouri.

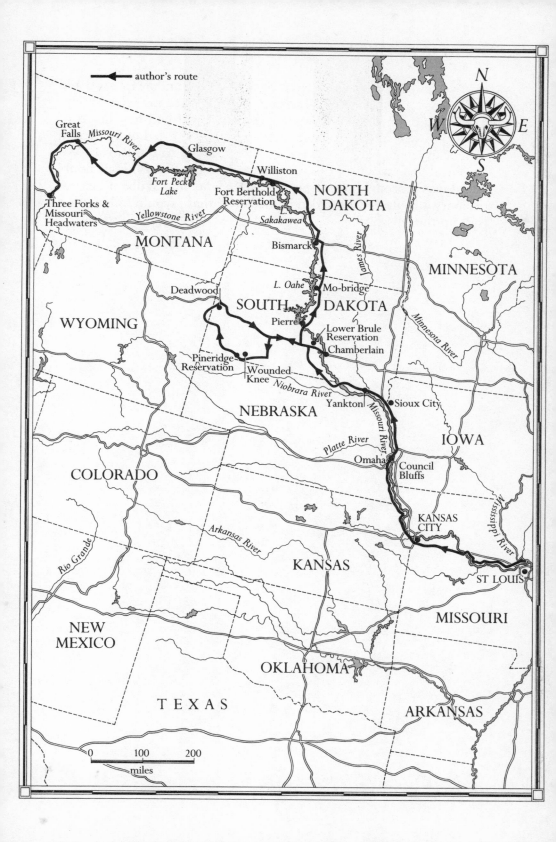

one

Ellen had strict words of warning about American girls. 'All they want is a man with money. Never believe a girl if she says she's marrying for love alone.'

Ellen was my neighbour on the flight to St Louis. She was a history of art teacher in her sixties with a wicked glint in her eye. She was quite schoolmistressy; short and neatly turned out in sensible tweed skirt, raccoon hat and brown brogues. She was on her way to stay the weekend with one of her former pupils, a self-made dog food tycoon. (Ah, dogs, I thought. Dogs were to play an important part in my visit to St Louis. But more of that later.)

'Don't you think it's a bit of a come-down making dog food having studied history of art?' I asked.

'No. There's a lot of money in dog food.'

Ellen was keen to talk about girls. Most of her former female pupils were desperate to get married. 'They're shopping around for someone with money and some of them are doing a helluva lot of shopping. They look for men in their early thirties because they are more likely to be making it.'

She did not have a high regard for her students' morals. 'Oh, those girls know what they want. They're not going to mess around with some 25-year-old, who's going to take maybe ten years to get rich. But they all say that good men are hard to find. I hear there's a terrible shortage of eligible men.'

She asked how old I was. I told her: thirty-four. She said she was surprised I had not yet been lured to the altar. I replied that perhaps English girls weren't as pushy as their American cousins. Ellen guffawed. She nudged me hard in the ribs. 'Don't you believe it. All girls are the same, American or English.'

The stewardess handed out in-flight midday snacks of roast beef sandwiches. Ellen's glasses hung round her neck on a chain. She took a hefty bite of her sandwich. As she did so, pieces of beef and potato salad slipped out from between the bread and dropped on to her spectacles. I tactfully pointed this out and she swiftly wiped them with a finger. She replaced her glasses and looked at me through horribly smeared lenses.

She warmed to her subject. The dog food tycoon, she said, was going out with a girl with two failed marriages behind her and two young children. 'He's hopelessly in love with her, but she's only after someone with money. If I was him, I wouldn't want to take her on.' I agreed that it all sounded most unsatisfactory, but if he was in love, then what could one do? 'What indeed?' Ellen said.

The plane landed at St Louis. A thin covering of snow lay on the runway. The pilot informed us the outside temperature was only just above freezing. I had told Ellen about my journey up the Missouri. 'Why on earth have you come to the Mid-West in January? It's such a horrible time of the year.' She pulled her raccoon hat hard down over her ears in preparation for leaving the warmth of the plane. 'Most tourists come here in summer or fall when it's much nicer.'

I explained that I wanted to see the prairies at the worst time of the year, at their most raw and rugged, in an attempt to understand the hardships endured by the nineteenth-century pioneers. I was quite happy if there were no other tourists around.

'You certainly won't have a problem there,' Ellen said. 'In fact, I doubt they've ever seen an Englishman in the places you're going to.' We said farewell in the airport. Ellen went off with her dog food tycoon and I took a cab into the city centre.

The first permanent settlement on the site of St Louis was established in 1764 by a young New Orleans Frenchman called Auguste Chouteau and his common-law stepfather Pierre Laclede. The pair found a thickly wooded site with easy access to the Mississippi river. It was a perfect spot for trading with the local Indians. Chouteau and Laclede's base prospered and by the early 1800s St Louis was a flourishing community.

The city's fortunes took off with the beaver trade. The beaver was a sudden accident of fashion worn by everyone from the smartest European ladies to the most backward drink-swilling yahoo. Almost overnight everyone wanted one of these highly-prized furs. Trappers flocked to St Louis. From there they made their way west to the Missouri's hunting grounds. Slaughtering the innocent beaver was no mean task. The creatures have to be trapped underwater – a cold, wet job that the Indians didn't like. The trappers were often in the mountains for years at a time. Death from starvation, drowning or exposure was common.

Then came tough times. The 1848 Californian goldrush brought a flood of people from the east. St Louis suffered a cholera epidemic followed by a fire that destroyed the city's business district. In the 1850s the fashion for beaver suddenly ended and the market collapsed. The mountain men vanished and with them went the last vestiges of French influence.

But all was not lost. Within ten years the steamboats arrived, heralding the great drive up the Missouri by land-hungry people. In that period the population of St Louis grew from 15,000 to 70,000 as the city took over the job of national expansion, becoming 'outfitters', supplying people with what they needed to move west.

The railroads arrived in the 1860s. Boat traffic died. And by 1874, Mark Twain, that most famous riverman of them all, sadly observed a drowsy St Louis riverfront with 'half a dozen sound asleep steamboats where I used to see a solid mile of wide awake ones'.

The railroads brought a new growth and there was a move to make 'the future great city' the nation's capital. By 1899 St Louis was the fourth largest city in America with the nation's biggest railroad station, brewery, shoe factory and hardwood lumber market. As local wags say, the place was traditionally 'first in booze, first in shoes and last in the American league'.

The city was good at firsts. The 1904 World's Fair held in St Louis is credited with producing the first ice cream cone and the first pitcher of iced tea. It was also here that visitors got their first taste of that American classic, the hot-dog. The Wainwright Building in downtown St Louis is recognised as the world's first skyscraper, and the first parachute jump happened here in 1912. In 1927 the city's businessmen sponsored Charles Lindbergh's *Spirit of St Louis* on the first solo flight across the Atlantic.

Present-day St Louis is a thriving industrial and commercial centre with a population of 2,400,000. The International Shoe and Brown Shoe companies have gone down in importance. But the world's biggest brewer, Anheuser-Busch of Budweiser fame, is still here (6.8 million bottles and 8.6 million cans produced each day), as is McDonnell-Douglas aircraft and an assortment of oil and chemical companies.

I checked into the Forest Park Hotel in the Central West End area of the city. It is a neighbourhood of tree-lined boulevards, turn-of-the-century gothic mansions, genteel nursing homes and wrought iron street lamps. Cats lay asleep on front porches enjoying the wintry sun. The Forest Park would have been quite elegant in the 1930s, but was now on the faded side. The entrance hall was all pillars and potted palms. The paintwork in my room was chipped and there was a profusion of stray pubic hairs in the bath – pubic hairs in baths were to become a regular feature in hotels and motels along the Missouri. Perhaps they said something about the hairiness of the Mid-Westerner.

I took a bus downtown to see St Louis's most famous landmark. The Gateway Arch is America's tallest and most extraordinary monument. It was completed in 1965 to symbolize St Louis as the starting point for the great westward expansion. 'You never get tired of looking at it,' was the view of St Louisans.

You certainly can't miss it. Constructed from concrete with stainless steel walls that shimmer in the sunlight, it towers 630 feet over the city and resembles an overgrown croquet hoop. I could not decide whether this was a work of understated magnificence, or vulgarity beyond one's wildest dreams.

When the arch was opened – a series of special passenger capsules inside the structure takes tourists to the top – the *St Louis Post-Dispatch* reported: 'The building of the arch has engendered a fresh confidence. The St Louisans . . . have made the arch not merely the symbol of 200 years gone, but also of a future, bright as the sky on topping-out day.'

The folk of East St Louis, the city's poor relation across the Mississippi, took a different view. With a refreshing lack of respect they suggested that St Louis be renamed the Wicket City and announced they would erect a mallet and ball of similar proportions.

After gazing in awe at this monster, I dodged legions of skateboarders on the walkways beneath it and strolled down to the riverfront to eat a pizza in one of the floating restaurants moored along the shore. At the next table was a party of girls, who were among several thousand speech therapists attending their annual convention. 'What do you think of the arch?' I asked them. Their feeling was that it bore a close resemblance to the McDonald's hamburger logo.

The girls wore badges with the words 'Speech Patrol'. After learning I was from England ('We just love your accent' etc . . .) we got onto the subject of English pronunciation. How, for example, should you say 'whale'?

'Well, it's just whale,' I suppose.

They tried to mimic me – 'waal, waeel, waail . . .' Then we tried 'mountain'. The girls made strange shapes with their mouths. 'Muntin, maontin, mauwwnten . . .'

One of the girls was from Kentucky. She said how awful it was that the state's schoolchildren all said 'ain't'.

Her friend was from Denver. 'We don't bother to correct "ain't" anymore. God, saying ain't is the least of our problems. Trouble is, you spend thirty minutes in class telling a kid not to say "ain't" and then he goes home and his parents say it.'

All the girls agreed that they hated 'ain't'. 'Gee, it's awful,' added one. I pointed out that perhaps 'gee' was not the best use of the English language. The girl blushed. I felt rather a cad.

St Louis made an apt choice as a venue for a conference on good speech, for it likes to maintain a reputation for being a gracious city. It is a place of wealth, culture and more than a touch of East-coast snobbery. Here originated the Pulitzer Prize, named after Joseph Pulitzer I, founder of the campaigning, liberal daily the *St Louis Post-Dispatch*; anyone who is anyone belongs to an organization called Downtown St Louis Inc., which includes fifty of the most important names in town – the latest Pulitzer, Joseph number three, an art connoisseur famed for his collection of Monets, is naturally a member. And in fall, teenaged daughters of the city's millionaires prepare for the debutante season. Rich daddies hire country clubs for grand private dances and there are $100-a-head balls such as the Fleur de Lys and the Veiled Prophet.

But St Louisans do not flaunt their riches like Beverly Hills *nouveaux riches*. Their wealth is carefully hidden away in quiet, leafy suburbs such as Clayton and Ladue. They do not drive flashy cars. Instead they will spend hundreds of dollars on charming French chintzes and on the thickest, embossed writing paper – there are an astonishing number of expensive stationery shops in the city. This is the subtle way of showing your friends you have old money and good taste. The St Louisan is a refined, cultivated soul. And it was with this in mind that I tracked down Maria Everding.

Maria was the city's self-styled First Lady of Manners. As well as running etiquette courses, she occupied a weekly radio spot telling people how they should, or should not, behave. I called her up and she suggested that I come to one of her monthly fashion shows that she ran in conjunction with a department store.

We met in a bar at Northwest Plaza, a gargantuan shopping mall on the outskirts of St Louis. I could hardly wait to ask her my first question: what is the correct way to eat a hamburger?

'A hamburger is finger food,' she pronounced. 'If it is very large you should cut it in half before picking it up.'

'But what about all the gunk like ketchup and gherkin that spews onto your hands?'

'Make sure it goes on the plate, not on you. And if it gets on your fingers? Well, I teach that *nothing* is finger-licking good. *Never, ever* lick your fingers. Always wipe them on a napkin.'

Maria was immaculately turned out. She was a petite, no-nonsense lady with a black bob of hair in the style worn by Lucy in the *Peanuts* cartoon strip. She wore a neat little white mink jacket over a blood-red figure-hugging dress; the hem fell just below the knee. Her fingernails were a deep crimson and beautifully manicured. On one finger rested a huge gold filigree ring. Her feet were daintily encased in black patent high heels, but certainly not high enough to be considered tarty. She drank a white wine cooler while I ordered a beer. She was very talkative.

Good manners were Maria's personal crusade against the rudeness of twentieth-century America. She was a graduate of the Patricia Stevens finishing school in St Louis and had gone on to create her own etiquette programme called 'Pretty As A Picture'. She charged parents $75 a course for the privilege of having their little darlings trained in social niceties.

'When my daughter was five I could see that children couldn't differentiate socially between right and wrong. I started with just a few young ladies and now I have over five hundred names on a waiting list. I've never had anyone flunk a course, not one rebel. You can hear a pin drop in the classes and I never have to raise my voice.'

Maria's course included poise, grooming and social etiquette. 'I teach them how to set a table and that a napkin should be put on your knee. But above all I tell them that saying 'please' and 'thank you' is okay and that they should stand up and shake hands if an adult comes into the room. As for sex, I teach them to be a lady. They should stick to what they feel is right and not be concerned with peer pressure. I even say if you're asked out on a date and a young man spends a lot of money on you, send him a thank-you note. What does it hurt?'

Maria's courses comprised six one-hour classes for a month. They culminated with a fashion show followed by a formal tea party at her house. 'I can't tell you the confidence the girls get. I put down my success to the influence of another voice. A mother can say anything she likes, but her daughter won't take the slightest bit of notice.'

Maria paused and delicately sipped her wine cooler. I asked what she considered was the worst fault in American teenaged girls. She stepped formally on to her soap box. 'They tend to be pretty awkward and uncouth. Many of these kids are children of people who were raised in the 1960s. The 1960s was the counter-culture era when everybody did his or her own thing, was anti-establishment and couldn't care less about good manners. So the parents can't teach their children anything. The one thing that really annoys me is bad telephone manners. Like when your daughter answers the phone and yells "Mom!" if the call's for her mother. And, can you believe it, some students even ask if they have to have good manners if they go to McDonald's? I tell them they should have good manners everywhere.'

She detested the way kids aped their parents. 'One little girl came to my tea party, grabbed some peanuts and stuffed them in her pocket. I told her you don't do things like that. She looked at me and said, 'But my mom always puts peanuts in her pocket.'

I looked around the bar. Most of the other customers were in their early twenties. They all looked quite well behaved. No one appeared to be stashing away the complimentary peanuts.

Maria took out a handkerchief, dabbed her nose and launched into a spirited discussion of good party manners. 'One of the most important things I teach my girls is how to pour punch. Do you know the proper way to pour punch? I bet you learn that automatically back in England.'

I said there wasn't a great demand for socially advanced punch pourers in England these days. 'Well, I'll tell you how. You hold the punch cup with the handle away from you over the punch bowl. You ladle it about three fourths full and then hand the glass to your guest with a napkin around it. After the first cup your guests can help themselves.'

Then there was the birthday party. 'If you receive a gift you don't like, let it be your secret and thank the person for her thoughtfulness.' Maria put on a naughty little girl look. She leaned closer to me. 'But if you really hate it,' she whispered conspiratorially, 'you can always give it away to to someone else next Christmas. But don't say I said that.'

Maria was keen to talk about table manners in England. We had a long discussion regarding the use of the knife and fork. It was a riveting conversation.

The American way of eating is to first hold down the food with the fork and cut it up with the knife. Then you put your knife on the side of your plate, transfer the fork to your right hand and eat using only the fork. I explained that in England we used the knife to mush the food onto the fork.

Maria was fascinated. She was in her element. 'But when you cut up the food and put the knife down, do you place the knife at the top of the plate?'

'Certainly not,' I said. 'We hold onto the knife at all times.'

'Why would you do that?'

'I've absolutely no idea.'

'This is really annoying me. I've been trying to find the history of this but I can't find it anywhere. I've gone back to the 1800s and I can only work out that when boys were at boarding school in England they ate like this because it was faster. But I hadn't a clue why in the United States we use the "transfer" method.'

'Maybe,' I suggested, 'it's because you always had plenty to eat in this country and you never had to worry about eating quickly.'

'Maybe,' Maria said. 'But I find it all very puzzling.'

Young ladies were not the only subject of Maria's attentions. She had recently launched a course for boys.

'The little ones come under duress, of course, but the teenagers enjoy it because they think they're going to meet girls. I teach them how to pull a chair out and how to help a lady with her coat. Then I take them for dinner at a French restaurant. That's too darling, all these eleven-year-olds in a French restaurant. One evening I had six little boys at dinner. There was a group of businessmen at the next table and they asked me what I was doing. I explained it was an etiquette class. At the end of dinner, one of the little boys helped me with my coat. The businessmen looked astonished. I have boys who call me later and say that I've really helped them in dating.'

'What? The secret of picking up classy girls?' Maria looked just the slightest bit stuffy. 'Well, put it that way if you must,' she sniffed.

Maria's most essential advice for young men concerned the hiring of limousines. I remarked that you wouldn't find many teenagers in Britain renting limousines.

'Well, I guess it's cheaper here, and anyway it's fun.' There were strict rules for ordering a limo. Certain questions had to be asked. 'For example, if you want to be left alone in the back with your date, does the rental company have a driver that doesn't talk too much? And remember you should always give your date the back nearside seat so she doesn't have to climb across.'

Finally, Maria added (and to this day I still don't know whether she was being serious): 'The colour is most important. Does the limousine have tinted windows? If so, make sure they don't clash with the colour of your date's eyes.'

This was enough etiquette for one evening. Maria glanced at her watch and announced it was time for the fashion show. I tried to attract the waitress's attention. She looked in the opposite direction.

'What should I do if I want the check in a hurry?' I asked. 'Is it okay to wave my arms?'

'That is just about acceptable,' she said. 'But *never, ever* whistle.'

We left the bar with that ubiquitous American farewell 'Have a nice day' ringing in our ears. 'Huh,' Maria said. 'I loathe it when people say that. Everyone in this country says it and sounds *so* insincere.'

We strolled through the shopping mall. Maria walked with the seductive wiggle of the catwalk, her right hand held out limply in front. We reached a closed door. I stepped forward and opened it for her.

'My, that's a nice surprise,' she trilled. 'A lot of American girls don't like men to open doors for them. I'm afraid I hate the new etiquette, that manners have changed and that a girl should open a door if they get to it first and not stand there and wait for a man to open it.'

I pointed out that most British women would expect a man to open the door for them. 'Oh dear no,' Maria said, 'executive women here don't like it at all.'

'I'd even open the door for a really tough London career woman and I doubt she'd mind,' I replied.

'Even at the office?'

'Certainly.'

'Well, I'm glad to hear it.'

The fashion show was being held in the centre of the mall. Anxious parents armed with video cameras were taking their seats beneath the catwalk. Maria showed me to a free chair while she scurried away to marshal her troops. There were nearly forty girls of all ages including the compere, one of Maria's ex-students. She was an exceedingly pretty girl of eighteen in a miraculously tight black cocktail dress.

Maria took the microphone. She spoke a few soothing words about her girls: 'As they begin to gain confidence, they blossom like a tiny rosebud does.' The parents nodded appreciatively. One by one her charges took the stage. They walked up and down with as much decorum as they could muster. The older they were, the more self-conscious they tended to be.

The girl in the slinky black number took over the microphone . . . 'This is Kerry. She is in seventh grade. She wants to be a model when she grows up. Her favourite animal is a cat and in her spare time she likes to watch TV.'

After each girl left the catwalk Maria patted her on the head and handed over a red rose. She looked on like Miss Jean Brodie. These were *her* girls.

'. . . Katy is in the sixth grade. She has won medals for tap dancing. Her favourite animal is a chimpanzee. Her favourite colour is turquoise . . . Alex enjoys talking on the telephone and her favourite animal is puppies.'

Animal? Puppies? English grammar was evidently not on the schedule.

'. . . This is Colleen. When she grows up she wants to be a lawyer.' Colleen was about eleven with a severe look on her face. She didn't smile once. This etiquette thing wasn't quite her bag. Pushed into it by mommy, I'll bet.

'. . . Tracy's favourite animal is a chipmunk . . .' Excitement gave way to boredom as the twentieth girl took the stage. A few shoppers, who had stopped to look, drifted away. The fathers in the audience began to yawn. '. . . Sarah's in her eighth grade and she's already won first prize in a fashion show so she's an old pro at this.' I felt this was an unfortunate use of the word pro. Sarah was fourteen, extremely pretty and knew it. Daddy was going to have problems with this one. '. . . Eliza's favourite food are carrots . . .'

And so the evening rambled on. Most of the girls admitted their favourite hobby was talking on the telephone. But it was indicative of the level of ambition in America that they all looked forward to high-profile, big-earning jobs: actresses, models, lawyers, fashion designers, interior decorators. Even a stockbroker. I wondered what had happened to little girls? For not one of them said that when she grew up she would like to be a nurse.

An exploding sluice of thick brown water, charging into the Mississippi with the urgency of a Seventh Cavalry attack; a relentless outpouring of water with a fierce wake vigorously battering the sandy shoreline. That is my first memory of the Big Muddy.

After nearly a week in St Louis I travelled a few miles out of the city to see the river that was to be my constant companion through the West for the next two months. The area around the confluence of the Missouri and Mississippi was dense with trees. In spring, the banks would be bursting with greenery with the first buds appearing on the apple trees. But this was winter and patches of ice covered the brown leaf-mould of the forest floor.

My guide to the spot was one of the locals. Nelson and Juliet Reed were my only contacts in St Louis, friends of friends from

Europe. I called them up and they asked me to lunch at their substantial bungalow that lay in an exclusive forest setting a few miles from the city centre. It was a comfortable house with acres of parquet floor and a vast conservatory that boasted an indoor waterfall and a jungle of exotic plants. The furnishings included some impressive oil paintings and pieces of Indian art. The furniture was most definitely antique.

The Reeds were typical St Louisans – gracious hosts and brimming with culture. Nelson was a gentle man with a lived-in face. He was in his sixties and had made a fortune in rubber and plastics. He could trace his St Louis roots back to 1818 when an ancestor arrived from Virginia.

'So the Reeds are an old St Louisan family,' I said.

Nelson considered for a moment. 'Old is not the right word,' he said, 'You're not an old St Louisan family unless you arrived with the first canoe.'

We lunched off artichoke stuffed with crab, washed down with a bottle of Pinot Grigio (none of your Californian Chablis here). Above the dining table hung an extraordinary electric wall sculpture with dozens of small lightbulbs that lit up at random.

Juliet was a petite, platinum blonde. She had been brought up in Belgium and, despite years in America, her voice bore traces of a husky Flemish accent. She and her husband were great Europhiles. They had spent many holidays on the Continent and had recently returned from a tour of the Loire châteaux. Juliet was heavily into self-improvement. She had started evening classes on the history of music. Last week it was Baroque. Tomorrow it was Beethoven. She was about to begin a course in Shakespeare's comedies. 'And she doesn't even like Shakespeare's comedies,' Nelson jibed. Juliet giggled. This was evidently a private joke.

We sipped the crisp Italian wine and I got a lesson in pronunciation. For example, you talk about St Louis with a hard 's'. It is never St Louee. 'I had an old aunt who talked about St Louee, but generally the French way of saying it went out before the First World War,' Nelson explained. Likewise, the way to pronounce Missouri, the state in which St Louis sits: 'Anyone who knows anything will *always* talk about Missour-a.'

I remarked that St Louis seemed a snobby city. Nelson laughed. 'We're a funny mix, but there are people here with French names who have every right to feel they have been here for a long time. People from the south think we're Yankees and people from the north assume that we're Southerners. Kansas City thinks we're sophisticated, but go east of Chicago and people think there are still buffalo out here.'

He looked at Juliet. 'I guess we're upright people with solid identities. A girl I'd known in High School went to live in California for a few years. When she came back she said, "It's incredible. People are still married to the same people here." '

Did St Louisans look down on other Americans? 'Oh, no,' Nelson said.

'I mean, I've been to Boston,' I said, 'and they're a frightfully snobby lot. They think they've got an awful lot of history.'

'We don't think,' came the quick reply. 'We know.'

Next morning Nelson picked me up from the hotel and we drove out in his Cadillac to the site of Lewis and Clark's base camp.

We left the city along a highway bordered by flat, bleak fields of the rich, ebony soil that locals call gumbo, like the Cajun soup. There was an inordinate number of squashed possums and skunks on the road. 'The skunks are incredible,' Nelson said. 'You can smell 'em long after they're dead.'

We turned off down a potholed track flanked by a thick screen of cottonwood and sycamore trees. In a clearing by the river was a monument marking Lewis and Clark's base camp. I left the car and walked down to the sandy shoreline for my first glimpse of the Big Muddy.

Since the first trappers paddled up the Missouri River in search of their booty of the wilderness, this powerful and tortuously winding passage of water has been treated with the greatest respect. Constantly shifting sandbanks and mighty currents combine to make this one of the most deceptive waterways on earth. The Missouri is a truculent bitch; she is not to be trusted. There are numerous drownings each year and you will hear stories of foolish folk who park their cars on sandbanks and go hunting. They return an hour later to find the river has changed course yet again and their vehicle has been swept away.

The Missouri's fickleness is legend. In 1868 the Sioux City Register reported: 'Of all the most variable things in creation, the most uncertain are the action of a jury, the state of a woman's mind, and the condition of the Missouri River.' The writer George Fitch called it 'a river that plays hide-and-seek with you today, and tomorrow follows you around like a pet dog with a dynamite cracker tied to his tail'. John G. Neihardt, who in 1908 descended part of the river by boat, was more flowery: 'I think God wished to teach the beauty of a virile soul fighting its way toward peace – and His precept was the Missouri.' In his gloriously irreverent 1946 book *Inside U.S.A.*, the writer John Gunther described it as an 'outlaw hippopotamus, this mud-foaming behemoth of river'. And another author, Stanley Vestal, put it thus: '. . . the hungriest river ever created, eating yellow clay banks and cornfields, eighty acres at a mouthful, winding up its banquet with a truck garden and picking its teeth with the timbers of a big red barn.'

The Missouri is a 'cutting' river, constantly slicing into the banks. And it is the yellowy brown water caused by an immense mass of loose sand and clay that has given the Missouri its nickname, Big Muddy.

'Too soupy to drink and too muddy to plough' is Meriwether Lewis's much-quoted epigram. 'Brave men drink it straight, cowards cut it with whisky', was the cowboy's challenge. And the Victorian geographer James Bell noted that 'in half a pint tumbler of the Missouri water has been found a sediment of two inches of slime'. But with a resolute Britishness, as if describing a jug of lemon barley water after a sweltering game of tennis, he added: 'It is, notwithstanding, extremely wholesome and well-tasted, and very cool in the hottest season of the year.'

For two centuries an argument has raged over which is the superior river – the Mississippi or the Missouri. I stood on the banks of the Mississippi and looked 200 yards across the water to where the Missouri's swifter torrent poured in. There was no doubt about it: the Missouri won hands down. I gazed in awe at the way her current seemed to nudge the Mississippi out of the way. A lone dredger at the mouth struggled to keep back the Missouri's silt; a line of sharp little white horses marked the spot where the two rivers collided mid-stream.

All the way up the Missouri I was to hear Mid-Westerners complain that the Big Muddy was the victim of a vile Southern conspiracy. Why did the Mississippi receive top billing when this relatively feeble band of water should be rightly called the Missouri right down to New Orleans? The Missouri has the bolder stream. And had the Big Muddy been discovered first then almost certainly this great river would have been called the Missouri from the Rocky Mountains to the Gulf of Mexico.

Our geographer Mr Bell agreed. 'At the confluence of these two streams,' he wrote, 'the Missouri rushes triumphantly across the Mississippi, its turbid waters seeming to disdain a connexion so inferior. In fact, from the junction down to the sea, the muddy waters of the Missouri completely discolour the stream; and every peculiar characteristic of the Mississippi, as a distinct river, is lost in the majestic volume of the Missouri.

'Of all the rivers, not merely of the United States, but of the whole continent of North America, the Missouri is the chief, whether we regard the continuity of its course, the velocity of its current, the immense volume of its waters, the number and magnitude of its tributary streams, the vast extent of its inland navigation, or the broad expanse of its periodical floods.' Bell's conclusion was that the Mississippi was little more than a 'subordinate' branch of the Missouri.

It had turned into a beautifully sunny day. A brisk winter wind ruffled the fallen leaves. Eagles circled over the riverbank and gulls dipped into the water. A flock of snow geese, tiny silver flecks in the broad blue sky, passed high above. I rejoined Nelson by the Lewis and Clark memorial.

It was near this site, at Camp Dubois, that Lewis and Clark spent the winter of 1803–4 preparing for their departure. It had been Clark's job to recruit the team, which numbered around thirty and included Lewis's negro slave, York. According to Lewis's brief, they were all 'good hunters, stout healthy unmarried young men, accustomed to the woods, and capable of bearing bodily fatigue to a pretty considerable extent'.

Their main transport consisted of a 55-foot 'keelboat' with twenty-two oars and a large square-sail. It drew an exceptionally shallow three feet and was open save for a small for'ard cabin. Lewis had commissioned the craft in Pittsburgh and sailed it down the Ohio River into the Mississippi. The vessel was long overdue thanks to the Pittsburgh boatwright, who, in twentieth-century parlance, had difficulty getting his act together. He was 'constantly either drunk or sick', according to Lewis. 'I spend most of my time with the workmen, alternately persuading and threatening.'

Later in the journey the men had learned how to make Indian-style dug-out canoes. This was a subject close to Nelson's heart. He had tried making canoes in his role as a semi-professional archaeologist – he had been partly responsible for the excavations at Cahokia, a collection of 1000-year-old Indian mounds outside St Louis.

'Cottonwood is excellent, but it not as easy as it sounds. I started out trying to do it with a stone tool as the Indians would have done in the old days. But I got out of that pretty fast. I moved into power saws and even then it was a monstrous job. You have to be very careful not to cut through the whole log.'

The expedition endured three arduous months of training at the Missouri's mouth. The camp was close enough to St Louis for the leaders to carry out last-minute official business, but distant enough so that the men would not be tempted by the city's saloons. By spring everyone was restless and bored. And on Monday, 14 May 1804, a stinking wet morning, the company set out for the unknown.

Nelson and I paused at the expedition monument. It was a bit of a let-down, a grubby concrete bandstand surrounded by flags of the states visited on the expedition. There was a fine collection of graffiti: 'Trust In Jesus' . . . 'For a free B. J. call Suzie on. . . .'

'What's a B. J.?' Nelson inquired. Come on, I thought. St Louisans couldn't be *that* polite.

I had one more visit to make before I left St Louis. It is said that despite the dreadful strain of two years away from civilisation, Lewis and Clark seldom quarrelled. Indeed, they disagreed about only one thing: eating dogmeat. There was little Lewis enjoyed more than a gently braised bow-wow. Clark, on the other hand, detested the taste.

With this faintly grisly idea in mind, I paid a visit to an elegant nineteenth-century Greek Revival mansion in the genteel St Louis suburb of Queen Park. Here is based the National Dog Museum of America, the only museum in the world dedicated exclusively to the history of Man's Best Friend.

On display was everything from dog paintings and sculpture to the collar once worn by a dog belonging to an eighteenth-century Marquis of Cholmondley. There were sketches of poodles, beagles

and papillons and a fireguard flanked by two brass boxers. There
was a wooden merry-go-round dog and silver tankards with dogs
on them. But, such was the regard in which the museum held Fido,
there were no stuffed dogs.

It was a Sunday, when the museum held their 'Guest Dog of the
Week' spot. This Sunday's featured pooch was the keeshond, a big
black and white furry thing used for guarding Dutch barges.

A keeshond owner was showing off three of her pets, who panted
a lot and sniffed the carpet. Their mistress was a lady in her fifties,
dressed in flared maroon Crimplene slacks and yellow top; she had
a bark as loud as her dogs. With her was her elderly mother who
had clacking false teeth.

I joined a dozen other people in an upstairs auditorium to watch
a video about the breed. The audience included a family of four
who had come along to see whether the keeshond would make a
suitable pet. We sat on metal chairs while the owner stood by with
her beloved mutts, Katy, Andrew and Pat. The trio refused to sit
still and snuffled around the room.

The video informed us that the keeshond is 'outgoing and
playful . . .' Andrew attempted to mount Katy . . . 'they are independent high-spirited dogs that make excellent pets . . .' Katy curled her
lip, Andrew retreated. One of the dogs wandered over to where I
sat. It appeared to take a great liking to me and pushed its snout
hard into my crotch. The lady tut-tutted and retrieved the thing.

The commentary continued: 'In general appearance the keeshond
is a natural, medium-sized handsome dog with a well-balanced body.
It is not allowed to be over or under eighteen inches not including
the woolly coat. Dogs underneath or above will be penalised in
shows. The head should not be too heavy or coarse or too small.
The muzzle must be equal in length to the skull. The nose should
be very dark in colour and provide the pleasing keeshond expression.
Lips should not be thick and there should be no wrinkle at the
corner of the mouth. Eyes must be well-placed, neither too close nor
too wide apart.'

Which meant that anything different to this and you had a keeshond with a massive inferiority complex.

I sat at the back taking notes. At the end the owner came up to
me. 'So you're interested in the keeshond,' she said.

'Well, no, not really. I really just wondered what they would be like to eat.' I don't know why I said it, it just sort of came out.

She looked horrified. Her mother's teeth clacked more than ever. One of the children, who had been patting the dogs, made a face and said, 'Ugh, gross.' I attempted to explain the Lewis and Clark connection with eating dogs. The owner did not get the point. It was time to leave.

On my way out, I tried the gift shop. Here you could buy dog watches, dog greeting cards and dog keyrings. By the door was a jar of complimentary biscuits for visiting dogs. There were books ranging from *The Dog In Art From Roccoco to Post-Modernism* to *The Four-Footed Therapist: How Your Dog Can Help You Solve Your Problems*. I bought a slim volume about Scammon, the dog that Lewis took on the expedition. Scammon was a Newfoundland that cost a hefty $20. Perhaps this is why Lewis was never tempted to eat him.

My earlier gaffe had preceded me. 'What's all this about eating dogs?' one of the gift shop ladies asked. She was immaculately groomed, tall and blonde like a saluki. I mumbled an explanation but she too was unaware of Lewis's strange culinary preference. 'The subject of eating dogs is not something that we would discuss here.' She was very firm about this. 'If I were you I would not bring up the subject of dog-eating here. Not ever. Period.'

I returned to my room at the Forest Park Hotel and relaxed in preparation for leaving St Louis the next day. I tried the television. There was little to watch except for endless public warning slots aimed at blacks about the dangers of the drug crack. I was mildly amused by a commercial for Life cereal with the heavy-handed slogan: 'Unless your kids are weird, they'll eat it.'

I swapped TV for the downmarket local newspaper the *St Louis Sun*. More dog news. There was a gruesome story about a mutt that had been found skinned and castrated on a construction site. Satanists were held responsible. Mindful of the city's pedigree-conscious folk, the reporter had added slightly unnecessarily: 'The dog appeared to be a mixed breed, but was predominantly Dobermann pinscher.'

A drive through the United States conjures up names like Chevrolet, Buick and Pontiac. You dream of cruising the highways in one of those outrageously uneconomical American automobiles where snappy road-handling is cheerfully sacrificed for soggy, armchair comfort.

I checked out of the hotel and took a cab to the Hertz rentacar offices in downtown St Louis. I had already booked a vehicle, but had failed to note the make. The Hertz man made me fill in numerous forms. He pointed through the office window to the car lot.

'It's over there,' he said.

'What? The grey Oldsmobile?'

'No. The white one.'

There was only one white car. A Toyota.

Japanese.

'But I'm writing a book about America, for God's sake. How can I pursue the American dream in a Japanese car? Haven't you got something that comes from the United States?'

'They build Toyotas in the United States,' the Hertz man said crisply. He failed to get the point.

The States was going through a crisis of conscience regarding the Japanese. Fifty years after Pearl Harbor, the little men of the Rising Sun were buying up everything from the car industry to skyscrapers. It was bad enough when they snapped up Columbia Pictures and Chicago's Sears Tower, but it was inexcusable when New York's Rockefeller Center, the world's greatest commercial address, fell to the mighty yen. Jap-bashing was the flavour of the day. Groups like

Help Save America For Our Kids' Future ranted that 'Japanism' had replaced Communism as the biggest threat. I was to hear anti-oriental sentiments right the way to Montana.

I was stuck with the Toyota. To be fair, it wasn't a bad car except for the seat belts that automatically slid against your body when you switched on the ignition. This was heralded by an odious electronic beep like an angry mouse. I felt I was strapped in for life.

The morning temperature was an unseasonally warm forty-five degrees as I left St Louis. I planned to spend all day driving to Kansas City, five hundred miles west along the Missouri. This part of the journey had taken Lewis and Clark a comparatively short time and formed only a minor part of their journals, so, like them, I decided to press on. I had intended to take a freight barge from St Louis, but despite endless phone calls, this proved impossible. These days, Missouri river traffic is sadly reduced. I had been in touch with one of the barge companies, who said they had a vessel leaving in a couple of weeks. But this did not fit in with my schedule. Instead, I agreed to catch one of their barges leaving Kansas City in a few days' time for the stretch of river up to Omaha.

Soon after leaving St Louis I came across the first of many road signs marking the official Lewis and Clark trail. They featured the silhouettes of our two heroes, dressed in frayed buckskins and beaver hats, with one of them (I never worked out if it was L or C) pointing the way west. I reflected that had communications been better in the twelfth century it might have been Prince Madoc on those signs. After all, wasn't *he* the first man up the Missouri?

Who knows? But there was a Welsh connection in St Louis. The Madoc theory was more or less alive, if not exactly kicking with the strength of a Merthyr Tydfil pit pony.

During my day out with Nelson Reed we had looked at various ancient Indian sites. One of these was outside St Louis near the town of Alton. An extraordinary dragon-like creature had been painted high on a limestone bluff overlooking the Mississippi just a few miles above the mouth of the Missouri.

Nelson explained that this was the Pisah bird, a mythical creature much feared by the tribe of Missouri Indians. The Pisah was an underwater monster with a long spiky tail that wrapped around his body. He had the face of a lion, birdlike feet and horns that made him a king animal, like Oberon. Get on the wrong side of him, and he swished his tail knocking you into the river. Victims were found drowned with mud in their nostrils.

'He was a very powerful manitou, or spirit,' Nelson said. 'You placated him by giving him sea shells and tobacco.'

But there was something about the Pisah bird that grabbed me more than anything else. I looked, and I looked again. There was no doubt about it. The Pisah bore a more than passing resemblance to the Welsh dragon. Perhaps an image left behind by Madoc and company?

I asked Nelson what he thought of the Welsh theory. 'Sounds like nonsense,' he remarked. 'But then America has long been the tramping ground of scoundrels . . .'

I ought to add that there was another link with Wales in St Louis, but it was hopelessly slim. A few hundred yards from my hotel in Euclid Avenue were two Welsh pubs. The first was called Llewellyn's. Welsh dragons were painted on the doors and there was a wealth of Welsh memorabilia inside. The bar had originally been started by a Welshman, but he had long ago sold out to his American partner. So that was no good. The second was called Dressel's. The owner, a real live Welshman (at last!), was on holiday back home in South Wales and therefore unavailable for comment. I asked one of his waiters what he thought of the Madoc business. 'Sounds like the most stupid thing I've ever heard,' was his reaction.

So as I drove towards Kansas City I temporarily put all Celtic thoughts behind me. Instead, I thought of the Germans. For this part of the country was little Germany – and of that, there was no question.

From the 1830s this part of the Missouri valley became home to thousands of settlers escaping the reactionary governments of post-Napoleonic Germany. Their legacy remains today. In villages like Dutzow, where emigrants from Bohemia first settled in 1832, there were German street names like Schomberg Road. I drove past a little clapboard farmhouse called *Das Schon Haus*. All along the road beside the river I saw mailboxes bearing German names like Moellering, Volkerding and Brandt. Their ancestors lay in cemeteries overlooked by white wooden churches topped off with neat little spires. I passed half-hidden wineries and Christmas tree farms. They nestled in hollows between undulating fields of rich soil that had been turned ready for drilling. I could have been in Bavaria.

Sixty miles out of St Louis I stopped for a coffee in the town of Hermann. Here the German heritage is taken to extremes.

Hermann was founded in 1836 by the German Settlement Society of Philadelphia. Appalled at the way that German immigrants were losing their native customs and language, the society established a colony of artisans and professionals that was to be the centre of the 'Second Fatherland'. Members bought shares entitling them to 40-acre farms around the town.

I drove into Hermann over the huge steel girder bridge that spanned the Missouri. The Germanness was unmistakeable: German shops, Weinkellers and a German Haus Motel; the German obsession for orderliness was evident in the meticulously clean streets. In the visitor centre a lady called Brenda Hoelmer told me that German was still the first language for a few elderly citizens.

'But there aren't many German-speakers left,' she said. 'My husband lived out in the country as a boy and when he went to first grade he couldn't speak English, only German. He had a real rough time. He couldn't play with the other kids because no one understood him.'

Hermann's streets were deserted. The town was all very twee and picture-book, but there was not much life. I walked along the riverbank to stretch my legs. The hazy sunshine glinted off the Missouri. The river looked cold and bleak with many of its treacherous sandbars in evidence. I found a bench and read a few more pages of Lewis and Clark's journals.

During this first stage of the expedition the leaders concentrated on sorting out troublemakers. Two of the men, Hugh Hall and John Collins, received a total of 150 lashes for insubordination and leaving their posts without permission. Clark, meanwhile, was complaining about the abundance of insects on the river. His spelling was worse than ever: 'The Ticks and Musquiters are verry troublesome,' he wrote on 17 June 1804. Poor William. The word mosquito was to cause him much aggravation. In the course of two years it was to vary somewhere between 'musquitor' and 'muskeetor'.

I returned to the Toyota, grappled with the seat belt and continued on my way past checkerboard fields and neat farmsteads. I left the river road for Interstate 70 where I joined a procession of thunderous chrome trucks stuffed with cattle. The animals' pink noses peeped from slits in the sides of the vehicles. Four hours later the light was beginning to fade as the smudge of Kansas City's skyscrapers emerged on the horizon. They did not appear to be scraping much sky and looked like a small outcrop of mushrooms in a very large field.

Eons ago, long before the Indians arrived, the land now known as the United States was home to a great God-fearing civilisation of cultured people and teeming cities. The capital of this empire was Kansas City.

At least, that is what the Mormons believe. But, bearing in mind that the Mormon Church also claims that the Indians were given their 'red' skins in divine retribution for starting a civil war in New York State, *circa* AD 500, perhaps we should not believe everything the Mormons say.

Today's Kansas City cannot be described as desperately godly. When I arrived the crime rate in this sprawling cattle town had hit an all-time high. The city was suffering from an unprecedented number of car thefts – joyriders had stolen 25% more automobiles in the past month than in the whole of the previous year.

Cars feature highly in the lives of Kansas Citizens. I was told that the best present you could buy an 18-year-old Kansas City boy was a new camshaft for his dragster. This is the home of 500-horsepower machines known as 'muscle cars'. Until a few years ago illegal Saturday night drag-racing went on in the car parks of every shopping mall in the city. The craze ended only after police objections and the increasing gas prices.

I opted to stay in the historic area of Westport where General Sterling Price's Confederate forces were defeated in 1864 after a three-day battle that ended the rebellion in the state of Missouri. The area is now the refuge of countless bars and nightclubs and the streets sizzle with loud rock music until the early hours.

I was feeling the first symptoms of a cold as I arrived at the Comfort Inn. It was one of those antiseptic American motels where they say breakfast is included, but 'breakfast' turns out to be a stale doughnut and coffee in a styrofoam cup. My immediate thought after the long drive was that I should go straight to bed and sleep off my cold. Curiosity won the day. To hell with it, I thought. I'll go and meet the locals. Biggest mistake of the trip so far.

I tried a place next to the motel. It was called the Flea Market Bar and Grill. One look inside confirmed that we were not talking sophistication. Five hundred miles west and the graciousness of St Louis was all but forgotten.

Plastic blow-up bottles of famous name beers hung from the ceiling. In one corner was a pinball machine called 'Bad Girls'. A television blared in the background. The clientele sat at plastic-topped tables swilling pitchers of Budweiser, most of which was going on the bare wood floor.

The barman was six and a half feet tall with a physique that suggested he ate sledgehammers for breakfast. Practically all his customers had a beard, including the women, most of whom were very drunk.

One of the gorillas at the bar grunted at me. 'You having a good evening?'

'Not really. I've got an awful cold and I've just driven all the way from St Louis along the river. You know, the scenic route.'

'Really,' he said. 'Didn't know there was one.' And with that he stared back into his beer. My cold couldn't cope with it. I left after one drink.

I walked further into the heart of Westport in search of a more salubrious joint. I passed bookshops and trendy boutiques. I eventually tried Stanford's, a bright English-style pub, almost empty and mercifully free of beards.

I ordered a beer. Down the bar a man picked up on my English accent. He was about my age with long, black hair. 'Well, howdie do,' he said stretching out a hand. 'Don't see many Englishmen round here. I'm Rick.' It was my introduction to Rick the Russian. The evening went badly downhill from that moment.

In his own words, the Russian was a 'melting pot'. His mother had been born in Minsk and his father came from a Greek island, but he was proudest of his maternal ancestry. A born and bred Kansas Citizen, he was dressed in jeans, white T-shirt and cowboy boots. A chunky gold chain hung round his neck. He was coy about his profession, which changed startlingly as the night progressed. He started off as a jackhammer operator on the roads before moving on to become an antique dealer. Much later, at about 1 am, he was a US Army explosives expert. Freelance. Hush-hush.

'What I do is classified. I was training those guys down in Panama. Hey, that invasion was big shit. Should never have happened.'

The Russian ordered more drinks. The barman was an Iranian

called Tommy. He had emigrated twelve years ago, but he still yearned for Tehran. 'Now that's a really beautiful city,' he said.

The Russian sucked on a glass of red wine. We talked about England. 'Wish I'd seen Hendrix back at the Isle of Wight festival,' he said wistfully. 'Now that's one place I want to see.'

I tried to tell him that the Isle of Wight was pretty sleepy these days. The most exciting thing was Sandown Zoo or hunting for cockles on Bembridge beach. But no, he really wanted to see it; this was his greatest dream.

I changed the subject. 'Tell me about Kansas City,' I said.

The Russian prided himself as a social scientist. 'What you have here,' he declared, 'is animal city.

'This is a seething volcano, a Harley Davidson town where Honda is a dirty word. Guys round here live for American bikes, football and drag-racing. You can do something twenty-four hours a day, it's better than Vegas. Trouble is, you're in the middle of the Bible Belt and they've got some of the country's toughest laws on drugs and liquor. But Kansas City is still the most cosmopolitan place you'll ever be in your life. It's crazeee.'

I agreed that it seemed a lot more worldly than St Louis. The Russian fired back. 'We are what St Louis claims to be – the true gateway to the West. Shit, St Louis is the gateway to the *East*. All the big cattle drives were to Kansas City, they weren't to St Louis and that's what the West is about. We are frontiersmen. Go to LA or New York and you'll see a lot of Kansas people there. This is where real Americans are born and raised. Your father can be from Poland and your mom from England, but if you're born here, you're full American. There's no ghettoizing here. It's what the word freedom is all about.'

When I arrived that evening I had noticed that Kansas City's downtown business area was deserted. The only signs of social activity seemed to be here in Westport. 'Everybody has moved to the suburbs in the last twenty years because downtown got too crowded,' my friend continued, 'Now there is no one downtown. We all moved to what we thought was going to be a nice quiet neighbourhood and the next day five thousand condominiums went in. Guess that's progress.'

It was after midnight. The Russian offered to show me some

nocturnal sights. 'Tell you what, we'll go to the best titty bar in town.'

Oh no, I thought. Still, the alcohol seemed to be doing my cold some good. For the second time that evening I said, 'What the hell.'

Tommy, the Iranian barman, waved us goodnight. We staggered into the street. The temperature had dropped alarmingly to well below freezing. The icy wind bit through my thick leather jacket.

The Russian had left his car in a deserted parking lot. The vehicle was a wreck, a massive, wide expanse of battered brown steel that looked exceptionally unroadworthy. Somewhere in this mess of makeshift welding was a 1979 eight-cylinder Mercury Cougar. But my host had great faith in it. 'In America you either spend $20,000 on a new car that breaks down next week, or you build one yourself and it lasts ten years.'

We got in. The Russian fired the ignition. The eight cylinders exploded with a roar. Beneath the front bench seat lay a pair of enormous household hi-fi speakers. The Russian slid a tape into the cassette deck. The British hard rock band Whitesnake hit us with a devastating wall of sound.

'Bloody hell, that's loud,' I yelled above the shrieks of Ritchie Blackmore's nerve-numbing guitar. The Russian flicked a lock of hair from his face and patted one of the speakers. 'Two hundred watts,' he bellowed back. 'Normally you have those itty-bitty car speakers, but they're the first things that break in cars of mine. These babies aren't going to blow.' He clunked the Cougar into gear and we rolled out of the car lot.

We headed across town towards the Kansas state line – the Russian explained that the clubs were better over in the state of Kansas where the laws on striptease were more relaxed than in Missouri.

He turned the music up. It was so deafening that we could no longer hear the groans of the Cougar's suspension. The glass in the cracked windscreen vibrated frighteningly and threatened to shatter. We paused at some traffic lights. The middle-aged occupants of the car alongside looked at us with deep distrust. The Russian was now headbanging the steering wheel in time to the music.

He really liked British hard rock. Led Zeppelin was his favourite. 'When I was growing up I looked for bands that would last. No one will ever beat Zeppelin. They're the epitome of my generation. Hang on!' He fumbled for another tape. Whitesnake was replaced by the album *Led Zeppelin II*. I tried surreptitiously to cover the speakers with my jacket. No good. The overpowering force of Robert Plant and Co. still managed to escape.

We rumbled past a girl in a mini-skirt walking along the street. She must have been freezing. The Russian gave me his view of America's womanhood. 'Now that's Kansas City for you – red tights and pink panties. Man, you should meet one of those Missouri farm girls with rich daddies who come to college here. She drives a red Japanese motorbike, wears her hair in a pony tail and thinks of her pussy as a big prize.'

By the time we reached our destination in Kansas City, Kansas, we were hoarse from shouting over the music. The neighbourhood did not look promising: grimy red brick tenement buildings and dismal warehouses. We pulled up by a club called Motions. The Cougar lunged onto the pavement with a crump. The Russian switched off the ignition. The music died. All was suddenly quiet. The numbing cold hit me as I stepped out of the car.

Motions was in full swing as we went in. A hot blast of air steamed up my glasses. I wiped them with a handkerchief and peered through the gloom. We were in a go-go bar of the tackiest kind, the sort of dive where cockroaches rearrange the furniture.

The stained, blood-red carpet stuck to my feet. At the far end of the room, a stage emerged through a smoky haze. Two dancers were strutting their stuff. They wore bikini bottoms and little starry tassels stuck on their nipples. The tassels were apparently demanded by law. They looked utterly absurd.

The girls were in their late twenties and very thin with gaunt, torpid faces. They attempted vainly to put some sex appeal into their act, twisting lethargically in mock copulation around a stainless-steel pole. Then they writhed up against a mirror at the back of the stage. It hadn't been cleaned for months and was smeared with lipstick and make-up. A juke box pumped out poundingly loud rock 'n' roll. Every so often the record selection ended, plunging the room into silence. The strippers left the stage and went round with a hat collecting more money for the machine. Evidently the management were too mean to provide free music.

The Russian found a table and I ordered beers from a sulky waitress. I looked around the club. The clientele sat round beer-sodden plastic-topped tables. They were impressive if only for their massive, button-popping bulks. Serious rednecks here: tartan check shirts, beards down to navels, hair in pony tails and all topped off with baseball caps. Judging by the number of mud-spattered four-wheel drive trucks outside, they were mostly farm boys on their night off. Some had probably driven 100 miles into town to see the show. They stared at the dancers with blank expressions. I didn't see one of them smile.

'These are the true frontiersmen,' the Russian declared. He launched into a vaguely incoherent discourse on the cowboy: 'The cowboy is freedom. The cowboy says to hell with everything so long as you have your individual freedom where no one can come and take what you've got. The whole point about being a cowboy is that no one is hurt in the process. You don't care about nobody else, you're just looking after yourself, trying to do the best you can.' Then he threw back the remains of his beer and with a nice line in simple philosophy he concluded, 'We're the last frontier and you don't want to fuck with the last frontier. A lot of people get freaked out by Kansas City.'

An hour later and I had bought three rounds of drinks. The Russian seemed reluctant to dig in his pocket. I was beginning to feel sponged upon. The Russian sensed my mood. He announced he had left his money in the car and would go and get it. With that, he hurried out of the bar.

I waited. And I waited. Ten minutes passed. I went outside. The Cougar was nowhere to be seen. The Russian had vanished into the night. Bloody marvellous, I thought. No transport home and I haven't a clue where I am.

Back in the club I tried to call for a taxi. I tackled the barman. He was a great brute of a bearded bruiser.

'Excuse me. Can you tell me where I am?' I asked simply.

The combination of my English accent and the absurdity of the question prompted a look as if the barman had just seen little green men in his garden. He informed me that we were on Kansas Avenue, a name that subsequently sent shudders through other Kansas Citizens I met. This was definitely not the place for an Englishman to end up with a total (and manically crazed) stranger.

'So can I call for a cab?'

'Nope. Ain't no cabs around here.' The barman looked disinterested. He began washing glasses. The strains of ZZ Top blasted through the club. I yelled above the din.

'Then how in the hell am I supposed to get back to Westport?'

'Walk?'

It transpired that Kansas City cab drivers studiously avoided this part of town at night. 'But I can't possibly walk ten miles at two in the morning in sub-zero temperatures.' I sneezed violently. My cold had returned with a vengeance. 'What do you want me to do? Sleep under one of the tables?'

The barman raised his eyebrows. He had no time for half-baked Englishmen. He picked up the phone. 'Okay I'll try and find a cab who's prepared to take the risk.'

I sat down with another beer. A voice from the table next to mine asked me for a cigarette. I looked round to see a girl of about twenty leaning back in her chair with her feet up on a table. She was quite pretty and petite, dressed in jeans and T-shirt with a wide-brimmed Janis Joplin hat. She had a wonderful smile.

We got chatting. She introduced herself as Becky. Here was my chance to use the oldest line in the book: 'Don't mind me for asking,' I said, 'but what's a girl like you doing in a place like this?'

'Bitches,' she replied. 'I like bitches.'

Becky was a lesbian. Now, I've been in a few dubious bars in my time, but this was the first lesbian I'd met in a strip joint.

A new dancer took the stage. Becky pushed her hat out of her eyes. She nudged me with her elbow as if she was one of the boys. 'Shit. Will you just look at that piece of ass? Man, I like the bitches here.' She turned back to me. 'Motions is a great club. They give me free beers because I fix the plumbing for them.'

'Oh Christ,' I muttered under my breath. The night was becoming impossibly bizarre. I longed for the sedate graciousness of St Louis. Bet they didn't have many lesbian plumbers there.

A black girl came through the door. 'Who's the guy for the cab to Westport?' I said a hurried goodbye to Becky, who was now in the process of pinching the waitress's behind. The black girl was the driver's girlfriend. She showed me into the cab outside. A fug of marijuana swirled round my head. The gleaming black face of the driver turned round. He offered me a joint. 'Thank you, but no,' I said. 'I've had quite enough to drink as it is.' The driver seemed baffled by my accent. His girlfriend curled up on the front seat next to him and we headed for Westport.

As we arrived at the hotel, the driver turned round again and looked hard at me. 'What I'd like to know,' he said, 'is what the hell were you doing on Kansas Avenue.' I replied that at this point in the evening I wasn't absolutely sure. 'If you ever meet a crazed half-Russian, half-Greek, who says he's an Army explosives expert, you can ask him.'

Kansas City is big on superlatives. It is said to boast more fountains than Rome and more boulevards than Paris; the Nelson Gallery has the largest collection of Oriental art outside the orient. The city was also home to President Harry S Truman, the man who has the distinction of ordering the dropping of the first atomic bomb. And you can't get much more superlative than that.

But first and foremost Kansas City has always been a cow town. The meat-packing houses have moved away, but the stockyards continue to do a million dollars worth of business a day. Here is the most important livestock exchange in America, a country that after China is the biggest meat producer in the world.

I'd been told that one of the greatest old-timers around was Jay Dillingham, septuagenarian ex-president of the Stockyard's Company, the body that runs the cattle auctions. I gave him a ring and he said he'd be 'tickled pink' to meet me.

As I drove across town and along the 'Jay Dillingham Freeway' I reflected that I was about to meet a powerful man. His office was in the Livestock Exchange Building, a redbrick monstrosity criss-crossed with fire escapes. It loomed threateningly, like a Victorian schoolmarm, over an undisciplined tangle of rusting cattle pens and weed-sprouting railroad sidings. In the distance an oily locomotive lazily shunted a line of goods trucks.

I pulled into a dusty parking lot alongside huge Buicks and Cadillacs, the sort of solid cars you expect stockbreeders to drive, and made my way to the second floor. A secretary showed me along a gloomy corridor to Jay's office.

The room was filled with clutter. On the walls were countless livestock awards, a signed picture of President Truman and a huge bronze cow mounted in a frame. There were tatty filing cabinets, a jumble of cardboard boxes, a complicated looking pre-war adding machine and the steel shovel Jay had used to dig the first sod of his freeway. In one corner sat an enormous safe that would have impressed Jesse James.

Jay was sitting in a beaten-up leather swivel chair behind a desk covered in papers; his wide-brimmed cowboy hat hung from a rickety hat stand. He slowly stretched an arm across the desk, and shook my hand. I sat down.

He was, in his own disparaging words, 'a broken down old cowboy'. He had been officially retired for sixteen years, but still came into his office each day. Why did he still bother?

'Hell, just to get away from home. Just hangin' out.' Jay was on the paunchy side. His hair was greying and there were a few liver spots on his distinguished face. But he was fit for his age.

His voice was a steady drawl. 'I don't have anything else to do, I don't chase women, I don't drink too much whisky, I don't shoot craps and I don't go to Las Vegas. I just come to the office and go for lunch with my friends. I used to come in every day, but a year ago I quit coming in Sundays. Hell, I thought it was time to slow down. I answer the telephone a bit, but otherwise I do nuttin'. Just keep my mind occupied.'

Jay was the granddaddy of the stockyards. He settled back in his chair and contentedly clasped his hands round his stomach. He had a glint in his eye and a smile that suggested he had been quite naughty in his younger days. Here was a man who knew his mind; the sort of man who always won arguments.

His family had been in Kansas City for six generations. He had worked his way to the top of the Livestock Exchange after starting as a seventeen-year-old clerk in 1937. The stockyards had been his life.

But things had changed in nearly half a century. And Jay wasn't happy. 'Aw, hell, it's a different ball game. When I first came here the damned market was just busier than hell. In just one day in 1941 we had sixty-four thousand cattle here. Now we don't see much more than that in a year. We started this auction thing about twenty years ago. In the old days it was sale by private treaty. A man had a certain number of pens allotted to him – we call them an alley – and a buyer would wait until the seller invited him in. You had to take your turn, couldn't all be in there at the same time. He negotiated for what they were worth and maybe he bought them or he just rode out and another guy came in to try. Now later, the seller might have not got the price he wanted and he might have to go all round town looking for the first buyer. Then in the meantime the buyer might have bought something else. Hell, damned auctions ruined the fun.'

Jay paused. No, he wasn't happy at all. The old days were definitely better. 'All them cattle came by rail in those days. Now it's all by truck. We built highways and put trucks on the road with rubber tyres and they could go anywhere at any time. So now cattle don't have to come to a central market like Kansas City; there are little markets scattered clear round the whole damned country. It's a lot cheaper and quicker for the farmer to use his own truck to go down the road ten miles to a market.

Kansas City's slaughterhouses had gone. 'We used to be the second biggest slaughtering centre in the country after Chicago. But they built these big feed lots all over the damned country and they're sold right there. That took all the fat cattle that used to graze on the pasture in Kansas and Oklahoma right out of this market. Then someone got the idea that when you feed cattle on grass the fat was yellow because of the carotene. They reckoned it wasn't as good as plain corn-fed. I look forward to the day to come when we go back to feeding cattle on grass, but that's just thinking out loud.

'It's one of those damn things, a change in the whole marketing picture. Some people call it progress. But like I told a young lady who was writing for one of those fancy books written out of New York or Chicago or some place – hell can't think – anyway she came here writing a story and she asked me, "What do you think of all this change?" I said it reminded me of what the chicken said about the egg, "That may be breakfast to you, but it's a pain in the ass to me." By God, she was just an innocent little thing, but she printed it.'

What did Jay think of St Louis's claim to being gateway to the West? He looked at me with steely cowboy eyes. 'Hell boy, what with that fancy accent of yours, I'd say you been in the East too long.

'Yeah, hell. St Louis.' He almost spat the words. 'They're too much damned Easterners to be Westerners. We're an altogether different breed of cats.'

But it was meat I had come to talk about: Kansas City steak, which, according to men like Jay, is one of the greatest delicacies known to man.

'It's probably the best-known piece of meat in the whole world. It's down to the particular cut and how we age it. We hang it for three weeks and that breaks down the fibre.'

'Isn't it going to be a bit high after three weeks?' I asked.

'No, sir. Hell, these days they put it in vacuum bags, but you don't get the same flavour. We used to age it on the carcass itself. You'd get a little mould on it, but, hell, that didn't hurt. I've eaten handfuls of it. But hey, boy, you ever hear how Kansas City steak should be eaten?' No, I hadn't. 'Raw, that's how.'

'God, that sounds disgusting.' Jay smiled tolerantly. What was this heathen doing in his office?

A dewy look filled his eyes. 'Fellow named Harold Dugdale ran a packing house up the river in St Joseph. I used to visit him once in a while and he'd take me out to his cooler. He always had a dozen or more loins hanging there just for friends and his own personal use. Temperature right at thirty-three Fahrenheit. He'd find one with a little bit of scum on it, and he'd take out a knife, cut a piece and say, "Eat it." It was a little green, but it was one of the most beautiful things known to man.'

So there weren't many vegetarians in Kansas City? Jay coughed as if a lump of Hereford gristle had stuck in his throat. 'Vegetarians? Hell, that don't amount to anything. We've eaten meat since the beginning of time. And if it's bad for me, how come I've lived so long?'

Before I left, I asked Jay how old he was. 'Well, I'm a day older than you. But if it all goes well and the Lord is willing I'll be eighty come spring.' I wished him a happy birthday.

'Hell,' he concluded, 'I'm going to hang one on that day.'

All this talk about mouldy steak had *not* made me hungry. I left the stockyards and motored up to Quality Hill, a tree-lined area of middle-class apartments on a high bluff overlooking the Missouri. It was on this hill that Lewis and Clark camped on their return journey from the wilderness. Here their men shot an elk and gathered custard apples, or paw-paws. I looked at the view while I lunched modestly on a bar of caramel-coated peanuts.

The Big Muddy curved and buckled below me like a piece of

discarded rust-brown ribbon. After the majestic sweeps of water through the valleys of countryside Missouri, she now looked dismally functional, like any river in any big city. Her grey banks were stacked with old warehouses and quaysides. A few wisps of gritty, industrial smoke spurted from factory chimneys. I could see no river traffic. A replica steamboat, complete with black, jagged smokestacks, the venue for dinner dances and drunken evenings afloat, sat sadly alone waiting for next summer's season.

From this height the river looked quite tranquil as it meandered muddily past the mouth of the Kansas River. But it was not always so.

The dam system that now keeps the waters in check was not completed until the 1950s. Before then, the river went on a rampage each spring as the snowmelt rushed down from the Rockies. No matter how hard people tried to corral the Missouri, it always broke out again.

1951 saw a flood that caused horrific damage throughout Kansas City. Everyone has a story about the Great Flood. Jay Dillingham remembered the water twenty-six inches deep on the *second* floor of the stockyards building. There was five feet of mud in the corridors. 'Water damned near tore everything out of the offices,' he recalled. 'We had had floods before, but that kinda put the icing on the cake. They got a lot more dams built pretty damned quick.'

I was learning why the Missouri was held in so much respect. Now it was time to leave the security of the land and meet this cruel leviathan for myself.

Three

They looked like a bunch of cut-throats. They had chipped teeth and scarves wrapped pirate-style around their heads. Grease-ingrained biceps exploded from ragged T-shirts and their oil-smeared jeans would have embarrassed a Hell's Angel. They were Missouri rivermen and they gave the impression that they could wrestle bears . . . and come off best.

Welcome to the crew of the *Dan C. Burnett*.

After numerous phone calls to various shipping agents I had managed to hitch a lift on one of the few vessels still plying the Missouri. Having been working the stretch of river south of Kansas City, the *Dan C. Burnett* was headed for Omaha. It was midnight when I eventually met her at a remote riverside fuelling depot on the eastern edge of Kansas City.

The *Dan C.* was lashed by steel cables like a giant cat's cradle to eight container barges: an eighth of a mile of rust-red steel with the acreage of a football field. What she might have lacked in dignity she made up in pure bulk. She wallowed like an elderly walrus in the murky, moonlit water, the lights from her wheelhouse casting a dim glow onto the riverbank. Her generators growled softly in the darkness.

Danny, the first mate, welcomed me aboard. He grabbed my bag and strode swiftly up the narrow gangplank. The wood was slippery. I followed gingerly. We reached the deck and I stumbled over a mess of ropes and cables.

Danny gave me a lecture. 'What we're on now, what we live on and what pushes the cargo is called the push-boat, or shove-boat.

45

Never call it a barge. Really gets me angry when people call it a barge.'

I promised faithfully that I'd always refer to it as the push-boat. I had no intention of getting on the wrong side of Danny. He had the look of one of those sinister gun-fighting preacher men in a spaghetti Western: a long, thin physique, piercing sapphire blue eyes, and shoulder-length hair. He wore grimy jeans and a thermal vest that after countless washes had ceased even to attempt to be white. He continued: 'The barges are the containers out in front. We call 'em a tow from the old days when they got towed behind.'

In the tiny mess-room below decks some of the crew were snatching a few minutes' rest while the *Dan C. Burnett* took on 10,000 gallons of diesel in preparation for her journey upstream. They were a surly lot. They lolled on bent metal chairs with their feet up on tables littered with crushed Coke cans. On the scratched lino floor was a brown-stained wastepaper bin that doubled up as a spittoon. In the background a television crackled with the canned laughter of a second-rate sit-com.

Danny introduced his colleagues. First came Fox, an evil-looking character in oil-smeared overalls with a baseball cap worn back to front. Then Ricky the engineer, squat and chubby, and digging the dirt from his fingernails with a penknife. Then Chris, the morose, moody type, gently slapping a flashlight against his palm as if it were a cosh. He spat a chew of tobacco into the bin.

Finally, there was Wayne. And Wayne looked terrifying. He resembled the classic circus strongman, with a thick red ribbon of beard that sprouted from beneath a triple chin. He was enormous and he was reading a publication called *Gun Magazine*.

None of them said a word. I attempted to break the ice. 'Hi, I'm Peter. I'm from England.' A pause, followed by what can only be described as a collective grunt. Danny turned to me almost apologetically. 'Don't expect much from them,' he mumbled. We left the room and climbed the stairs to the wheelhouse. A few minutes later we cast off and headed sluggishly upriver towards the lights of central Kansas City.

After the weary crew, the *Dan C. Burnett*'s pilot, Pat Gerlach, presented a picture of go-getting enthusiasm. He greeted me like a long-lost friend and announced he was delighted I had joined the boat.

Pat was a short, stocky extrovert. He was in his mid-thirties and wore a loud check shirt. Whenever something amused him he clapped his hands loudly and yelled, 'Whoo-ee!' He came from an Arkansas farming family, but the river was his life. He had started out as a deckhand and had worked his way up to become one of the youngest pilots on the Missouri.

Pat warned that we could be in for a rough ride. There was a good chance of running aground. Due to the shortage of water on the Missouri the river is open to shipping for little more than six months a year. The season had only just opened and the *Dan C. Burnett* was the first vessel of the year to test the waters on the Kansas City–Omaha stretch.

'Guess you could say we're guinea pigs.' Pat adjusted his cap. It bore the logo of Arkansas Game and Fish Conservation. He concentrated hard. From the wheelhouse window we could see the crew scatter on to the deck. They cast off the mooring ropes. The miner's lamps on their safety helmets threw eerie shadows across the containers. Pat eased forward the throttles on the two 4000 hp engines. The hydraulics gave a ghostly hiss and we moved sluggishly upriver at three miles per hour, our path lit by a powerful zion searchlight on the wheelhouse roof.

Pat softly hummed a few bars of 'Greensleeves' to ease the tension. As the lights of downtown came up ahead he moved onto a more spirited rendition of 'Kansas City Here I Come'. I settled back in my seat and wondered what the Big Muddy, one of the world's most feared waterways, had in store for me.

'Yeah, guinea pigs. That's what we are.' Pat gently tugged the steering arms and the *Dan C.* slowly changed course. He kept one eye on the depth sounder. 'Our draught is about seven feet and the river bottom's about nine.' He noticed the look of horror on my face. 'That's right, Pete. Just two feet between steel and mud. And it's a pretty long ole tow. This is the biggest I'd want to bring up in this water. More than that and you run right out of room. Yeah, could be a mighty adventuresome trip. Whoo-ee!'

'What's the worst that could happen?' I asked.

'We could hit a sandbar and break a couple of barges off. Anything worse than that would be a total disaster. Like we sink. Whoo-ee!' Pat spluttered with laughter. I am not sure that I found this awfully amusing. Missouri pilots seemed to have a bizarre sense of humour.

Pat had just returned from leave in Arkansas where he was building a new house. This was his first trip in three months. He had rejoined the *Dan C.* only that morning. 'I'm a little rusty. Takes time to get used to this big ole boat reacting.' He delicately touched the steering arm that controlled the four rudders. 'You never forget how to drive it, but it takes a little bit of work to get good again.'

'Thanks for telling me,' I replied. 'Shall I put the lifejacket on now?' Pat emitted a roar of laughter that ended in a coughing fit.

Each barge contained dry fertilizer bound for the corn fields of Nebraska and Iowa. After they had been emptied they would be cleaned and refilled with grain for the return trip. The total cargo amounted to 10,000 tons, the equivalent of 400 truckloads.

'If the river's good to you, you can move a hell of a lot of stuff at one time,' Pat explained. 'That's the big advantage. But things ain't what they used to be. In the last eight years the water levels have been real bad and the towing industry has really gone down. The railroads took a lot of our freight. It should be cheaper to use the river than road or rail, but the goddam government subsidises the railroads.

'They don't have the same problems on the Mississippi. It's not treacherous. There are more boats and you can work quicker so the towing rates are lower. The Mississippi's like an interstate compared to the Missouri. We're just an old dirt road. Yeah, an old dirt road. Even at maximum there are probably no more than ten boats on the Missouri at one time. We're becoming a rarity, a dying breed. The next few years is gonna be a big fight. Might have to get me a new job.'

The crew rotated in six hour shifts. Some were asleep down below, including the *Dan C. Burnett*'s captain, Vic Thompson.

'A fine man, Vic. From down Louisiana way,' Pat said. 'Though an Englishman like you might have a trouble understanding his accent. Guess it's a little broad.'

The lights of Kansas City were around us. The riverbank was a jumble of decaying quaysides and the corroded hulks of abandoned sand barges, the victims of one grounding too many. They were half-sunk into the mud and speckled with graffiti.

There were many wrecks round here, including the remains of steamboats from the last century. This was Kansas River Bend, a particularly bad part of the river. 'Us pilots treat it with great respect,' Pat went on. 'There's this great hairpin turn. The Kansas is dumping sand out in the Missouri making sandbars. Then there's the current that can push you right on to one of them. The stream's running against us at nine miles per hour and the wind doesn't help neither.' Strong easterly gusts were buffeting the boat. 'It can be a bitch. Lose your concentration for a minute and it'll blow your ass right back round. You gotta compensate. Then the channel can change overnight. The US Coastguard patrol boats put down marker buoys and twenty-four hours later they can mean nothing. It's what we call a lot of variables. Yeah, that's the word. Variables.

'Luckily we've got radar so we can spot trouble. But those steam-boats didn't have no hope. I got this theory that the first boat up the Missouri got to this bend and crashed. Then the people said, 'Fuck it, we'll build the town here.' And that was Kansas City. Whoo-ee!'

We left Kansas City under a rail bridge. There was some question over whether the boat would clear it. Pat cut the engines and we passed underneath with only a foot to spare. He grinned. 'Close thing. Wouldn't have looked too good on my record. Been on the boat hardly twenty-four hours and I tear the goddam top off.'

'Don't you ever get bored?' I asked.

'Hell no. Always something going on and the pay's good. Gets a little lonely sometimes though.' The crew worked a month on, fifteen days off. Pat saw little of his wife and family during the season. 'A month's a long time to be away from home. Do you have a family?'

'No, but I've got a girlfriend, who's pretty pissed off that I'm away so long.'

'Yeah. Women are kinda funny about that sort of thing.'

Once on board, the crew were stuck there until their next leave. It was constant work with no breaks. Excursions into towns were forbidden. 'It's strange because you're so near to civilization and yet so far away. Like being in prison.' There was also a strict alcohol ban. As Pat said, 'Boats like these are dangerous places. Wouldn't be too good if I was up here all fuelled up with tea 'n' Scotch.'

Outside the cosy warmth of the wheelhouse the temperature was around freezing. Earlier in the evening there had been a thin splattering of rain. Sheet ice now covered the steel decks.

'It must be dangerous for the crew,' I said.

'Certainly wouldn't want to fall between the barges.' Pat was now swivelling the searchlight to pick out the channel. 'Makes you smart a little. Years ago a friend of mine fell between two barges. Luckily he had enough sense to turn sideways. It hurt him bad, but it didn't crush him. Then there was another guy, Billy, who fell off the head of the barges and went under 'em. He popped up again further back and hung on. His lungs were full of water, but he made it. We got him out and said, "Billy, you all right?" And he said, "Yeah, I think so. But I'm tired." Then he smoked a cigarette, but he couldn't puff it 'cos his lungs were so full of water. Whoo-ee! Billy was a lucky guy.'

I found my cabin. A sign above the door said it was for the use of guests only. I had expected the worst. At best I thought I'd be sharing a sweaty hole with three others, but I was astounded by what I saw: *en suite* shower, fluffy brown carpet, and guest towels and a bar of soap laid out on the bunk. I was only reminded that I was on a Missouri riverboat by the lifejacket on the wall and the monotonous grumble of the engines. They slowly lulled me into sleep.

By this stage of the journey, Lewis and Clark were getting to grips with the wilderness. They were in reasonable spirits although some of the party were suffering from sunstroke and boils. Clark's spelling and punctuation was as eccentric as ever. On 14 July, he reported how a vicious gale nearly upturned the boat: 'The storm . . . would have thrown her up on the Sand Island dashed to pics in an Instant, had not the party leeped out on the Leeward Side and kept her off with the assistance of the ancker & Cable . . . In this situation we Continued about 40 Minits. when the Storm Sudenly Seased and the river become Instancetaniously as Smoth As Glass.'

All good pioneering stuff. But if the expedition was yet to provide the maps for the settlers of the future, then the transport for the great westward expansion was already in the development stages.

On 20 July 1786, a gunsmith and clock mender named John Fitch launched an extraordinary craft on the Delaware River in New Jersey. Bearing a resemblance to an overgrown beetle, it was a small skiff with a jumble of chains attached to paddles. The crowd on the shore jeered as this ludicrous object juddered and jolted through the waves. It was the first steamboat, and John Fitch was its inventor.

The steam revolution took a long time to grab America's imagination. And it was not until 1819 that the first steam-driven vessel appeared on the Missouri. It took fifteen more years before steamboats were making regular journeys up the river.

The typical Missouri steamboat was 130 feet long. It was equipped with stern-wheels and was flat-bottomed so that it could navigate in exceptionally shallow waters. Unlike the Mississippi steamboats, which were all velvet and chandeliers, the Missouri River packets were crudely equipped. They befitted the status of their passengers – usually a raggle-taggle collection of trappers, fortune hunters and Indian traders. And passengers were forced to endure frequent stops while the Big Muddy's mud – 120 tons per million gallons of water – was cleaned from the boilers.

'No craft on Western waters, if upon any waters of the globe, displayed more majesty and beauty, or filled the mind with more interesting reflections, than these picturesque vessels of the early days in the boundless prairies of the West.' This was the Missouri steamboat, according to Hiram Chittenden in his 1902 epic, *The American Fur Trade of the Far West*. 'In the midst of this virgin wilderness a noble steamboat appears, its handsome form standing high above the water in fine outline against the verdure of the shore; its lofty chimneys pouring forth clouds of smoke in the atmosphere unused to such intrusion, and its progress against the impetuous current exhibiting an extraordinary display of power.'

These 'fire canoes', as the awestruck Indians dubbed them, were magnificent craft. But they were also very dangerous with an average life expectancy of little more than five months. Even in that short time they could make a profit, such was the cheapness of their construction.

Captains often pushed their boats' boilers to their limits. They were inclined to explode without warning, killing anyone unfortunate enough to be in the vicinity. By 1850 there had been at least 150 major steamboat disasters. Around 1400 people died after being hit by flying wreckage or scalding water. This gave rise to the much-repeated black joke that passengers who had not yet paid their fares were put in the stern of the vessel where they would be in least danger from explosion. If you were really unlucky, your bunk was next to the cages of mewling cats on their way to rat-hunting duty at the cavalry forts.

The 'impetuous current' was also a perpetual hazard. Chittenden recalled an incident involving a boat called *The Miner* that ran into trouble near Sioux City, Iowa: 'The whirl of the water was so swift that the center of the eddy was nearly twelve feet below its circumference. The boat was trying to pull itself by with a line when it was caught by the eddy, swung out in the stream, whirled violently around and careened over until the river flowed right across the lower deck.'

The other problem was food. Steamboat fare was unremittingly dull, consisting almost entirely of fat pork, beans, corn and coffee, and brightened up by the occasional flapjack. By the 1840s most boats employed hunters to supplement meals with game. While the vessel tied up at night and the passengers slept, the hunter would go off after deer, duck and buffalo.

The *Dan C. Burnett* did not have the services of a hunter, but she did have an excellent cook.

I awoke at 8 am. After a shower I followed the smell of baking bread down to the galley. I was too late for the crew's breakfast, which had been two hours earlier, but Marilyn the cook fixed me coffee and doughnuts.

Marilyn was like a mother to the crew. She was a quiet, matronly woman in her sixties with grey hair, spectacles and an air of serenity. At mealtimes she would sit at the head of the table saying little. She would push food towards her boys and mildly scold them if they did not eat enough.

Her ex-husband was a riverman, as was her son Tracy, the *Dan C. Burnett*'s second engineer. Marilyn had worked the Missouri for seventeen years. 'I don't know any different life,' she explained. 'Cooks get paid so badly on dry land, but you get decent money on the boats. I wouldn't trade 'em for the world.' Did the crew ever give her a hard time? 'Nah, they're like a big family to me. I get mad once in a while but they're mostly good boys.'

The day was dull and overcast. We were making four miles per hour. Through the galley window I could see the bank slowly drifting past. I remembered a remark of Pat's from the previous evening: 'You know you're not going too fast when the tractors in the fields are outrunning you.' The muddy shore was a chaos of rotting logs and twisted roots. Above the banks rose thick plantations of cottonwood trees. The autumn winds had long since scattered their leaves, leaving twisted branches swinging listlessly in the wind. Here and there the cottonwood was broken by the skeletal frames of sycamore, and willow boughs lazily reached down to touch the freezing river. I swallowed a couple of doughnuts and went up to the wheelhouse.

Pat had left his shift. Vic Thompson, the captain, was at the helm. I introduced myself and we began talking. And for the first half an hour I understood virtually nothing that he said.

Vic's Louisiana accent was as thick as the Big Muddy. I could just pick out a few 'Lordy me's' and 'I'll be darned', but that was about it. (I mentioned this to Marilyn later and she cheered me up no end. '*You* find him difficult to understand? I've worked with him five years and *I* don't understand him.')

Vic wiped the sleep from his eyes and concentrated hard. He was fifty-two but looked older. Nearly thirty troublesome years on the river had taken their toll. He was quite short with a well-sated paunch that attempted to burst out of a creased blue denim shirt. The belt around his sagging trousers was stretched to its limit. He chain-smoked cigarettes and spoke in between puffs with a slight stutter. He had a gloriously vague manner about him.

'D'ya sleep well? Yeah? Well, I'll be darned. That's good. Damn, that's good you slept well. First time I ever got on one of these here push-boats, took two or three days before I could sleep.' Vic turned away, unzipped his trousers and peed into an old tin. He kept one eye on the river and the other on the tin. 'Wouldn't like to crash the boat just because I've drunk too much coffee.'

Vic had been a Missouri pilot for nearly twenty years. He had started as a deckhand long before that. 'This is a mighty ratty, raggedy river. Shucks, when we get a lot of rain an' all this river jumps up in an hour, and then it's pretty dangerous. Sometimes you get big ole logs coming down and you tie up real good and let it run by. Mebbe two days. Sometimes a week before it runs out. But it's real low now. Lowest I ever seen it.' He paused, and added with great feeling, 'I've been on the Mississippi, but the Missouri has my respect. Never know what she's gonna do to you.'

He was a born riverman. 'Before I got married my wife said she didn't like my being away so I quit the river. Worked three or four jobs in factories an' all but didn't like it. She told me you want to go back on the boats ain't you, and I said yes. I was just sitting around getting in her hair. Been back since '69 and never quit since. I'll get me another five years in and then I'm off. Got two sons to get through college and then I'll retire. Seemed like they'd just growed up overnight on me. That's the worst thing about working out here. You're gone from home so much.'

A flight of duck took off in our path. The birds flew a few hundred yards and settled on a sandbank. The day showed no sign of improving. It began to rain. Out on the tow the deckhands washed down the deck. Vic poured me a coffee from his thermos and launched into his Missouri horror stories.

'It's the cables you wanna watch out for.' He pointed through the wheelhouse window to the hawsers that joined the barges together. 'They get real tight and if you go aground they can snap. Can whip right through the wheelhouse. The barges rear up like a bronco. The first thing a deckhand has to do is get away from the rigging or it'll hit him.

'Few years back I was on watch just up from Kansas City and I got grounded. A cable popped and the whiplash caught one of the boys. He had to have his leg off.' Vic's hands briefly left the controls. He hitched up his trousers like a small boy. An expression of resigned sadness clouded his face. 'That's the worst thing that's happened to me out here. It's sort of hard to take. You think of a thousand ways you could have avoided it. It bothered me for an awful long time. I really hated myself, but I don't know what else I could have done.' Vic looked at me and sighed. 'It's the old story. It's you against the river, and sometimes the river wins.'

He pointed at four red buttons on the control panel. They activated an emergency release system in the event of going aground. 'It lets the tow go and you pick 'em up later. You can always get a barge back, but you can't get lives back. Yeah, this can be a dangerous place to work.'

'And that explains why there's no alcohol allowed on board,' I remarked.

'Right,' Vic said. 'A man's got a job to do and if he's all stoned out you can't depend on that man if you get into trouble.'

He began a long reminiscence about the old days. 'When I started twenty-five years ago the river people used to drink real hard. People used to get boozed up on shore. A lot of towns didn't like to see the river people. Police would see you comin' over the levee and they'd know you'd been on the boat for ten days. They'd let you get a couple of beers and then they'd nail you for being public drunk. Reckon we had a hell of a wild look in our eyes.'

'And did you cause trouble?' I asked.

'Hell, no.' Vic winked. 'Always somebody else who'd start it.'

Vic touched the steering arms and eased the boat around another bend. To the east a lone freight train clattered down the track that ran alongside the river.

'Yeah, wild 'n' woolly, that was how it was. And you should've seen some of the captains. I was cleaning the wheelhouse one day and the captain passed out at the wheel. He was on his second bottle of whisky and he kinda keeled over. Put the boat right in the bank.

'I was pretty green back in them days. Another time I was getting on with him and I reached out to pick up his suitcase and all it did was rattle. When we opened it up he had no clothes, just bottles. He was loaded. So the owner said, "Captain, why don't you wait a coupla days to straighten out a little?" He was one of the best captains, who's ever handled a boat. But he wouldn't last now, I can tell you.'

Vic was well into his memories. 'Good ole boys some of those captains. I remember one who always complained because his coffee was cold by the time I got it up to the wheelhouse. He complained once too many and I thought I'd fix him. I put the cup in the stove and heated it up real good. Then I got my heavy leather gloves and carried it up to him. I said to him, "Better watch it Captain, this is a hot cup of coffee." He said, "Hell, boy, you ain't never brought me a hot cup of coffee yet." And he grabbed it. Burned right through his hand. He was mad as hell, but he never did complain again. Guess he thought it was funny 'cos he told everyone up and down the river 'bout it. Lordy, I've had fun on this ole river.'

At midday Pat appeared from his slumbers and took over his watch. I went below with Vic for lunch. The crew were helping themselves to huge wedges of meatloaf. I noticed that everyone ate very slowly, savouring the moment. Meals were sacred affairs that broke the monotony of the journey.

I tried talking to the deckhands. I soon realised that my first impressions had been wrong. They were not the miserable pirates that I'd been led to believe. The conversation was admittedly rather stilted at first, but during the next couple of days I was to discover that the tough-guy manner was little more than a front.

I settled down on my chair with a plate of pork chops and sweet potatoes. Ricky, the engineer, was subjecting the frightening-looking Wayne to an unmerciful ribbing.

Wayne had joined the boat only a week earlier. He had spent five years in the US Navy, but this was his first experience of rivers. He had presumed that life on a Missouri push-boat would be similar to that on the aircraft carrier USS *Saratoga*. So he had arrived complete with a set of smart clothes – including a tuxedo – for going ashore at towns.

Ricky thought this hysterically funny. 'Didn't know you were going to spend thirty days in your greasy blue jeans, did you?'

Wayne cut himself a third helping of chocolate cake. He blushed. 'How was I to know we wouldn't be allowed off the boat? People don't tell you nothing before you come aboard.'

I sympathised. 'I didn't know what to expect. Frankly, when I saw you lot last night I thought I'd end up getting my throat cut for a dollar.' They all laughed.

'Guess we looked pretty bad,' Wayne said. 'But I don't go looking for trouble; I'm not as tough as I look. Keep myself to myself.'

Later, when we'd got to know each other, Wayne told me about the last fight he'd had. It was a year ago. He'd been on a date in a bar when a drunk sat down next to him. 'Sat right down on my tux. I asked him very politely to move. The guy said, "Do you want to get hit?" I didn't wait for him to hit me and he ended up in hospital with eighteen stitches. I felt pretty bad about it, but these things have got to be sorted out quickly. No good wasting time.' All this was said with an angelic look on face as if he was about to kiss his grandma goodnight.

Lunch over, Vic retired to his cabin. I climbed back up to the wheelhouse to keep Pat company. The afternoon drifted on. Then Pat decided to liven things up.

'Wanna drive?' He left his seat and indicated that I should take the controls.

'Do you think this is wise?' I asked.

'Why not? Like I told you, just remember there's only two feet between the boat and the river.'

'Thanks a bundle.'

The steering was surprisingly sensitive. I managed quite well for five minutes. Then I began drifting towards the sandbars.

'What the hell do I do now?'

Pat wasn't in the slightest bit concerned. He hooted with laughter. 'Just tease her back, don't steer too hard. Just gradual movements. Let the weight of the boat pull you over. You got so much current out there if you let her swing you'll break the cables. It's difficult, but it's a nice feeling, ain't it?'

I wasn't so sure. My previous river boating experiences had been confined to larky weekends on the English canals. A million-dollar, 960-foot barge-load of fertilizer was an entirely different proposition.

The boat swung alarmingly. The current tried to force me into the bank. I couldn't take my eyes off the river for a moment for fear of hitting something. Pat twittered on.

'Bit more rudder. Hear that vibrating noise? That's the propellors sucking mud.' Vibrating? What was the man talking about? The whole boat was juddering like hell!

'I hope we don't run out of water,' Pat continued. 'Wouldn't look too good on my record if you ran this ole boat aground. Whoo-ee!' I managed for another thirty minutes until my nerves could stand it no longer. 'Well, Pete, you ain't done too bad, but I think you's gonna crash us.' And with that Pat retook the helm. He gently tweaked the rudder controls and readjusted the throttle. Within thirty seconds the tow ceased to swing and we were back on a steady course. The engines settled back into a comfortable hum.

And so we plodded on up the Big Muddy. That night I went to bed early. I woke at 5.30 am. After Marilyn's breakfast of bacon and eggs I joined Vic and Danny in the wheelhouse. The morning mist was rising from the river. We were now nearly 100 miles from Kansas City. In the night we had passed the town of St Joseph.

St Joseph, established as a fur trading post in 1826, is thick with history. The rivertown was home to that Western legend, the Pony Express. 'Wanted,' ran the newspaper advertisements, 'Young, slim, energetic men under eighteen. They must be consummate horsemen, ready to risk their lives every day. Orphans preferred.' This privately-run $5-a-letter mail service, whose fearless young riders included the teenaged Buffalo Bill, was the only link between Missouri and California. But it lasted only twenty months. Four days after the first transcontinental telegraph line opened in October 1861, the Pony Express went out of business.

Twenty years later, St Joseph hit the headlines again, this time for rather more sinister reasons. For this was the place where the outlaw Jesse James finally met his maker.

3 April 1882. It is a warm morning and Jesse is in the sitting room of his hide-out planning yet another bank raid with two of his gang, Charles Ford and Bob Ward. Jesse is aged thirty-four and responsible for the deaths of at least sixteen people. He has hidden his guns so as not to arouse the neighbours' suspicions. Jesse turns away to look for something. His cronies seize this opportunity and draw their revolvers. Ward shoots Jesse in the back of his head. He falls to the floor dead.

Ward and Ford leave the house and attempt to collect the $10,000 reward. Instead they are charged with murder. They are pardoned shortly before they are due to hang, but within two years Ford's conscience gets the better of him. He commits suicide. Ward is killed eleven years later in a bar-room brawl in Colorado.

St Joseph – and, indeed, America as a whole – still takes Jesse James very seriously. His former home, a small clapboard house, is one of the town's big tourist attractions. You can still see the dent in the floor where the dying Jesse struck his head. In the wall is the hole where the bullet ended up. (Although over the years souvenir hunters have chipped away pieces of wall so it now looks like a small bazooka shell has blasted through it.)

On display in the house is a knife with which Jesse was planning to slaughter his seventeenth victim. By the end of his short life he had developed a taste for slitting bank cashiers' throats *after* he had robbed the bank. I felt that this was not very sporting, and, as irritating as bank cashiers may be, hardly in the tradition of a local hero. Do in the manager if you must.

The US flag flies outside the house thereby giving James some sort of official recognition. And in these violent days of Los Angeles street gangs it baffled me that the American public – let alone a morally crusading Republican government – would want to be associated with such a homicidal maniac.

I put this to Danny and Vic. Danny said I had got it all wrong. It turned out he was a keen amateur historian and had read much about the gunfighting days of the Wild West.

'Jesse was a sort of Robin Hood figure, who helped poor farmers,' he declared. 'If a bank was going to repossess your farm because you hadn't paid your debts, Jesse would give you the money to pay the mortgage. Then he'd go and rob the bank and get his money back and more. A lot of people sympathised with him because of the way the sheriffs came after him, blowing up houses and the like. He'd fought for the South in the Civil War and people thought the law was picking on him. The cult grew from there.'

'Okay,' I replied. 'But I'd hardly put him in the Robin Hood category. After all, Robin didn't go around indiscriminately butchering the Sheriff of Nottingham's pikemen.'

Danny looked grim. He didn't want to argue this one. 'Well, he was like Robin Hood to start with. Don't know what went wrong. Guess he went a little crazy and ended up a mad-dog killer.'

We changed the subject. Vic wanted to talk about girls. During the summer the crew were frequently subjected to young ladies on the banks brazenly flashing their breasts.

'Man, titties everywhere! Now that's what I call real tough.' Vic readjusted his trousers. 'They know we're stuck on the boat and there's nothing we can do but look. There's always a big tussle over who's going to get the binoculars.'

At night the banks were alive with courting couples. 'Use the spotlight to catch 'em. Dozens of them making out on picnic tables.' Vic was in his element. 'One time I light up this pair real good. Ain't got a stitch on. The guy looks mad and grabs a hunting rifle. Man, I turned out that light quick.' Vic bellowed with laughter and gave a phlegmy cough.

'And d'ya remember the hermit?' Danny asked.

Vic smiled at the memory. The hermit was a man who lived in a cliffside cave above the river at Atchison, a town we had passed the previous evening. 'Haven't seen him in years,' Vic went on. 'He'd come down the bank with no clothes on. Man, he was well hung. Looked like he had a third leg. We had a woman cook on the boat and that old girl would be out on deck so quick. Couldn't keep her eyes off of him.'

But the summer months could be dangerous. Vic became serious. 'Everybody's out in their little boats drinking. They get half-brained and it's a bad deal, really is. Never hit a boat, though I've come mighty close.

'Remember one Fourth of July down near St Louis. This cat came by water skiing. The boat whips right in front of me and he falls right off the skis. I call down to the engine room and we try to stop. At the last minute before we hit him the little ski boat runs in and drags him out. I hit the bank and rammed a hole in one of the barges. Spooked me bad. I guarantee people can be real stupid in boats. Need the law they got in Oklahoma. Get caught drunk in a boat and they take it from you.'

We saw no other boats all day. Vic and Pat changed over yet again – six hours on, six hours off. The sky became dark and the first few drops of rain began to fall. It was turning into a miserable evening.

It was lonely on the river. I was beginning to understand how Lewis and Clark must have felt. The state of Kansas gave way to Nebraska. There was little sign of life in the sweeping ploughed fields that lay behind the choking lines of cottonwood: only a few isolated farmhouses and wooden barns in danger of collapse. We were heading into America's Great Plains, a vast spread of flat, open country that was to continue with relentless monotony until I reached Montana and the mountains.

It was raining hard by the time Vic took the evening watch. The rain pattered on the roof and streaked down the windows. The temperature dropped and the rain turned to ice. The deck became a skating rink. The deckhands, dressed in yellow oilskins, scattered bags of salt and sand to make the steel less slippery. We watched them from the cosy, smoky fug of the wheelhouse.

There was a sharp whiff of cold. The rain turned to snow. In the bright glare of the spotlight the flakes resembled bits of tinsel.

'Well, this is very Christmassy,' I said.

'Ha!' Vic snorted. 'It's Christmas come too late.'

And then the fog came. It descended with a frightening suddenness. 'Wall-to-wall carpet,' as Vic put it. Fog is the great enemy of the Missouri pilot. For as soon as the searchlight is unable to pick out the riverbanks and the lurking sandbars you must tie up and wait for the weather to improve.

By 10 pm we could go no further. Fog swirled around the wheelhouse creating unearthly shadows. What phantoms lurked here? Sherlock Holmes would have loved it. I could almost hear the Hound of the Baskervilles howling through the trees. Vic steered into the bank. The hydraulics gave a spectral hiss as he cut the engines. 'This can be a lonely part of the world when it's like this. I remember being up here when one of my children was born. We were completely cut off for three days.'

We sipped coffee and talked about anything to get our minds off the appalling weather. 'I really like your British actors.' Vic was a fan of the television series, *The Avengers*. 'Really liked that British gentleman of yours. What was he called? Patrick..?'

'McNee?' I offered.

'Yeah. And the girl. You know, the first one.'

We managed Diana Rigg and Joanna Lumley, but we simply couldn't manage the 'first one'. It took us over an hour – during which time we discussed David Niven, Peter Lawford and every James Bond movie ever made – before Vic remembered the name of Honor Blackman.

We were a few miles south of Brownville, home to one of America's many nuclear power stations. Through the fog we could see the sinister orange glow of the plant's perimeter lights.

'They patrol the hell out of those places, reckon they've got more guards than workers.'

Vic told me about an incident at another nuclear plant further upriver at Blair. He had narrowly escaped jail after a jolly little stunt went terribly wrong. It was a wonderfully anarchic story.

'I figured those lights were automatic. Like they came on when it got dark. Well, we came cruising past one night and I figured that if I played the searchlight on 'em I'd have a bit of fun. Lordy, those lights suddenly thought it was daytime. Went out one by one.

'Man, there must've been twenty guards, all came out with dogs an' all and they were hot! Rubbin' their eyes and thinking they're about to get hit by a bunch of terrorists. Damn, it was funny. Dogs were barking and people were running around mad as hell. Whole crew's in the wheelhouse and boy, were we laughing. Next day I knows about it. They got the name of the boat and I was in bad trouble. Police come aboard and tell me that it ain't funny to put out the lights at a nuclear power plant. They gave me the worst time of my life. Shit, I'm not going to do that again.'

I went down to the galley to raid Marilyn's chocolate chip cookie jar. Wayne and Fox were munching corned beef sandwiches. Fox was winding up Wayne about the 'green-eyed fog monster' that lurked in the mist outside.

Wayne wasn't having any of it. He might have been raised in

superstitious, small-town America, but after five years in the Navy he was wise to stories like this. Fox was disappointed. 'We had one boy who believed every word. He was terrified, wouldn't go out on the tow.'

New deckhands like Wayne were the constant butt of jokes.

The crew had already kidded him that one of his jobs was to stretch the cables – manually. It couldn't be long before they had him waterskiing behind the boat.

By 1 am we were underway again. I marvelled at Vic's piloting skills. As far as I was concerned it was still as foggy as ever. I could only just pick out the banks through the spotlight. The fog created the illusion that the shore was much closer than it really was.

Despite the immense mental strain of navigating in these conditions, Vic was a picture of cool. He had one eye on the depth sounder as we glided through the mist. I said that I admired him. 'That's mighty kind of you,' he replied. 'Reckon I'm only half-way crazy.'

We eventually reached Brownville where we were dropping off two barges. We tied up by a grain elevator. Vic lit a cigarette and slumped in his chair. He was shattered. 'Well, Pete' – he took a long drag of tobacco – 'now you know what the Missouri can do. You're seeing her when she ain't at her best. I guarantee it.'

Layer upon layer of fog came down around us. I went outside for a brief stroll around the push-boat's deck. The quayside loading floodlights shone dully through the grey swirl throwing their glow onto a ramshackle collection of concrete office buildings. Occasionally the fog would clear for a minute or two so that I could see the banks across the river. The gnarled, petrified stumps of cottonwood trees sprouting from the sandy shoreline appeared as blurred shapes through the gloom. The grim weather seemed to have quietened even the mighty Missouri. The stream was now slow. Ripples of icy water gently splashed and bounced against the tow.

It took twenty-four hours longer than expected to reach Omaha. Fog and snow continued to delay us. For the next two days I either slept, read on my bunk or sat chatting in the wheelhouse. Pat and I had some ridiculous conversations. I suppose it had something to do with the lack of anything much to do. Or, as Pat said, 'This river sends you a little weird after a while. Like, I've developed this bad phobia of spiders. In the summer they get through the wheelhouse roof and drop right down in front of my nose. We can be right in the middle of the river for thirty days and I don't know where those spiders come from. Man, I hate 'em.'

He had decided to call me Pizza. There is something in the way an Englishman with a public school accent says Peter that completely and utterly confuses the Americans. They could never get it right. 'Whadya say? Pizza?' So Pizza it was.

My last afternoon on the *Dan C.* we passed a flock of 1,000 pelicans bound for the migration grounds of Canada. As the boat approached, they took off, their black wing-tips languidly cutting through the hazy, grey sky, ungainly beaks stretched out before them. They flapped upriver, no sense of urgency to their flight.

Pat was very excited. His face lit up like a little boy's. He was a great wildlife enthusiast – 'I'm a country boy through and through; raised in the cottonfields; hate cities.' We had already seen geese, herons, cormorants and the occasional pheasant, but the pelicans made his day.

We talked about shooting. Whenever he was on leave Pat would spend hours prowling the woods around his home in search of game. He liked to eat deer. But nothing beat a good squirrel.

'Southern fried squirrel,' he declared. 'Now, Pizza, if you had everything laid out on a platter that would be the first thing I'd grab.' This absurd discourse began after we saw a red squirrel scamper up a cottonwood tree.

Pat gave me his gourmet guide to squirrel eating. He reckoned that grey squirrel tasted better than red. 'The grey's slyer, more difficult to hunt. It's best to kill 'em off hickory nuts and then they taste real good. Never touch 'em if they've been on cypress or pine. I fillet 'em, sprinkle 'em with seasoning salt and then throw 'em in flour and fry 'em in a skillet at a very low temperature with maybe quarter an inch of grease. Boy, they're delicious, real gamey. The heads and tongues are the best.'

I interrupted him. 'If I was going to eat squirrel I'd remove the head first. I think the idea of eating squirrel head would be a bit too much of a good thing.'

'Well, I guess you could pretty him up and stick a horse chestnut in his mouth.' Pat howled with laughter. 'The Old Testament says it's sacrilege to eat anything with paws. Gotta have a split hoof or chew its cud or something. So I guess I'm a heathen. Whoo-ee!'

We moved on to bullfrogs. Pat liked bullfrogs' legs for breakfast. 'But you gotta remember one thing. Never microwave a bullfrog. They explode real bad.' We both collapsed into laughter. Tears ran down our cheeks.

And so the black humour continued. By the end of the afternoon we had discussed everything from sautéed hedgehogs to whether Dobermann or Airedale would make the better pâté.

Vic took over the watch. We passed the grey, gaping mouth of the Platte river, one of the Missouri's major tributaries. Due to large amounts of sand and silt, the Platte long ago ceased being navigable to large craft.

Much of the Missouri's so-called muddiness comes from this river. 'A mile wide, an inch deep,' is how the writer Stanley Vestal described it. 'Stand it on end and it will reach to heaven, so muddy that the catfish have to come up to sneeze.'

The water was clearer above the Platte. The holiday homes along the banks became more frequent. We were getting closer to civilization. I went down to my cabin and packed my bag.

The *Dan C. Burnett* was heading on up to Sioux City, but Vic agreed to drop me off at Bellevue, one of the oldest towns in Nebraska, now a sprawling suburb a few miles south of Omaha. From there I would take a cab into Omaha city centre.

After four days I was sad to leave the boat. My initial misgivings about the crew had proved wrong. I had warmed to them. I did not envy their life. Despite high rates of pay, it was a tough job with constant pressure and only snatched bouts of sleep.

We reached Bellevue at midnight. Vic steered the boat into the bank and I said my goodbyes. As I left, he recommended a bar in Omaha where they used to serve something called a Pink Cadillac. I discovered later that it had closed years ago.

I walked to the end of the tow with Danny and Fox. They accompanied me down the gangplank. A road ran parallel to the river. There were street lights and a few houses in the distance. But otherwise, there was no sign of life.

A few minutes later a car drove by. We attempted to flag it down. The occupants took one look at us and sped past. I was not surprised.

With their unshaven faces, unkempt hair and greasy boiler suits Danny and Fox must have presented a threatening sight.

Five minutes later a police car rolled up out of the night. 'Fox, he's smelt you,' Danny jibed.

'Very funny,' Fox replied.

The black and white drew up by us. The officer cautiously wound down his window. His face was a picture of suspicion.

Danny explained I needed a lift into town. Suspicion turned to puzzlement. Finally the policeman agreed. I said goodbye to the two deckhands and got in next to a massive pump-action shotgun. On the way into Bellevue the cop introduced himself as Tim. And yes, he conceded, this was the first time he'd met an Englishman getting off a barge tow on a deserted Missouri riverbank at midnight.

'You've come from *where*?' Tim asked.

'That's right. Kansas City.'

'Wow. Never realized there was still commercial river traffic up here.'

Tell that to Vic and the crew, I thought. Oh yes, they'd really appreciate that.

Tim dropped me at an all-night grocery store in Bellevue. Inside a couple of girls were giggling over pornographic magazines by the newspaper rack. They were being eyed up by a sleepy, spotty assistant slouched behind the counter.

I announced I had just arrived via river from Kansas City and could I use the phone to call a cab. My English accent shook Spotty from his slumbers. He looked at me with wide-eyed surprise – the little green men syndrome all over again. I thought of all those Western movies. It was wonderful. I felt like the stranger who's just ridden into town.

Four

Unkind folk call Omaha 'a cornfield with lights'. You will hear jokes about backwoods hicks, who have made their fortunes in this prairie city. They move into $250,000 houses in leafy, lakeside suburbs. But the farming instinct is so deeply inbred that they will buy a tractor and replace the flower beds with rows of corn. Then they will turn the garden into a hay field. What pleasing view they might have had from their terrace is now obscured by huge round bales.

Now that I had left the *Dan C. Burnett* I rented another car. It was a hard slog finding a vehicle that I could eventually drop off at Great Falls, Montana, the final town on my itinerary. Hiring a car in America is not always easy. The companies all have different rates and it can take great patience finding the best deal.

I tried them all. I rang National: they wouldn't let me drop a car out of Nebraska. Nor would Thrifty. The girl at Hertz refused to understand my accent.

'I'd like to hire a car and drop it off at Great Falls.'

'Where?'

'Great Falls, Montana.'

'Can you spell that?'

'G-R-E-A-T F-A-L-L-S.'

'I'm sorry sir, I don't understand you.'

'Great Falls – as in bloody great waterfall.'

'Water what?'

'Arghh!'

I eventually settled for Budget who came up with a reasonable rate and had an operator who had heard an English accent before, even if it was only in Sherlock Holmes movies. I went to pick up the vehicle. There were about thirty cars in Budget's parking lot, twenty-nine of which appeared to be of American manufacture. They gave me the thirtieth – another white Toyota, the same model, the same throttle-you-slowly seat belts. I was developing a complex. Was there something in my manner that made rentacar people believe I would only drive a Japanese car?

I spent my first day in Omaha recovering from my days on the *Dan C. Burnett*. My head still reverberated with the relentless shudder of the diesel engines. I pottered around the Old Market area, which lay a few blocks from my hotel. A skin of snow lay on the freezing sidewalks. Once home to a thriving meat-packing industry, the Old Market's warehouses spent many neglected years before being tarted up during the Eighties. The market buildings were now an enclave of snazzy bars and antique emporia selling everything from battered trumpets to 1930s Coca Cola bottles.

In one of the many secondhand bookshops I bought a nineteenth-century etiquette and sex manual. It was a well-thumbed little volume titled *Safe Counsel*, packed with hellfire and damnation warnings. For example, Wasp Waists: 'Marrying small waists is attended with consequences scarcely less disastrous than rich and fashionable girls. Am amply developed chest is a sure indication of a naturally vigorous constitution; while small waists indicate small and feeble vital organs, a delicate constitution, sickly offspring, and a short life.' And for 'curing' masturbation, coyly described by the authors as 'the secret habit', parents should make their children 'hoe the garden or work on the farm . . . and if the patient is weak and very much emaciated, cod liver oil is an excellent remedy.'

That evening I tried the bars to see what Omaha had in the way of conversationalists. In a place called Mr Toad's I was buttonholed by a man called Eddie. He was standing alone at the bar swilling Guinness.

Eddie was in his late sixties. He wore a bobble hat over a boyish face. Our conversation got off to a rip-roaring start. 'So you're from England,' he said. 'Hey, tell me one thing. Do English hookers still fuck standing up?'

'Er, I beg your pardon?'

Eddie had been stationed in Britain during the war. He was

referring to the old urban myth that whores could not be prosecuted if they attended to their clients while remaining upright.

'I've absolutely no idea,' I added.

'Sure made us laugh at the time.' Eddie wasn't letting this one drop. 'You could tell how long a guy had been in England from how bad his watch was scratched. You know, all that screwing up 'gainst stone walls.'

Eddie was keen to share his wartime reminiscences. 'I was with the armoured division in '43 when the goddam invasion started. Can't remember where. They kept us out in the boondocks, all goddam mud 'n' shit and wouldn't let us out. We had so much equipment that the British Isles must have sunk six inches.'

Eddie lowered his voice to a conspiratorial whisper. 'We were all punk kids, eighteen or nineteen, hell, I don't know. We had one guy who was a virgin. One night we get hold of some old English broad and she takes him down a coal bunker during an air raid and lays him. And when he comes out of that goddam bunker he looks like he's been shovelling coal for six months. All you could see was his eyes. Looked like a fuckin' panda.' He shook his head and sighed. 'What a goddam way to lose your virginity.'

And with that, Eddie returned to his Guinness. I muttered an excuse and left. I wandered up the street. The next bar was called Billy Frogg's. A haze of smoke greeted me. Ancient English railway signs from little halts like Eltham hung on the walls. The cavernous room was packed with braying, trendily-dressed yuppies, most of whom were in the advanced stages of inebriation. I squeezed on to a bar stool and ordered a beer. The noise was dreadful and I thought about bed. I was about to leave when I noticed a man hovering behind my shoulder.

He had a broad beatific grin on his face and was rocking unsteadily on his feet. He was much older than the other customers and his elderly, scuffed anorak stuck out among the expensive leather jackets. His hair had not seen a brush in several days and his splendid handlebar moustache was in a state of severe disrepair. It drooped forlornly at the ends. Some of the customers near us moved away as if they weren't sure what the cat had dragged in. Two girls, whom I'd been attempting to engage in conversation, edged away as the man pushed his way to the bar. My first reaction was that he was a vagrant, a down-and-out. But on closer examination he seemed to have that happy-but-stranded look after an exceptionally epic night (and most of the day) on the razzle.

In fact, he turned out to be the one and only Quite Famous Person I was to meet on my journey.

He was a cartoonist. His name was Howard Shoemaker and for thirty-one years his spindly drawings had been appearing in the pages of *Playboy* magazine.

I was surprised that a cartoonist of such distinction chose to live in Omaha. Surely richer pickings were to be found in, say, New York? 'Never wanted to leave Omaha,' said Shoe, as he liked to be known. 'Born here, raised my kids here and got everything I need. Love it to death.'

Nor had he been tempted to settle in Chicago, headquarters of Hugh Hefner's *Playboy* empire. 'Hated the place, and Hefner's parties weren't much better. Dick Calvert once said that the only nude he saw in the *Playboy* swimming pool was Norman Mailer. I certainly never saw any orgies. The girls worked hard, their feet hurt and those dreadful costumes cut them right up to the crotch. The last thing on their minds was sex.'

Shoe explained that he had been out earlier with a group of friends, an itinerant drinking club who called themselves the Slime Dogs. He stuck out his hand and wiggled it as if he was suffering from a bad case of alcoholic jitters. 'And that,' he said, 'is the Slime Dogs handshake.'

'Why the Slime Dogs?' I asked.

'Guess we're kinda like the dog next door who does nothing but shit.'

There was no sign of Shoe's fellows. They had all gone home and he was the last one still standing. He had popped into Billy Frogg's for a nightcap. We chatted for a few minutes, but it was getting late. The rigours of the push-boat were catching up with me. We arranged to meet the next day when Shoe promised he would introduce me to some Omaha characters.

Lewis and Clark reached the bluffs of present day Omaha at the beginning of August, 1804. The weather was hot, the insects unbearable. 'The musquitors so thick and & troublesom,' Lewis complained, 'that it was disagreeable and painful to Continue a moment still.' Clark was putting on a brave face: 'The air is pure and helthy so far as we can judge.'

The expedition landed on the east side of the river, at what is now the town of Council Bluffs. They named the area after the meeting – or council – they held with members of the Oto and Missouri tribes, who were among the first Indians they met. Lewis delivered a rather pompous speech about 'the great white father' (Jefferson), who lived in Washington. Lewis requested the Indians' loyalty, adding that Jefferson would much appreciate it if they ceased squabbling among themselves. He then rewarded them with various medals and, more significantly, a bottle of whisky. It was their first taste of liquor, the white man's firewater that was in the years to come to wreak such havoc among the Indian nations.

With the coming of the steamboats, people began to settle in Council Bluffs. Some moved across the river to establish the trading post of Omaha. The town grew into one of the great centres of westward migration. First came the Mormons who wintered here in 1846 on their way to Utah. The first transcontinental railroad arrived in 1863 and with it thousands of fortune-seeking immigrants. By the end of the century Omaha was a booming agricultural and industrial centre with a gambling underworld that was the talk of America.

These days Omaha is best known as Nuke City. For out in Bellevue – the suburb where I had left the *Dan C. Burnett* – is the headquarters of Strategic Air Command, the control centre of the United States' nuclear missile system. In its own words, SAC is the 'backbone of the nation's security'. The President may give his orders in Washington . . . but the button is pushed here.

Since I was in the area, I decided to pay SAC a visit. Understandably the military authorities were more than a little wary of a British writer telephoning for an appointment at such short notice.

I got through to a Major Suzanne Randle in the media relations department. Such is the serious nature of nuclear weapons that SAC prefer to run extensive checks on journalists before admitting them onto the base.

'Why do you want to come to SAC?' Major Randle asked not unreasonably.

Lying in bed in the hotel watching early morning TV with half an eye on a *Flintstones* cartoon, this was a question I had not expected. I stuttered something about interviewing local people about what impact the Missouri had on their lives. That was it. Impact. A good American word.

Major Randle sounded distinctly unimpressed. It was very short notice, she explained. No, she did not think an interview could be arranged.

I pushed on. I had a tight schedule and was only in town for a few days. After much cajoling, the major gave way and agreed that I could visit the base briefly that afternoon.

For much of the drive down to Bellevue I was stuck behind an elderly Plymouth with a bumper sticker that read 'a nuclear bomb could ruin your day'. I stopped at a McDonald's and ate a Big Mac while surrounded by groups of fresh-faced, off-duty airmen. I was early for my appointment so I decided to take a short detour and kill some time in the SAC museum next to the base.

The museum was a veritable supermarket of bombs and missiles. Here the public could learn where all those taxes went.

Exhibits included the 1950s Mark 36 thermonuclear hydrogen bomb and all manner of intercontinental ballistic missiles. There was Peacekeeper, Titan and Minuteman. And how neat and tidy the Cruise missiles looked – surprisingly small at less than twenty-one feet long. Kiddies, who love to push buttons (just like the nice Mr President), could have terrific fun with a light-up model of a Minuteman silo. There was also a model of the E-4B Airborne Command Post, the 747 jet that would take to the air with the chiefs of staff (and lucky Mr President) in the event of nuclear attack. Near the entrance was a plastic wishing well with all proceeds to the museum. I wondered how many people had dropped their coins and wished that nuclear missiles would go away.

SAC were as frank about their failures as their achievements. I paused at a jolly little photograph of launch complex 374–7 in Arkansas a few hours after it was obliterated by an explosion that destroyed a liquid fuel Titan 2 ICBM in its silo and killed one airman. The blast was so powerful that one of the silo's heavy concrete blast doors was hurled several hundred feet. The missile's nuclear warhead ended up in an adjacent field. But the blurb told us that there was no nuclear 'mishap'. I felt that this was a quaint use of the word.

Outside the museum more historic missiles were lined up by

disused snow-covered runways. I could hear the rumble of a jet engine in the clouds overhead. I returned to the car and made my way to the SAC headquarters along a road flanked by barbed wire.

A young, cherubic sentry guarded the main gate. He was dressed in combat fatigues and armed with pistol and walkie-talkie. He noted my British passport and remarked that not many foreigners visited the base. So I was curious when he appeared to mistake me for someone else.

'Have you come for employment?' he asked.

'Hadn't thought about it, although I suppose I could probably let off a missile as well as anyone.' The soldier did not find this desperately funny.

'I was expecting someone else,' he explained stiffly.

'What? Another Englishman?'

'Can't tell you. It's classified.'

Perhaps any moment a British secret serviceman was about to turn up to do business with the Americans. As I pondered on this, the guard filled out some forms, took the Toyota's number plate, lifted the security barrier and waved me through. To my surprise he never even bothered to search the car.

The base was like a small town. I got hopelessly lost and drove around for ten minutes before a passing soldier directed me to the main building. I parked the car by a decommissioned Titan missile. This towering monster sat at the building's entrance like an ornamental statue outside a stately home.

I walked inside to a security desk staffed by a posse of soldiers armed to the teeth. Major Randle was already waiting for me. And with her was the senior media relations officer Colonel George Peck.

Peck fancied himself as a joker; the life and soul of the party. He presented me with a special pass and declared, 'You'd better wear that at all times. Otherwise you'll be on your stomach counting the carpet threads.' Following this example of SAC humour, he uttered a guttural laugh. 'Huck! Huck! Huck!'

The two officers presented a sort of knockabout double act. Peck was a born public relations man. Had he worked for ACME he would have been the Mid-West's biggest brush salesman. He sold his product with the fervour of the soap powder tycoon as if to say, 'Sincerely folks, nuclear missiles are good for you and your family.' The Major – 'please call me Sue' – was in charge of the statistics;

hard facts that, while a little on the dreary side, were vital to the cause of nuclear salesmanship. Did I know, for example, that SAC personnel numbered 12,500 with 25,000 dependents? Or that SAC expenditure (building programmes etc.) generated $1.4 billion a year for Omaha?

Colonel Peck suggested that I conduct the interview over coffee and cake in the canteen. The Major giggled. She was an attractive woman in her mid-forties with immaculately permed black hair and wearing neatly pressed regulation slacks. 'But I mustn't have cake,' she protested. 'I'll put on so much weight.'

I cynically suspected that this was the beginning of a familiar Randle-Peck conversation; a mild bout of 'aren't we being human?' flirtation laid on specially for visiting journalists.

'Oh, but you've got the body beautiful,' Peck gushed. 'Come on, you don't have to worry about things like that.'

'Yes, I do.'

'Aw, no y'don't. I'm the one that has to worry about my weight. Huck! Huck! Huck!'

We walked along a grey corridor. The Major confided to me that the Americans were very into 'body fat' at the moment. I made a comment about how much Americans seemed to eat. She looked rather surprised. I said that I'd been in a McDonald's earlier and had seen people eating three burgers at a sitting. She made no further comment. Perhaps all Americans ate their burgers in threes.

We reached the cafeteria. I began to wonder what I was doing there. I suppose it had been enough just having a look inside SAC headquarters. But I hadn't a clue what I was going to ask my hosts. I have never cared for military installations ever since spending two barbaric, foot-slogging months in my late teens as a would-be Army officer at the Guards Depot, Pirbright. The Army subsequently failed me on the grounds that I 'panicked under pressure'. Now, all these years later, as I sat in the SAC cafeteria, I began to do just that. I felt a nervous attack coming on.

We all lined up for coffee. A Chinese serving lady filled my cup and pointed me towards an extraordinary-looking cream machine. I was unfamiliar with the gadget. I pushed a lever and most of the cream went over my sleeve. Major Randle looked at the mess with distaste. I smeared it away with a handkerchief.

The room was crowded with servicemen on their afternoon break.

The Colonel found a spare table and the three of us sat down. My nervous attack worsened. I brought out a packet of cigarettes.

'No smoking!' the Colonel and Major chorused.

'Ah, okay.' I returned the cigarettes to my pocket and fumbled for my pen. In my embarrassment and confusion I brought out a lighter by mistake. The Colonel looked at me as if I was deaf. The Major said 'No smoking!' again. This interview was getting off to a great start.

They would not let the matter rest. 'You can't smoke in this building,' the Major said quickly.

'I wasn't going to. I was just trying to find my pen.'

'Just warning you.' For a moment she reminded me of a particularly aggressive Latin mistress I was forced to suffer when aged eight.

The Colonel twisted the knife. 'We have a very healthy commander, General Chane, who has banned smoking – and I say more power to him. He is very concerned with the whole fitness aspect of our job.' (Smug, self-righteous prig, I thought. How fit, for God's sake, do you have to be to push a button?)

The lighter went back into my pocket. The pen came out. I cleared my throat. The interview began.

'Is it fair to say,' I asked, 'that if the Russians, or whoever, got twitchy and launched a nuclear strike, Omaha would be the first place to disappear in a puff of smoke?'

Major Randle and Colonel Peck exchanged nervous glances across the table. The Major cleared her throat. 'I think . . .' She paused. 'I think you're probably right. Yes, I think you're probably on to something there.'

The Colonel struggled for an answer. 'That is a valid question. But because SAC have such great confidence in our deterrent ability we feel that this is actually the safest place in the United States.' He leaned back and smiled. He was pleased at how he had parried the question.

'No,' the Major said, 'no, I think Peter's right. If the balloon ever went up then . . .' She struggled for the right words. 'Then . . .'

'Bye bye Omaha?' I suggested.

'Exactly.' And then she laughed. I was beginning to like Major Randle.

The Colonel's initial sense of humour seemed to have disappeared. With a small sniff of disapproval he launched into a hard sell. 'We are a very important organization and we have an impact on the entire world as a consequence. Our missiles are stationed all over the States, but the tip of the pyramid is here.'

'And you let the things off with the red phone?' I asked. (The most talked about item in the SAC underground command post is the 'red phone' with which the SAC controller can scramble more than 150 missile control centres throughout the world.)

''Fraid it's no longer red,' the Colonel explained. 'It's a regular, business phone with a lot of little buttons. You pick it up and it goes straight through. It's got multiple backups so you never get a breakdown.'

'You can't get crossed lines, you mean?'

'That's right.' After our initial hiccough the Colonel was back on his joke-a-minute public relations form. 'At least, you'll never hear Aunt Mildred on it. Huck! Huck!' I was glad to hear it. Wouldn't want Aunt Mildred blowing Cuba to bits.

He got serious again. 'We've recently upgraded the command centre. It's a bit of a disappointment to some people who expect to see great boards with little airplanes being moved round like in a Bond movie. Actually it looks like a corporate boardroom.'

Major Randle interrupted. 'But we do have a button that we push and the computers come up out of the desk. That's quite James Bond.'

'And is it strictly necessary?' I asked.

'Not really,' Major Randle trilled. She brushed a strand of hair from her face. 'But it looks nice.'

The Colonel raised an eyebrow at the Major. Oh yes, it was necessary, he said. He was not keen on projecting the image that SAC introduced new-fangled gadgetry simply because it 'looked nice'. It gave the controllers extra desk space without the computer screen always getting in the way.

We talked a little more, mainly about the women who demonstrated against the Cruise missiles at Greenham Common airbase. 'Filthy people,' the Major sniffed. She herself had been briefly posted there.

After half an hour my time was up. Colonel Peck saw me out of the building. A cluster of junior soldiers were on their knees scrubbing the entrance hall – SAC were preparing for an official visit by President Bush the following week and a massive clean-up operation was in progress. All personnel had been assigned extra duties. The Colonel nudged me in a man-to-man sort of way. 'You could say,' he leered, 'that we're running up and down out of every orifice that God gave us.' And, with a final 'Huck!', he marched away.

I returned to Omaha and met up with Shoe later that afternoon. I asked him how Omahans felt about having SAC on their doorstep. 'Guess we don't think about it much. When the time comes, give us a bottle and a girl. We'll go out on the street and boom, boom, boom – you got fifteen minutes to take me to heaven, baby!'

'So that's how you think about nuclear catastrophe?'

'What other way is there to think?'

We met in the Dubliner, an Irish bar on the edge of the Old Market. It was a long, thin subterranean dive reached by a steep flight of battered wooden steps. There was a darts board at one end and a string of paper shamrocks hung above the bar. The Dub, as it was known, conveyed the impression that only serious drinkers were welcome.

Shoe had tidied himself up since his excesses of the previous night. His grey hair was smoothed back and he had attended to his splendid moustache. It now twirled up cosily around his cheeks like a rare piece of sculpture.

He was with a friend, a paunchy lawyer called Pete, another member of the famous Slime Dogs. Pete was a roly-poly man with a poker face. He wore large tortoiseshell glasses and a striped sweatshirt in garish pink and blue.

We talked about the Missouri and how the river had changed since the US Army Corps of Engineers introduced the system of dykes and dams that had stopped the great floods of the early 1950s.

Shoe munched on a hot dog as he remembered the childhood fishing expeditions with his father. 'We'd get a railroad spike, the nail they hold the track down with. We'd put the spike on a heavy cord, put on about fifteen hooks and bait it with the stinkiest fish bait we could find, usually rotten chicken liver. The river wasn't fast then and we'd catch these big catfish that were feeding on the bottom.'

But the dykes changed all that. 'The flood of 1951 was horrendous, almost washed our home away. Practically overnight the Corps of Engineers built all these banks. From being almost a mile wide during the spring floods the river turned into a high-speed sluice.

Wouldn't go near it now. It's too fast. Scares me.' Shoe sipped his beer. A line of foam clung to his moustache. 'They say the Corps of Engineers have screwed up more rivers than they have ever saved. But I suppose the Missouri had to be controlled.'

Shoe had been brought up across the river in Council Bluffs. He did not hold the place in great affection 'Now, that's a shitty place, a tough, blue-collar town. Sucks hind tit on Omaha. It's the end of the Earth. Nothing happens there.'

'Yeah.' Pete shared Shoe's prejudices. 'If the United States had an enema,' he joined, taking a long suck of beer, 'Council Bluffs is where they'd put in the nozzle.'

Shoe remembered the story of an Oklahoma trucker, who stopped off at a topless bar in CB called The Razzle Dazzle. 'Three yo-yos grab him, one of them pisses in his hat and puts it back on his head. The cowboy goes out to his car, gets a .32 automatic, comes back and shoots six rounds in the ceiling. The police come down and arrest him for discharging a firearm. They don't do anything to the locals. That's Council Bluffs for you.'

We left the Dub for M's Bar, another of Shoe's drinking haunts in the Old Market. We went through a narrow litter-infested alley. The walls were splattered with obscure graffiti like 'Eno's a prefabricated turd' and 'War Kills' alongside ban-the-bomb signs. Colonel Peck had his 'media relations' work cut out for him.

As we walked, Shoe and Pete moaned about how developers had demolished so many Victorian warehouses in the Old Market. Much of the property in downtown Omaha was owned by the giant food processing corporation Konagra. Konagra had scant regard for Omaha's heritage. During the 1980s, the company was said to have destroyed sixty-one warehouse blocks, replacing them with concrete high-rises.

'I don't know what it is that makes some Americans hate old buildings,' Pete sighed. 'These big corporations don't appreciate history, they only look for dollar signs. Why have dusty old nineteenth-century brick when you can have plate glass office blocks instead?'

The evening drifted on. We stayed in M's Bar for a couple of hours. Shoe spent much of the time admiring the girls. He projected a laddish image. 'Mmmm, look at that lady,' he muttered. He preened his moustache and pointed at a blonde in a short, white leather

skirt. 'That's baby's a jackal. Mmm, over here, pussy, over here.'
The girl studiously ignored him. She was used to more sophisticated
chat-up lines.

Peter left for an early night, but Shoe wanted to continue drinking.
He had a couple more hours to kill before his wife expected him
home. He offered to show me the bars uptown.

We took a cab forty blocks north. On the way we talked about
Britain. Shoe had never been there, but he longed to see Scotland.
'Always listen to bagpipe music at home,' he admitted. 'Love those
weepy wails, but it's really difficult to make love to.'

We embarked on a beery bar-hop. Shoe dragged me from one
establishment to another. They were all very similar: plastic decor
with a profusion of Formica table tops and Miller Lite signs on the
walls. Jukeboxes blasted out ancient Elvis songs. Middle-aged men
crowded round pool tables. Shoe cruised the customers, shaking
hands with nearly everyone. He was well-known in Omaha. A
character.

We ended up at a place called the Veterans of Foreign Wars Club.
It was a drab, wooden building reached across a dusty parking lot.
The railroad ran nearby. A freight train hooted. A chain of clanking
boxcars passed through the night.

It was warm inside the VFW. I squinted in the sharp glare of neon
strip lighting. The clientele were mostly old soldiers dating from the
Second World War and Korea. Soft country music came from a
radio. A few people sat alone at the bar staring into space. Others
huddled round tables playing cards.

We joined a trio in the corner. They were old friends of Shoe's
and they welcomed him fondly. Shoe introduced me to Leroy and
Morrie. They were approaching their seventies and dressed in
checked shirts and Stetson hats. Their bear-like hands threatened to
crush mine. They had sleepy eyes and grizzled, weather-beaten faces.
With them was a handsome grey-haired lady whom they called Miss
Dotty. The trio had obviously been drinking hard since early evening.

'This is Slime Dog Leroy, Slime Dog Morrie and Slime Dog Miss
Dotty,' Shoe said.

'How dare you, Shoe?' Miss Dotty replied in mock indignation.
She sipped a lemonade schnapps and looked at him down an aristocratic nose. 'I'm not one of your Slime Dogs.'

'Aw, Miss Dotty. You may be a woman, but you're a Slime Dog like the rest of us.'

We embarked on a primitive discussion about Mid-Western culture. I asked Morrie and Leroy why they wore such big cowboy hats. They thought about this for a moment and looked at each other like a pair of naughty schoolboys. Then Leroy screwed his face into a grin. 'So the rain don't fall on your eyeball.'

'Naw,' Morrie said. 'It's so the birds don't shit on your leg.' They broke out into hacking laughter. Shoe joined in. Miss Dotty looked disapproving.

Leroy made a feeble attempt at sobriety. He straightened his face. 'I'll tell you why I wear this hat.' He fingered the rim. 'It's because I've worn it all my life and I'm just gonna keep wearing it.'

'No, it's not.' Morrie slapped his friend on the back. 'It's because we're gettin' bald, asshole.'

Like so many Mid-Westerners, Morrie was a gun fanatic. He owned an impressive collection, including an M1 automatic rifle and antique British sporting pistols. He launched into a lecture about firearms.

'I don't have guns to kill people, I like 'em because that's the way I was born and raised. I was taught to have respect for firearms. They were hanging on the porch and they were always fully loaded, and when you grabbed one the dog would get really excited. When I was seven years old my father got me a gun and he told me what not to do with it. He said you don't aim it at anybody.'

I quoted a rhyme that *my* father had told me as a small boy:

> 'Never never let your gun
> Pointed be at anyone,
> That it may unloaded be
> Matters not the least to me.'

Leroy growled approvingly. This was the first time he had heard the verse. 'Yeah, like it. That's very good. You hear that Morrie?'

'Huh?' Morrie was unimpressed. 'Tell that to the dumb motherfuckers in New York.'

We were all fairly drunk, except for Miss Dotty. This gun talk bored her. She switched to genealogy.

Miss Dotty was convinced she was descended from an English aristocratic family.

'It's nice meeting somebody from England.' She smoothed down her pinafore dress and teased her hair. 'My grandfather came from England when he was two. From the time I was a little girl I was always told that he was an English lord and that he could have gone back home and claimed his title.' I listened politely. I suggested that she contact a genealogy outfit like Debretts. Maybe they could trace her ancestry.

'Don't overload the man with bullshit now.' Leroy set about another whisky and soda. He nudged me. 'Know that expression, boy? Overloaded with bullshit?' I explained that I was familiar with the term.

Miss Dotty was most indignant. 'I'm not overloading anyone, Leroy. Maybe I should go to England and trace my roots and maybe there's a title there. Maybe I'm a lady. Maybe there's a big castle with land waiting for me. Ain't that right, Peter?'

I ummed and erred. Perhaps she was being a little optimistic. I tried to be as tactful as possible. 'Well, who knows?' I said. 'Perhaps it's worth a try.'

Leroy spluttered. 'All you'd find over there is a rhubarb patch.'

'Or a cow turd,' Morrie joined in.

Miss Dotty looked hurt. 'I don't think that's very nice, Morrie,' she said primly.

Shoe and I left just as the evening was in the final stages of disintegration. Having exhausted all conversation, Morrie and Leroy were making farting noises into my tape recorder. Miss Dotty chattered wildly, but no one was listening. She was now certain she was related to the Queen.

Outside the VFW Shoe presented me with a leaving present. With a sly grin he dug into his pocket and brought out an oblong object. He was like a schoolboy showing off his prize-winning conker. I peered at the thing.

'What on earth is it?' I said stupidly.

In Shoe's hand was a life-sized, plastic replica of a vagina. It was designed like a piece of jewellery that could be worn on a chain around the neck.

'It's a pussy pendant.' Shoe lovingly stroked the plastic curves and crevices. 'An artist friend makes them. He takes a cast of the real thing and sets them in plastic. Can't take casts of men's parts because they don't stay up long enough.' He pressed the thing into my hand. 'Ain't that great to wear at family parties? Every time you look at it you can think of the Slime Dogs.' I thanked him. It was certainly the most unusual souvenir I had ever picked up on my travels.

If Armageddon wasn't going to arrive courtesy of Strategic Air Command, then America was being destroyed from within. The degeneration of the American family was leading the country towards apocalypse.

That was the gloomy view of Father Valentine Peter, director of Boy's Town, America's legendary children's home and one of Omaha's best-known landmarks.

In 1917, a young Irish immigrant priest named Father Edward Flanagan took in five homeless boys off the streets. He was horrified at the way the youths had been abused and neglected. And, as more wayward youngsters turned up on his doorstep, Father Flanagan began what was to become a life's work. By the 1930s Flanagan had raised enough money to buy a small farm on the western outskirts of Omaha.

Boy's Town was born. The charity's logo depicted a teenaged youth carrying another child piggy-back with the slogan: 'He ain't heavy, father . . . he's m' brother.' Flanagan's fame spread and his endeavours were immortalised in the 1938 film *Boy's Town*. The movie starred Spencer Tracy as Flanagan. Mickey Rooney played one of his troubled charges.

After Flanagan's death in 1948, his project continued to grow. Today there are Boy's Town programmes all over America dedicated to the welfare of 12,500 wayward boys and girls each year.

I visited the home on my way out of Omaha. Thanks to Shoe I was suffering from a snarling hangover. A talk with a priest might invigorate my addled brain.

It was snowing hard as I reached the parkland campus dotted with a dozen neo-Tudor houses that were home to the 700 permanent residents.

I met Father Peter in his office in the administration block. He was dressed in dog collar and black priestly vestments. He was a well-built man with greying hair and eyes that locked contact with mine. He was obviously a great thinker, though I suspected he would take a tough stand against any of his charges who stepped out of line.

Father Peter was on a crusade against America's social problems. He expounded his views like a man with a mission. The single most important reason for the country's spiritual decline, he declared, was the breakdown of the family unit.

The priest clasped his hands together. He delivered a fiery sermon. 'The reason for this family breakdown is that America is becoming an increasingly materialistic society. Everyone needs more money to pay for their possessions, their mortgages. So the mother goes out to work and the children get neglected.'

Was this not an unfashionable argument in these days of feminism and career women? 'Perhaps. But if children are not brought up with traditional family values, like sitting down to meals with at least one parent, they will go astray. No argument about it.'

Father Peter's voice was firm. 'Once you see family life beginning to disintegrate then civilization is in peril. There is a spiritual decay and neglect at the root of everything from physical and sexual abuse to drug dependency and suicide.

'This is particularly the case with children. If you do not provide your child with a sense of who they are and who they belong to, is it possible for that child to trust the world? Is it possible for that child to have reason to hope even in dark times? If you do not provide a child with family life, it is like not providing him or her with something to eat. But it is much more terrible than hunger because hunger can be overcome with food. That darkness cannot. Once it enters the soul then it abides in the soul.'

Father Peter's family came originally from Bavaria. They emigrated to America in 1938 shortly before Hitler's *anschluss*. But he was ashamed to be American in the 1990s.

'This country has a lack of spiritual values, and that is the great cancer that will kill American society. It is interesting to note that the United States has exported the worst of our culture and none of the best. The worst of our culture is the crass materialism, it is the worst of our music and television. It is sad that most people outside the United States think of us in terms of what they see on the telly.

'The trouble is that we have had it too good for too long. After the Second World War the British people sacrificed much more than we did. You still had rationing for seven years after the war. And you lost your colonies.' He clapped his hands together and laughed. 'You had great upheaval, but we had virtually none. None of our cities got bombed. Except for our dead, the war changed us very little. Perhaps that was bad for us. Now we have problems that people in authority insist on ignoring.'

I had met a rare, and none too welcome bird in America – a socialist. 'You are right,' he conceded. 'I am not popular when I talk like this.'

Many of American industry's policies were anti-family. Families were transferred from one end of the country to the other without warning. A company would close all its plants in one town without warning. Social conscience did not rank high in the United States.

'Of course we would benefit by more socialist policies and higher taxes. Our taxes are absurdly low. The rich hardly pay any tax at all.'

Boy's Town's annual budget was $87,000,000. Most of the money came from individual donations. 'We get a little Government funding and hardly anything from big business.' The priest smiled wanly. He expected no different. 'It's just the way things are. But I feel that a little philanthropy wouldn't go amiss.'

Before I continued on my way north, Father Peter inquired whether I was enjoying the Mid-West. I replied that everything was fine and dandy.

'I may have painted a dismal picture of America as a whole,' he added, 'but generally there are good people in Nebraska. I have something that I always say to visitors. If you live by the sea you can hear it speak to you because it speaks very loudly. If you live in the mountains they are so powerful that they shout at you.'

He lowered his voice. 'But if you live on the Great Plains all you can hear is the whisper of the prairie. It is a beautiful message of courage and hope; that the seasons will return over and over, that you must be courageous enough to last through the winter until the spring comes.'

And so I set out to find Father Peter's whispering prairie. I left the city on Highway 75. The road conditions were dreadful. The snow continued to fall and the Toyota's wheels skidded on the ice. Spring was going to be a long time coming.

My talk with Father Peter had sobered me up. Here was a highly spiritual man, utterly dedicated to his work. Before we parted he had gently admonished me for my lifestyle. At the age of thirty-four, I should be settling down rather than cruising America in search of a story.

'As a boy I read about the Seven Wonders of the World,' he said. 'I never saw them all, but I spent nearly ten years travelling. After a while you have seen everything you want. You must settle down and sink roots deep into the soil. Man cannot be a tumbleweed all his life.'

I found a country station on the car radio. The singer Loudon Wainwright III was belting out an enthusiastic little ditty called 'Dead Skunk In The Middle Of The Road'.

Everyday America had returned with a jolt.

Five

I was not having much luck with the Welsh theory. The only Welsh clue in Omaha was two Llewllyns listed in the telephone directory. In an idle moment I tried ringing them. No answer. I consoled myself with the story of John Evans.

By the end of the eighteenth century the Welsh were thoroughly fed up with snide Scots and Englishmen, who persistently questioned Madoc's alleged exploits. In 1791, the London-Welsh literary society, the *Gwyneddigion*, published a feisty little pamphlet. In it they attacked snide Welsh-haters like Dr Robertson, the man who claimed Madoc could never have discovered America because no Welshman was capable of such a deed.

'It is evident by their belchings,' the boyos raged, 'that there remains still some latent malignity in the bottom of their stomachs which sometimes affects their brains.' But what more could you expect from Englishmen descended from 'bastards, arrant thieves and murderers whether Saxon or Norman'?

The fight was on. Swift action was called for. And the following year the *Gwyneddigion* produced a secret weapon in the form of the Reverend John Evans.

The Reverend Evans, twenty-two-year-old Methodist clergyman from Caernarvon, was a remarkable man. His brief was to find Madoc's Indian descendants and reconvert them to Christianity. With little more than a couple of guides for company, Evans made a canoe journey up the Missouri arriving in what is now North Dakota. He spent the winter of 1796 with the Mandans, the tribe said most likely to be related to Madoc.

85

Although the journey was an incredible adventure in itself and Evans returned with new knowledge about this little-charted area of America, the Welsh link died on him. Upon his return to civilization he was forced to admit to his sponsors: 'Having explored the Missouri for 1,800 miles . . . I am able to inform you that there is no such people as the Welsh Indians.'

The weather improved as I left Omaha. The snow stopped and a hint of sun appeared in the grey sky. I headed into rolling prairie, overtaking farmers in slow, elderly Buicks spewing smoke behind them. Balls of tumbleweed, carried by an easterly wind, bounced lethargically across the road. It was if they came from nowhere and were going nowhere. Bald eagles hovered a thousand feet up, seeking their prey.

There was a raw magnificence to the countryside; a sprinkling of snow lay on the vast ploughed fields, which in summer would be a swaying mass of corn. So quiet is the prairie that farmers swear that they can hear the corn growing.

The highway ran parallel to the Missouri. I caught glimpses of the river to the east. The stream did not seem so swift in this part of Nebraska. The torrent seemed to have been stemmed by occasional patches of sheet ice that were dotted here and there like gaps in a jigsaw puzzle. There were less trees. The waterline led to wide grassy banks that crept up into the ploughed fields. I drove through little frontier towns like Fort Calhoun and Tekamah. They all looked depressingly similar. Grain elevators and harsh, stainless-steel silos loomed over untidy railroad sidings. Weeds grew between the tracks. There were endless tractor showrooms and gas stations with 'Cold Beer' signs. Collapsed armchairs, stuffing falling from the seats, sat on the rotten front porches of wooden houses. Perhaps Grandpa would doze there under the peeling paint on a summer's evening. In Decatur (population 720) nearly all the houses were pastel green. Green was evidently the local hardware store's paint of the month.

Between the towns were great tracts of emptiness. Water towers dotted the horizon. Dilapidated cattle pens stood rotting in the fields. There was little traffic and the countryside became less and less populated. I passed the entrances to ranches marked with rotted wooden cross-bars bearing the owners' names and topped off with ancient pairs of cow horns. I caught glimpses of half-hidden farms lying deep in the prairie several miles from the road.

For the time being I put the Welsh out of my mind. Instead, I concentrated on the Indians. For I was entering Sioux country.

The Sioux are one of the largest American Indian tribes. Sioux is an abbreviation of Nadowessioux, a French corruption of Nadowe-is-iw. The name was given to them by their long-time rivals, the Chippewa. Roughly translated, it means 'snake'; in other words, 'enemy'. They led a nomadic existence and with their long, braided hair and muscular features, they enjoyed a reputation as one of the most warlike and aggressive of the Western tribes.

For centuries the traditional Sioux hunting grounds extended over a vast area from the west of the Mississippi, north from the Arkansas River to the Rocky Mountains.

But the arrival of the white man changed all that. European aggression and diseases such as smallpox ravaged their numbers. And by the first quarter of the nineteenth century the Sioux were being squashed into smaller and smaller territory, mainly in the Dakotas, Nebraska and Montana, on what were to become official reservations.

Lewis and Clark were among the last white intruders to have half-way decent relations with the native Americans. Their patron, Thomas Jefferson, had insisted that they respect their Indian hosts. 'It may be taken for a certainty,' he declared, 'that not a foot of land will be taken from the Indians without their consent.'

Jefferson's words were soon forgotten. Settlers swooped into Indian country. They took the land and embarked upon the destruction of the sacred buffalo herds. The Indians could not understand all the fence posts in the ground. For the earth was their mother. Would you drive a stake into the heart of your mother? The cultural shock upon these virtually stone age people must have been enormous.

The US Government made treaties that they promptly broke. Native American culture was based on the oral tradition. Nothing was written down. Therefore the Government realised they could promise anything they liked. Pathetically sad though it may sound, the Indians trusted every word, because for the Indians your word was your bond.

'They made us many promises, more than I can ever remember,' one elderly Sioux warrior recalled. 'But they never kept but one; they promised to take our land, and they took it.'

Land disputes proliferated. The sabre-rattling military established forts to protect white interests. And in 1854, the Great Plains erupted into bloody violence.

The immediate cause was hardly in the Hollywood tradition of bareback redskins whooping it up over the prairie. To the contrary, it was all started by a cow which was found, apparently abandoned, by a Minneconjou Sioux a few miles from Fort Laramie, Wyoming. The Indian killed the animal and took the hide back to his camp. The cow's white owner took great exception to this and demanded $25 damages. The Sioux elders could afford only $10. This was not enough. And with a heavy-handedness that even Clint Eastwood would have balked at, a lieutenant rode out with thirty-two men and two howitzers to apprehend the alleged thief. An argument broke out and, in a fit of pique, the lieutenant had the Sioux chief shot. The officer had badly misjudged the Indian strength. In the fight that followed all the soldiers were killed.

The American public demanded retaliation. The following summer, 300 US soldiers massacred 86 Sioux in another village. And thus began the subjugation of a once proud nation: a deliberate destruction and genocide led by oafs like General Philip Sheridan, the man who casually remarked, 'The only good Indians I ever saw were dead.' No, tact, brains and perception did not play a large part in the US Army of the nineteenth century.

I turned east across the Missouri into Iowa, heart of the nation's breadbasket; a hog-rearing, corn-covered agrarian state that induces much mirth in Americans. Many Scandinavians settled here and there are numerous jokes about unsophisticated, small-town 'Iowegians'.

My next stop, Iowa's rivertown Sioux City, did not look promising. Flat, dull prairie gave way to an industrial sprawl peppered with advertising hoardings. As I drove through the outskirts I was struck by the sickly, rotting smell of the meat-rendering plant that has given this ugly metropolis the nickname Sewer City. Even in zero temperatures the stink was appalling. God knows what it would be like in summer.

It was here that Lewis and Clark suffered the only fatality of the expedition. For nearly a month their young second sergeant Charles Floyd had been complaining of stomach pains. On 19 August 1804,

Clark reported: 'Serjeant Floyd is taken verry bad all at once with a Biliose Chorlick . . . we are much allarmed at his Situation.' Floyd died a day later in great pain from what seems to have been a ruptured appendix. His friends buried him on a windswept cliff above the Missouri beneath a simple cedar post bearing his name.

I took a detour to the site known as Sergeant's Bluff. Floyd's resting place was marked by a stone obelisk bearing the homily: 'Graves of such men are pilgrim shrines, shrines to no class or creed confined.' It was a lonely spot. Wind buffeted the monument. A thousand feet below lay the roaring Interstate 29 that ran alongside the Missouri. The river was coated in a blue sheet of ice. It looked exceptionally unfriendly.

A police car was parked near the monument. It contained two state troopers, who were looking out for speeding motorists.

'Just waiting to catch a few yo-yos,' one of the officers explained with an evil grin. 'It's easy. No one can see us from the road.'

I drove into Sioux City over a bridge spanning the Floyd River. I felt that perhaps Lewis and Clark could have found a more impressive river by which to remember their colleague. The mouth was dry and flanked by grimy factories. It resembled a large, polluted drain.

Accommodation in Sioux City was a problem. I was trying to make a point of staying in the centre of each city I visited, but the cheap hotels of Sioux City's infamous Fourth Street had been demolished long ago. The only place to stay downtown was the Hilton. I gritted my teeth, upped my budget, and took a room on my credit card. The hotel may have been part of the famous chain, but guests were advised not to be confused by the name. The decor was cheap 'n' tacky with hideous Spanish-style furniture and fluffy, puce green carpet.

The hotel summed up the intense ugliness of the city. I opened my window . . . and was promptly assaulted by the dreadful smell of the meat-rendering plant. From my room I had a view of a concrete plaza where a drunk clutching a bottle bellowed insults at passers-by.

Sioux City has long enjoyed a reputation as a rough, brawling town. During the 1930s corruption was rife; the big Chicago racketeers moved their minions down to run new operations. But the town was most famous for the great cattle drives that began in Texas or Wyoming and ended at the railroad sidings. Once the hired hands had been paid off, they would obliterate the memory of those hard weeks in the saddle with almighty booze-ups. The bars were wild and dangerous, giving rise to the expression 'Saturday night in Sioux City'. The phrase is still used across the States to describe a night of shameful excess and debauchery.

Back on the *Dan C. Burnett*, Captain Vic had warned me about the place. 'Fourth Street was real bad,' he said. 'Fights like you've never seen.' He remembered going into a bar where a shabbily-dressed Indian demanded a whisky. 'He swallowed it down, but I guess he didn't like me. He walked out saying, "Know what? I wish I'd scalped your ancestors." I was flabbergasted.'

I found it a curious city. There were some fine Gothic villas on the outskirts. But the centre had become a victim of bad, indiscriminate planning: the original concrete jungle. I explored the series of first-floor enclosed walkways that connected the downtown stores, offices and apartment blocks. Theoretically, you could live in climate controlled conditions without stepping outside all year – an advantage in a place where the winters are long and vicious and summer temperatures reach well into the hundreds. The long white corridors were mostly deserted except for a few shoppers who scurried by like rats in a tube. The only noise was the hum of air-conditioning and the echo of footsteps. It was a mugger's paradise. And attached to the ceilings were mirrors to warn people if anyone was approaching from behind.

But Sioux Citizens were fiercely protective of their home. That evening I shared a few drinks with a lawyer called Bob whom I met in a bar across the road from the Hilton. He had whitish hair, thick black spectacles and looked like an owl. He was seated alone at the bar, his hands either side of a vodka and tonic that had evidently been replenished several times: his glass contained about six slices of lemon.

I made a remark about the smell. Bob laughed. I should have been here before they removed the Everest of manure in the stockyards. 'When I first moved here I'd gag on the streets. Don't notice it now. Reckon it's dulled my sense of smell.'

Bob had had a hard time when he'd arrived from Cleveland twenty years ago. 'This is a complicated place, the last stronghold of the independent man. There are plenty of millionaire farmers, but they don't spend money in fancy restaurants. This is strictly meat 'n' potatoes country. And they don't like being told what to do.

'It can be a really clannish place and extremely difficult for out-of-town lawyers. Unless you're a native the judges and juries can give you a hard time.'

Bob scratched his ear. He smiled. 'I remember a story about a farmer from Minona County who's in court for something or other. He gets in the witness stand and the lawyer asks where he lives. He says Minona County. The lawyer says, "Have you lived there all your life?" And the farmer replies, "Not yet, I ain't." People are like that round here. Straight talking, with a sense of humour.'

I left Bob to his vodka. I moved on to Sioux City's premier nightclub, the 201. The bouncers scrutinised my passport to ensure I was over the legal drinking age of twenty-one. This seemed a fairly pointless exercise. All around me, girls of little more than fifteen were getting in with barely a second glance. I learned later there was a booming local market for fake ID cards.

Middle America was in full swing. The club was the size of an aircraft hangar with bare, whitewashed walls and a few multi-coloured neon strips on the ceiling. The owners probably liked to describe it as 'minimalist'. I called it cheapskate. The clientele was mainly young. The dance floor was crammed with a press of people attempting to move to Bruce Springsteen.

I found a spare seat at the bar. 'This is a meat rack,' the girl next to me drawled. She introduced herself as Shelley. She was about thirty.

Shelley had been married at eighteen, divorced three years later, and had five daughters, two by her ex-husband, and three more by a boyfriend who had since deserted her. She came to the 201 a couple of nights of the week for a brief break from her family. She usually came alone and enjoyed just doing nothing and watching the crowds.

'Yeah, the biggest meat rack in town,' Shelley repeated. She had a pretty, freckly face with a figure that was on the large side. In Mid-West parlance, she was what they call a 'corn-fed-girl'.

She went on: 'Three girls for every man. Do you know that feeling when you wake up in the morning and you've got your arm underneath a woman and you look at her and you want to chew your arm off? I wonder how many of these people will feel like that tomorrow.'

I remarked that her domestic set-up seemed somewhat – how should I put it – chaotic? 'You'd be surprised how many girls are in the same situation. It's all divorces and kids round here.'

Her parents had given her several thousand dollars on her eighteenth birthday. She made some bad investments, the worst of which was her husband. 'I paid his way through college and when he smashed up his car I paid for that. Then he smashed up another and I paid again. When I was twenty-one we split.'

Her parents had been married thirty-five years. They strongly disapproved of their single-parent daughter. 'I'd like to find a new man, but most of them round here are oafs. Stupid farm boys. I have boyfriends, but I hate to take them home because my girls check them out. If they don't like him, they'll sit right between us on the couch.'

So, did Sioux City deserve its rough reputation? Shelley said there were still fights, but these days they were usually between women over a man. 'The other night I saw a girl take a beer bottle, smash it over the bar and slash another girl on her face. That's pretty commonplace.

'These little girls get tanked up on two beers. It's kinda funny watching them. They fall into the arms of the first man they can find. Unfortunately it's usually someone who's already got a girl.'

I left before the fights broke out. Back at the hotel, I watched a late-night horror movie. It featured a long, gory scene in which a baddy (or goody?) had his heart ripped out. America can be strange. They say you must be twenty-one to drink, yet public television screens repulsive satanistic nonsense that can be watched by schoolchildren.

Tell a New Yorker or Californian that you're off to South Dakota and they are likely to guffaw with laughter. 'Poor you,' they'll say. For this is the heart of the North American prairie stuck halfway between the North Pole and the equator. Why should any reasonably sophisticated person want to visit this state that, together with its neighbour North Dakota, makes up a sort of North American Siberia? The Dakotas are not on the way to anywhere and the weather is ghastly, either blizzards or droughts. It is the coldest part of the country in winter and the hottest in summer.

'When you reach South Dakota,' goes the old joke, 'set your watch back twenty years.' And when I arrived, the inhabitants were in a lather because map publishers Rand McNally had omitted the state from their latest road atlas on the grounds that no one went there. The good-natured South Dakotans are used to jokes at their own expense. They had come up with a T-shirt bearing a US map with a vacant lot towards the north and the slogan: 'The land that Rand forgot.'

But more seriously, young South Dakotans were deserting the state for richer pickings in cities like Minneapolis. Indians I met later claimed that by the year 2000 they would be in the majority. Demographically, South Dakota is a state of old white women and young Indians. In 1990 the average age of white South Dakotans was fifty-four; the average Indian age was fourteen.

Like all the Plains states, South Dakota is a place of traditional values where the biggest industry is ranching and farming: the state is the nation's biggest rye producer; she is in the top five for sheep, wheat, sunflower seeds, alfalfa, oats and honey.

Like all agricultural communities, this is a sturdy bastion of patriotism where nationalistic instincts run deep. Back in Omaha I had been warned that strong anti-Indian feeling lurked beneath the surface like a pustulate wound.

Perhaps I was lucky, but I encountered little racial bigotry during my stay. But a businessman friend of Shoe's had told me how he was attempting to sell fertilizer in a small town on the eastern edge of the state. 'These farmers showed me round and pointed out the statue of the first local white woman raped by an Indian. I asked them where they had put the statue of the first Indian woman raped by a white man. They ran me out of town.'

One night in Sioux City was enough. The next morning I crossed back over the Missouri and motored north towards South Dakota. The temperature had risen sharply and the snow was beginning to thaw. The sun shone in a magnificently blue, clear sky. I was lucky: it was February, a time when the Great Plains are usually snowbound. But unseasonably good weather was forecast. For the rest of the trip I was to enjoy bright, sunny skies. The Toyota clattered over the South Dakota stateline across the steel girder Meridian

Highway Bridge into the town of Yankton. Below the bridge the waters of the Missouri seemed to be a little clearer; the famous muddiness of the lower reaches was beginning to fade.

Yankton, the original capital of Dakota Territory, was one of the most important steamboat landings on the Missouri. The name was a corruption of a Sioux word, 'thanktonwan', meaning 'end village'.[1]

The Missouri paddle steamers were restricted to a very limited season. After the ice cleared in April they had only until July to ply their trade before the water level dropped. After that, the rivertowns would be cut off until the following spring. By the 1860s, up to thirty boats were docking each week at Yankton with settlers and gold prospectors. The settlement grew into a lively little town and the paddle steamer captains built themselves fine homes along gracious tree-lined avenues. Experts in social niceties swore that the hotels were even better than some on the East Coast.

The historic houses are still there, but present-day Yankton cannot be described as a particularly lively place. Indeed, the town seemed to be best-known for the state mental hospital. There was hardly anyone around and Main Street was deserted except for bundles of lolloping tumbleweed.

I found a motel on the outskirts and checked in for one night. The restaurant was closed and I was forced to eat dinner a few yards up the road in something called a Happy Eater. It was running a German sausage promotion. I ordered a selection of bratwurst. They arrived decorated with little flags saying German Sausage Festival. I wondered what on earth induced people to stick flags in sausages?

A few miles outside Yankton, is Gavin's Point, the first of the Missouri's dams and hydro-electric plants. Here is the start of the series of lakes that tame the Big Muddy's flow all the way to Montana.

The next day I drove out to the dam to meet the project engineer Al Munch. He was a serious man with a red face and slicked hair over a balding head. He had spent most of his life working on the Missouri with the Corps of Engineers.

---

[1] Lovers of ephemera will note that Yankton has nothing to do with the term Yankee. This was a contraction of Jan Kees, or John Cheese, a contemptuous nickname given by the Dutch to the New Englanders in the seventeenth century.

Al held the Missouri in deep affection. 'It's the greatest river in the country. As a youngster I lived about fifty miles from it in North Dakota. I remember my dad taking me to see it for the first time. In Britain you take the sea for granted, but I hadn't seen anything like this river. I thought, what an incredible body of water.'

Gavin's Point is the most important of the Missouri's six dams for navigation and flood control. 'We are the ones who decide how much water to let through to keep the boats floating in St Louis,' Al explained. 'And it's usually our water that keeps the lower Mississippi running as well.'

Lack of water was a growing danger. The Missouri was into her fourth year of drought. 'We've got enough in the reservoirs to last for eight years. After that we'll be in a crisis. On one side we have to keep water back for the hydro-electric schemes and recreation on the lakes. But the navigation companies have tremendous political clout and keep hustling Washington to make us release more water. The Corps are stuck like pigs in the middle. We're blamed for everything – right down to the fact that there ain't been no rain!'

I was shown round the dam by the operations supervisor Dennie Spark, an enthusiastic man with a pockmarked, weather beaten face. Like his boss, Dennie adored the river. 'I really and truly believe that the Missouri is the life blood of the Mid-West. But it's so sad. The old river's really hurting now. The reservoirs upstream are down thirty feet and it will take six years of normal rainfall to refill them.'

Dennie led me through a maze of corridors past the shuddering hydro-electric turbines. We climbed a steel staircase and came out on to the dam's spillway. I looked across the concrete. Jagged sheets of sparkling ice lay untidily on the first of the Missouri's lakes, named after Lewis and Clark. The explorers had camped on one of the bluffs here on their way north.

Dennie pushed a button to open one of the spillway gates. 'This'll give you an idea of the power of this ole river,' he said. The water flooded out with a roaring, foaming rush breaking up the ice around the base of the dam. The noise of flooding water was deafening.

'That's nothing,' Dennie shouted. 'Perhaps 1,000 cubic feet of water per second. Seven years ago we had so much water we were spilling thirty times as much. Now, that *was* a sight.'

A couple of men were fishing from a boat 100 yards downstream. Dennie shook his head. 'The fishermen can be real stupid. Sometimes they get out of their boats and start walking on the ice. Now that's real dangerous. We have to open a gate and spill a little water to break up the ice so they're not tempted to do it.'

We strolled across the dam. Dennie pointed out a high cliff fringed with cottonwood trees. It was a favourite suicide spot. 'An Indian boy jumped and landed down in them rocks,' he said. He put a stick of gum in his mouth and rolled it around with his tongue. 'Don't know what it is about this dam, but people like to kill themselves here. Last summer a guy shot himself in the parking lot and then someone did a head dive right into the concrete at the bottom of the dam.'

And with that cheerful snippet of information, I left Gavin's Point and continued onward. The road ran through undulating prairie high above the river. The sun shone in an icy blue sky streaked with aircraft vapour trails. Sixty miles later I crossed Fort Randall dam, the next of the Missouri's hydro-electric enterprises. I turned the Toyota down a dirt track to the site of the old fort that lay a quarter of a mile from the river.

Now I was truly in cowboys and Indians country.

There was little left to remember Fort Randall except for a ruined church. The parade ground and buildings had disappeared years ago. They were marked by a few signposts erected for the benefit of tourists. I climbed a grassy knoll to the cemetery. A white picket fence surrounded a cluster of lonely wooden crosses. The freezing wind ripped through my clothes. Pockets of snow lay on the coarse grass. It was deathly quiet with not even the sound of birds. I could imagine parties of marauding Indians swooping down over the hillsides. It must have been a miserable place to be stationed.

The military outposts on the Dakota frontier were far removed from the glamorous forts of Hollywood legend. They were roughly built with log walls, earth roofs and dirt floors. They deteriorated rapidly, lacked proper ventilation and lighting and became infested with rodents. They were almost impossible to heat. Wind and snow howled through cracks between the logs. Washrooms were a rarity. And such was the overcrowding that bunks were packed closely together. Until the 1870s soldiers often slept in pairs head-to-toe in one bunk.

Life was a tedious routine beginning at 5.30 am and ending at 9.30 pm. The men worked hard on construction projects, cutting firewood, hauling water and guarding cattle and horses. The forts were far from civilization and come evening soldiers had to make their own entertainment. This usually involved consuming large quantities of alcohol and spending their time with the prostitutes that trailed round the forts. Poor hygiene, rampant alcoholism and an unhealthy diet resulted in ill-health and low morale. Desertion was common.

Officers were occasionally joined by their wives, who valiantly organized dances and ice skating parties on the Missouri. Women did not last long. There were bad medical facilities for childbirth, the constant fear of Indian attacks, and limited schooling for children. Far from flouncing around like Maureen O'Hara in bodices clenched to the bosom, many wives worked as fort laundresses to supplement their husbands' meagre incomes.

Fort Randall's graves told their own stories: 16 March 1869, Private Elias A. Pratt – 'killed by Indians'; 14 March 1864 Private John Folck – 'killed by Indians'. By the cemetery entrance was displayed a copy of a letter to Folck's widow Mary from another soldier, Nathaniel Johnson. He described how Folck was helping to load wood on to a wagon. Suddenly they were fired on by seven or eight Indians.

'They shot John with guns and arrows and cut him up with a tomahawk,' his friend wrote. Folck was rescued by a negro called Tap, who managed to get him back to the Fort. He was wounded in fourteen places. He died a few hours later having requested that his clothes be sent to his wife.

'The day was very disagreeable being windy and chilly,' Johnson wrote. 'Men that have been here for five or six years say that he had the most respectful burial of anyone that has been buried here. John and I have bunked together for fifteen months. During that time no angry word or ill feeling ever passed between us . . . I feel that I have lost my best friend.'

There were the graves of infants like William J. Smith, a baby who died from Indian gunshot wounds on 1 September 1878. Others succumbed to whooping cough, pneumonia and tuberculosis.

Bad alcohol was also a danger. I stopped by the grave of a coloured man called David Dezaire. According to the fort surgeon he was a heavy drinker who had contracted pneumonia from 'traders' whisky'

– raw alcohol, gunpowder and a spit of tobacco for colour. He had died aged seventy leaving a Sioux squaw wife and five children.

The light was fading as I left Fort Randall. With the dying sun came a sharp drop in temperature. I turned up the Toyota's heater as I took the road for the rivertown of Chamberlain, my next overnight stop. I remembered a quote by a nineteenth-century soldier, Captain Gerald Russell: 'I was first a bogtrotter [in Ireland], din a cobbler, din an immigrant, din a weary [private soldier], din a corporil, din a sargint, and now I'm a commissioned officer and Captain fur life . . . and gintleman, by act of Congress.' The likes of Russell may not have been the brightest of souls. But life in godforsaken outposts like Fort Randall must have been sheer hell.

It was nearly dark by the time Chamberlain appeared on the horizon. The flat countryside was becoming increasingly monotonous. There were so few other cars around that passing motorists waved at me. The first time it happened I thought they were trying to tell me there was something wrong with my car, that a wheel was about to fall off. I was the cynical Londoner, unable to believe that people would wave simply out of friendliness. I learned to return the greeting. I waved back. You have to make your own entertainment on the prairie.

In an attempt to liven things up I played around with the radio. I couldn't find anything on FM, and AM was all tractor commercials and tripe pork prices.

But I did get a laugh out of the South Dakota Beef Industry Council commercials. They were firmly aimed at health freaks worried about the cholesterol levels in meat. 'Beef! Real food for real people' ran the slogan – the state's cattlemen didn't want anyone having silly ideas about vegetarianism.

One advertisement featured a chap who had given up eating kelp because he realized beef was just as good for him. Then there was a 'beef line' featuring a nutritionist saying that beef was essential for children's health. Nice touch, that. Pile on the guilt. You're a bad mom if you don't give your kids beef.

At Chamberlain I checked into an another anonymous motel that made up for its garish, golden nylon carpet with splendid views of the river. Through the window I could hear the howl of coyotes. I dined next door in a huge barn of a restaurant called Al's Oasis.

The customers were mostly truckers, who had no qualms about piling into great slabs of cow.

Al, whoever he may be, had decorated the place in cowboy chic. Ropes and wagon wheels hung from the ceiling. A menagerie of stuffed furry animals squinted at me through glassy eyes. The waitresses were dressed like extras in *Annie Get Your Gun*. I ordered the house speciality – buffalo burgers. 'BUFFALO – LOW IN CHOLESTEROL!' the menu screamed in big red letters. Hurrah for buffalos! Won't catch a buffalo having a cardiac arrest.

Six

'They'll treat you with disdain on the reservations, white boy.' I remembered the bleak words of the Cherokee back in Chicago. So was this how all Indians treated their white guests? I was about to find out.

For my first excursion into Indian tribal territory I chose Lower Brule, smallest of the reservations on the banks of the Missouri. What's more, there was just the slightest sniff of a Welsh connection.

Over a breakfast of pancakes in a Chamberlain café, I picked up an intriguing nugget of information. An old-timer sitting on the next table started talking to me. I mentioned my Madoc quest. He looked baffled. 'Don't know about no princes,' he said, 'but you should check out Michael Jandreau at Lower Brule.' Jandreau was chairman of the reservation's tribal council. 'Heard that he likes to talk about having Welsh blood.'

To say that I could hardly contain my excitement would be exaggerating. But I was intrigued. I used the café's telephone to call Jandreau. He was very chatty. There was no hint of 'disdain' in his voice and we arranged to meet later that morning.

Driving onto an American Indian reservation for the first time can be a shock. Suddenly you leave the clinical tidiness of white America for another world. At the reservation boundary the road surface changes abruptly. The smooth ribbon of tarmac becomes neglected and cracked. You pass drunken roadsigns that have been knocked askew and never replaced. The verges are strewn with litter; packs of scabby, scavenging dogs rush out to bite the wheels of your car.

Rusting, abandoned cars and agricultural equipment lie rotting in the fields. Many of the shops are derelict. You are likely to see a boarded-up motel that went bust years ago, its car-park overgrown with weeds. The rickety houses are a product of half-hearted workmanship: shabby, chipped paint, holes in the roofs and outside privies. In the backyards are flapping washing lines, broken down caravans and more redundant machinery. (Although outside the most rundown shack you will see a TV satellite dish.)

The Lower Brule tribe of Sioux were better off than most. The population numbered 1,250 and the reservation covered 130,000 acres. They had a strong agricultural economy mainly in popcorn and butter beans. At one time they were the largest single producer of popcorn in the United States. (Today Lower Brule's entire bean production goes to Heinz UK.)

The tribe also had a lucrative bloodsports sideline. Here you could shoot a buffalo or an elk. And, of course, pheasants. South Dakota is *the* pheasant state of America. Come fall and everyone goes hunting.

The Chinese ring-necked pheasant was first introduced to the state in 1898 by a Dr Zitlitz, who released ten birds into the wild. Surprisingly enough, they flourished, despite the extremes in weather and egg-eating vermin like wildcats, skunks and raccoons. Pheasant shooting is now one of the state's biggest tourist money-spinners. As one local wag remarked, 'We have more pheasants than Republicans . . . and you can't count the Republicans.'

I met Michael Jandreau at the tribal office, a bright yellow prefabricated steel bungalow in the centre of Lower Brule village. I walked up a path littered with burger wrappers and Coke cans. Inside was a glorious muddle of cardboard boxes piled high with paper and half-open overflowing filing. Plastic sports trophies covered the shelves. On the walls were posters calling for a drug-free America.

Michael was a small man of forty-six with a kind, squashy face. His sparkling eyes suggested a nervous restlessness. He was dressed in a startling red windcheater, an even brighter red baseball hat, black jeans and cowboy boots. He spoke quietly, often gesticulating with his hands.

Later, when we had got to know each other, I asked him if he had a tribal name. Michael was coy. After much prodding he revealed that it was *Tatanka Waka* – Buffalo Feather. 'It came about because I was responsible for introducing the tribe's buffalo herd a few years back. The feather connection comes from my grandfather who was called Long Eagle.'

He had been chairman of the tribal council, Lower Brule's governing body, for eleven years. 'Is being tribal chairman the equivalent of chief?' I asked. Michael chuckled at my naïvety. 'Remember,' I added hastily, 'you're talking to a dumb Englishman who's been brought up on cowboys and Indians.'

'Okay, I get you. But no, the chairman is a political position for business purposes. Chief is a position of honour that is granted to you by the people. Traditionally the Lower Brule band don't have a chief. We have an individual who *claims* to be a headman because of him being a full-blooded Sioux . . .' and here he curled a lip and sniffed loudly, 'but he took that on himself. I will say no more.'

Michael suggested that we drive out into the hills to find the tribe's buffalo herd. I grabbed my camera and joined him in a beaten up four-wheel-drive Chevrolet. It had a cracked windscreen and hadn't been swept out in years. A layer of yellowy-brown prairie dust covered the floor.

As we left the village Michael pointed out a wooden corral surrounded with white wooden benches. 'That's where we have our rodeos in the summer.'

'I thought it was only the cowboys who had rodeos.'

'Ha!' Michael's mouth moved into a wide grin. 'Hey, you gotta remember something. There's quite a bit of cowboy in us Indians.'

He coaxed the Chevvy up a potholed track into the hills above the village. The vehicle threatened to rattle itself apart. He lazily caressed the steering wheel with one hand. With the other he helped himself to handfuls of sunflower seeds from a bag on the dashboard. 'I quit smoking five years ago and I need something like this to occupy me.'

I could wait no longer to ask the big question. 'So what's all this I hear about you being part-Welsh?'

'Sure.' Michael spat a sunflower husk into a styrofoam cup wedged between his legs. 'That was from my great-grandmother. Pure-blooded Welsh she was. Think she was from – what do you call them? – the valleys.'

His paternal great-grandfather was the result of a union between a French trapper named Jandreau and a Sioux squaw. It was a good story of the Old West.

The little boy was born at a camp at Crow Creek about thirty miles west of Lower Brule. The trapper fell ill and his fellow Frenchmen decided to take him back to St Louis. The boy, aged three, insisted on going with his father. Rather than leave her people, his Indian mother elected to stay behind. The party set out south, but the trapper died after only a few days' journey. When they reached Missouri Valley, Iowa, his friends handed the boy over to a couple of homesteaders who raised him. The boy grew up and married Michael's Welsh great-grandmother, whose parents had emigrated from Wales a few years earlier.

'There's been a lot more Sioux blood in the family since then, but I kinda like having the French connection,' Michael added. 'There are a lot of us Indians round here with French surnames.'

'So do you feel particularly Welsh?'

'At school I used to get real sad when I read about how children worked down the mines in Wales. Perhaps that was a part of my own background crying out. I'm pretty short too. Guess that makes me Welsh.'

'But can you sing? The Welsh are supposed to have great voices.'

'Uh, uh. No way. Can't even dance, so I'm not much of a Sioux either. I've got a pair of beaded moccasins, but that's about it.'

The Chevvy bumped across the prairie. It was cold and windy. The sun struggled to break through the clouds. We reached the brow of a hill. Michael stopped the car. We gazed down at the Missouri.

'It always makes me sad when I look at her,' Michael whispered. For what had once been a twisting, snake of water was now a wide, placid lake. Thanks to the Corps of Engineers and their dams the whole character of the Sioux's beloved river had been changed forever.

Lower Brule reservation lost 28,000 acres of rich, flood-irrigated soil when the two neighbouring dams – Big Bend and Fort Randall – were completed in the 1950s. The reservation was forced to move its village two miles. The Indians received $5,000,000 compensation for the loss of their most productive land. There was resentment in Michael's voice. 'It seems a lot, but we had a hard struggle financing new irrigation projects. We had a great deal of poverty in those early years.'

The Missouri's hydro-electric plants had generated millions of dollars. But the reservation had seen not one penny more than the original payment. It had taken twenty years to get even a reduction in the cost of electricity for their irrigation project.

But far more importantly, the Sioux had lost an old friend. The force of progress had destroyed part of Mother Earth's gift to her people. The Sioux believe that a river is as much a part of life as land. Water, land, animals are all intricately part of one another. They are all created by God for man's use. Everything should be in harmony. Major disruptions are viewed with extreme trepidation.

The Indians also claim a scientific argument. They say that man-made change in a river invites disaster. Before the dams were built, the Missouri was a fast-flowing stream of cold water which was thickly over-shadowed by trees. But now the stream has slowed down and the banks are barren so that the water has warmed up. It evaporates faster and creates changes in the weather. The Sioux say that this explained why the region was now four years into a drought and the Missouri was at its lowest ebb yet. The news was not good for the Corps of Engineers. For, according to Sioux legend, such droughts could last for twenty-eight years!

'To create a lake where a river should be is very bad news for our people.' Michael stopped the car near the water. 'Okay, we have come to terms with it – what else can we do? We understand that we need electricity and that the white man's cities must be protected from floods. But it has created great feelings of resentment, feelings of being used and abused.' His eyes met mine. 'They've torn the heart out of the Missouri but it still keeps beating. You can't keep things down for ever. Dams can be broken and the glory of God keeps living on.'

He cheered up a little as he remembered his childhood. 'I grew up and ran these hills as a boy, lived on choke cherries and wild turnips and plums.

'Aw, it was beautiful. A big bottom land where the river ran swift and muddy.' As a boy he collected frogs and sold them to a store-keeper in Chamberlain. 'He gave me a nickel for each one. I usually handed it back and traded it for penny candy.'

The wind gusted around the car, ruffling the prairie grasses. Michael changed the conversation to the subject of Britain. 'Now that's somewhere I'd like to see. I've read a lot about England. I really like that writer of yours. What's his name? Herriot?'

'What? You mean James Herriot, who wrote *All Creatures Great and Small?*' The last thing I had expected was to be discussing James Herriot, that most English of writers, while in the company of a Sioux tribal chairman on the South Dakotan prairie.

'Yeah. Got all his books. I'd really like to see those Yorkshire Dales. The way he describes them makes them sound just like this country. We're a bit bigger out here, but the colours are the same, aren't they?'

I looked across the rolling, russet brown landscape. 'You know, I think you've got a point there,' I said. 'Put up a few stone walls and you could be on Ilkley Moor.'

'Yeah, that's exactly what I thought.' He paused for thought. 'Mother Earth's not so selective after all.'

We cruised around the hills for another hour looking for the buffalo herd, but they had moved to another part of the reservation. 'Always the same with buffalo.' Michael spat a sunflower husk out of the window. 'You can never find 'em when you need 'em.'

As we drove back through the hills we talked about the social problems facing the Indians. There are an estimated four million native Americans, the majority living away from their reservations.

To put it bluntly, the majority of white Americans complain that the Indians are lazy good-for-nothings. They will tell you that the Indians grab large hand-outs of Government cash, which they fritter away on cars that are never serviced and are left to rot where they break down. And, of course, alcohol. Talk to reasonably well-educated people in New York or Los Angeles and you'll hear that reservation Indians are permanently drunk. The impression I got is that Americans regard the reservations as a cluster of nasty pimples they would rather forget about.

The Indians reply that for 150 years the white man has been engaged upon a methodical obliteration of their culture. He does not understand their ways, never did and never will. Why can't they be left alone by what they see as destructive, decadent white America? As for alcohol, it is always a few that give the rest a bad name.

Michael was refreshingly frank about Lower Brule's shortcomings. I heard later that he was well-known in South Dakota for blunt talking. He did not allow his emotions to cloud his judgement.

The reservation's only bar was closed several years ago. But the bootleggers still sold out of the back door. 'Sure, we have an alcohol problem like on any reservation. Drugs as well. We'll never be able to stop that; I guess it's just a question of education, a balance.

'I believe that biologically there is an inherent weakness to alcohol in my people. I've been around non-Indians and Indians. I've never seen an Indian who's been able to hold alcohol like a non-Indian. Indian drinkers will end up with cirrhosis of the liver more quickly than non-Indians. I believe it has to do with the whole dietary process. Historically, we never had alcohol. We never even had sugar to speak of, and sugar and alcohol are so closely linked. That's why we also have such a high incidence of sugar diabetes.'

'It's all very well *you* talking like that,' I countered. 'Trouble is when us whites suggest anything like that we're accused of racialism.'

'Yup. That's too bad, I suppose.' Michael spat out another husk and wiped his mouth.

He dropped me back at my car. We said goodbye. We had enjoyed each other's company. As an afterthought I asked what he thought was the future of the native American. Could we look forward to a new era of Indian pride?

Michael thought so. Moderates like himself believed the years of US Government nannying and oppression were finally at an end. 'Our image is looking better, and frankly it wasn't very good what with the alcohol and drugs. But we spend a lot of time pointing out the dangers and we're winning the battle.

'I believe that some day the reservations, if only they'll put their mind and heart to it, will be self-sufficient. We will not need the federal government. In the past so many educated people have left reservations and never returned. But now we have professional people like doctors who are willing to return and look at their responsibility to their people without saying "I've got to make it for me." If people want to leave the reservations, sure, let them go ahead. But the people here will be independent. That is my dream.'

The most emotive name in the history of nineteenth-century Indian sacrifice and struggle is Wounded Knee. Here, on the bleak prairie in the south-west corner of South Dakota, all hope of reconciliation with the white man died on 28 December 1890.

By the end of the 1880s the US authorities had stripped the Sioux of their remaining dignity. The humiliating defeat in 1876 of General George Armstrong Custer's Seventh Cavalry at Little Big Horn prompted a wave of anti-Indian feeling. The 'savages' could not be allowed to get away with it. So-called civilized newspapers like the *New York Herald* called for extermination and Indians all over America were hunted down and killed without mercy.

As far as white Americans were concerned, the Indian was a dangerous creature no better than the wolf or the rattlesnake. 'The tales that first awakened the attention of childhood,' wrote Thomas L. McKenney, a nineteenth-century administrator of Indian affairs, 'were of the painted savage, creeping with the stealthy tread of the panther, upon the sleeping inmates of the cabin ... of bleeding scalps, torn from the heads of gray-haired old men, of infants, and of women ... and of the dreadful scenes of torture at the stake.'

So when news arrived in early 1890 of an Indian religious revival sweeping across the Great Plains, America reacted with horror and hysteria. It was called the Ghost Dance and it was led by a dubious self-styled Indian messiah called Wovoka. He preached that the ghosts of dead Indians were rising up to help living Indians in the hour of greatest need. The craze spread like fire. Normal life on the Sioux reservations stopped. No work was done and the schools were closed. And while Wovoka claimed his message was one of peace and love, the authorities were nervous.

Three days after Christmas 1890 a Seventh Cavalry unit detained a party of about 350 suspected Sioux ghost-dancers at Wounded Knee creek. They were on their way to the nearby reservation at Pine Ridge having trudged from Standing Rock reservation on the northern edge of South Dakota.

Five hundred cavalrymen surrounded the Indian camp. They set up four Hotchkiss guns – large calibre, quick-firing artillery pieces. It was a freezing night and the Indians huddled patiently in their teepees.

At first light the next morning the soldiers lined up the Sioux men and ordered them to hand over the few ancient weapons in their possession. No one really knows what exactly happened in the next few minutes. There was a disturbance and it is said that a shot rang out. The troops panicked and opened fire at point-blank range. Their carbines were joined by the Hotchkiss guns rattling off shells at the rate of one a second. Flying shrapnel tore into the teepees. Young girls knelt and covered their faces with shawls so that they could not see the troopers walk up and shoot them. The slaughter continued until not one of the Indians – men, women or children – remained standing. 'We tried to run,' one of the women said later, 'but they shot us like we were buffalo.'

By the time the smoke cleared and the snow was settling on the blood-soaked mud, more than half the Sioux camp was dead. Many of the wounded crawled away to die later. The final death toll was estimated at more than 300.

White America claimed a great victory. The US Government described the action as a 'battle' and handed out medals to the victorious troops. After all, they said, were not twenty-five soldiers killed? True. Although nearly all of them were killed by their own bullets or shrapnel.

With the centenary of Wounded Knee only months away, I decided to see the place for myself. I temporarily abandoned the Missouri and drove west to Pine Ridge reservation, home to 25,000 Oglala Sioux, largest of the American tribes. Another 175,000 members are scattered around the country, living off the reservation.

After the relative tidiness of Lower Brule – admittedly tiny by comparison – Pine Ridge was a run-down, squalid mess. Locals had warned me not to expect too much, but this was the sort of Indian shambles that right-wing rednecks make jokes about.

Trash, empty bottles and wrecked cars littered the roadside ditches. I turned on the radio and found the local Pine Ridge station. A pest control commercial gave way to ethnic Sioux music – discordant yah-yahing voices accompanied by frantic war drums – that was continually interrupted by coughing disc jockeys. Every so often the music disappeared altogether. It sounded as if someone in the studio had tripped over and accidentally pulled out a plug.

The road into the main town of Pine Ridge, nestling in a bowl in the prairie, was pitted with craters. As I reached the outskirts, the tarmac fizzled out completely. The Toyota's suspension creaked as I plunged on to a rude gravel track. There were one or two parked maintenance trucks and signs that indicated roadworks, but I suspected that there had been little progress for months.

In the centre of town I joined a chaotic assortment of battered, ancient cars that trundled over the potholes. Their wheels churning up the road surface. I quickly closed the windows as a clogging cloud of dust swept over the Toyota. It was like being in a Missouri fog. I could hardly see in front of my face. There was a dreadful feeling of hopelessness and deprivation: tatty, grey houses and dilapidated shops. Children hung about at street corners; haggard, toothless old men in ragged anoraks sat on the pavements staring at their feet.

I stopped the car to ask the way to the tribal council offices. I tried an Indian with a leathery face. His breath smelled of alcohol. He didn't seem to understand me and I remembered that, in Pine Ridge, English was the second language to the Sioux dialect of Lakota. (And anyway, there wasn't much chance of him understanding my British accent!)

I parked by the police station and walked inside. Holes pitted the floorboards. At least one of the officers was drunk. Another man – apparently nothing to do with the police and just passing the time of day out of the cold – gave me the right directions.

The tribal council building was quite smart from the outside: red brick and one of the few half-decent constructions in town. The Stars and Stripes fluttered from a flagpole. I walked inside to a marvellous muddle. Bits of linoleum were missing from the floor like stray pieces in a jig-saw puzzle. Foam stuffing poked through the seats of ripped vinyl chairs. The noticeboards were a jumble of scraps of paper relating to tribal business. Posters warning about the dangers of drugs and alcohol: 'Sioux For Sobriety', 'It is better to build children than to repair adults.' They hung next to leaflets requesting entrants for the Miss Indian contest to be held in Mexico later that year.

Earlier that morning I had telephoned the offices asking to speak to the tribal council chairman. He was unavailable. After a certain amount of confusion, the operator put me through to someone called Alex White Plume. Mr White Plume was a member of the council's executive committee. He sounded a little harassed, but agreed to spare me a few minutes during his lunch break.

A girl at the reception desk pointed me down a corridor. There was an unholy hubbub about the place. All the doors leading off the corridor were wide open. A mêlée of people, old hunched men, mothers and toddlers, wandered casually in and out of rooms petitioning council members. It was the antithesis of United States Government offices I had visited, usually places of orderly calm. I eventually found Alex White Plume in an office at the rear of the building. He was surrounded by a mountain of files.

Alex was in an awful state. He had been elected to the tribal council only that very morning. He was now bogged down with paperwork. Outside the door a noisy queue of people waited to see him. Old women with grizzled, leathery faces jabbered loudly in Lakota. 'Wish they'd go away,' Alex muttered. He complained of a headache and asked me for an aspirin. I was very sorry, but I did not have any on me. If he wanted, I could get some from the car. Alex waved a hand and told me not to worry. He would stick it out.

Alex was in his early thirties. He had long, straggly hair and wore cowboy boots and jeans ripped at the knees. I asked him what plans the tribe had for celebrating – if that was the right word – the centenary of Wounded Knee.

He explained that 1990 was the year that the Sioux would finally come out of mourning for their slaughtered dead. About five hundred horsemen, including representatives from other countries, were planning a seven-day ride from Standing Rock reservation 160 miles to the north. The journey would end with a ceremony at the mass grave at Wounded Knee. There had been similar rides for the past five years, but this was the grand finale. Other tribes around America also planned ceremonies to expurgate their grief.

'We will pull the mourners out of mourning. According to our tradition, the children of those who died on that terrible field are born with that horrendous act against them. So are their children and so on. Now, it is time for us to be purified. Our people have had one hundred years of sadness and no direction. We have just been existing. By doing this we will build unity amongst our people and move into a happy new life.'

What was the US Government's reaction to all this? 'Jesus,' Alex said softly. He put his head in his hands and gently rubbed his aching forehead. 'I don't even know that they care.'

I learned that native Americans were divided into two camps: progressive and non-progressive. The progressive were happy to integrate into American society and to follow the white man's ways. The non-progressives wanted nothing to do with the US Government. Their dream was to be left alone on autonomous, self-governing reservations. They disapproved strongly of mainstream education. They did not want their children leaving the reservations to be educated and then returning home with the white man's way of thinking.

Alex was a non-progressive. So were his Pine Ridge colleagues.

'In the reservation we are in our own world. We have our own language, culture and our government. For years, the United States Government tried to get us into their mainstream, but still they treated us as apart from their society.' Alex smiled. 'Know what? I'm thankful because otherwise we would all be white people now. Because of this racism our culture is intact.'

But were they not cutting themselves off by taking backward steps? Wouldn't this attitude actually damage their children?

'Not really. Our kids get confused when they go to white schools and then come back here. If we teach them our language and culture they'll stay on the reservations and will work to make the reservations better places. Then we can increase industry, make ourselves self-sufficient and self-governing. We hope to be independent by 1992.'

'How independent do you mean? Will you issue passports?'

I suspected Alex was becoming a little impatient with my questioning. He stood up. 'I don't like to predict the future. We used to do that before the white people came, when life was orderly and predictable. But it's not like that any more.'

He was about to show me out. At that moment a woman stuck her head round the door. Alex looked relieved. He spoke to the newcomer. 'This guy's from England. Wants to learn about us. You can talk to him.' And with that, he introduced me to Charlotte Black Elk.

Charlotte was highly educated, a lawyer and a molecular biologist, and one of the most respected people on the reservation. She was a petite woman in her late thirties with long brown hair that tumbled down to her waist. Behind black-rimmed spectacles lay an exceedingly pretty face. She was dressed incongruously in a button-up woollen cream overcoat, knee-length skirt, black stockings and smart, white shoes. I had noticed that everyone else on the reservation, both men and women, favoured jeans and sweatshirts. Charlotte, with her immaculately manicured, blood-red fingernails, could have been on her way to a debutante cocktail party.

I thanked Alex for his time. Charlotte led me down the corridor to another office. We settled under a glaring neon strip in a room furnished with a battered table and chairs.

Charlotte was not to be messed with. She was an extremely single-minded woman with eyes that seemed to mock me. Perhaps this was the Cherokee's famous disdain. Whatever the case, Miss Black Elk appeared to regard me with the confidence of a rattlesnake about to devour a baby rabbit. I felt relieved to be British. At least she couldn't pin any blame on *my* forefathers.

Charlotte was a deeply committed Oglala Sioux. Her late grandfather had been the distinguished Ben Black Elk, who, in his war bonnet standing by Mount Rushmere, was the most photographed Indian of all time. His had been the first image to be broadcast worldwide by the satellite *Telstar* in 1963. When asked to give the world a greeting in his own language, he had drily announced: 'We are still here.'

Charlotte was maintaining the family tradition as one of the most learned members of the tribe. She may have looked like the epitome of the westernized Indian, but she possessed radical views. Indeed, she was responsible for the eponymous Black Elk Rule, a piece of US Government legislation that has chilled the hearts of capitalists hoping to profit from sacred Indian lands.

The Black Elk Rule concerned the Black Hills, the range of mountains sixty miles from Pine Ridge in western South Dakota. This exceptionally beautiful expanse of grassy ridges and flowery valleys gets its name from the dense, black-green covering of pine and fir. They are said to be the oldest mountains in the world – six billion years old.

But there is more to the Black Hills than being one of the nation's most popular national parks. The area serves as a monument to the history of the white man's greed. For beneath the surface of the hills lies the mineral that has turned friend against friend.

Gold.

The Sioux hate the sight of gold. They believe it should stay in the earth. The earth is the Sioux's mother, the trees their brothers and sisters, all of whom have as much right to a dignified existence as human beings. As Charlotte said, 'When you rape the earth and destroy trees you are defiling our relatives. What really hurts is that over ninety per cent of the gold taken out of the earth is used for jewellery. Why should humans devastate our mother to decorate their bodies?'

With the discovery of gold in 1874, a wild rush of prospectors flooded into the Black Hills. The mining enterprises were centered around Deadwood and Lead, which grew into hell-holes of vice and bloodshed as more seekers of 'pay dirt' flocked in. The writer James Bryce provided the most colourful description of the hell that was gold-mining on the western frontier: 'an industry which is like gambling in its influence on the character, with its sudden alterations of wealth and poverty, its long hours of painful toil relieved by bouts of drinking and merriment, its life in a crowd of men who have come together from the four winds of heaven, and will scatter again as soon as some are enriched and others ruined, and the gold in the gulch is exhausted'.

The Black Hills were rich with gold and the countryside became scarred from the jabbing of pick-axes. The mining has continued to this day and the Homestake Mine at Lead remains the largest single producer of gold in the United States.

But there is more gold in them thar' hills. Tons of it. The mining companies would dearly love to tear even more out of the heart of the landscape. And that is where Charlotte, the lawyer, stepped in.

Charlotte argued in court that the Sioux were the rightful owners of the Black Hills. The mining companies had no right to be there. The Government refuted this, claiming that the Sioux had no historical connection with the area. Only when the white man moved in had the Indians staked their claim. 'I had to prove that the Black Hills were sacred to us, that they had been stolen from us and that we wanted them back. The Government said this was nonsense and that we had been reading too much tourist literature.'

To establish Sioux ownership, Charlotte closely studied the ancient stories to see if they were scientifically verifiable. She discovered that 2,000-year-old legends had a sound scientific basis. Far from being a bunch of painted savages, the Sioux possessed a high degree of scientific knowledge with a measuring system similar to the metric scale.

I nervously fingered my gold signet ring as Charlotte launched into her thesis. 'One of our stories tells of part of our traditional, sacred land. It says that, having been soft, the earth became solid. The water separated from the land and some of the liquid was tossed upwards to make the sky.' (The Sioux name for blue sky can be translated as, 'I am the difference tossed upwards.') 'The legend goes on to say that there was a desire for a heart for the earth. So material was pushed from the core to the surface.

'This land that our ancestors were talking about can only be the Black Hills. The legend fits the geology of the area and meets biological test. Putting it simply, the hills were created when the core of the earth pushed material upwards.'

Charlotte's argument was good enough for the courts. Thanks to her, there is now a moratorium on expanding the mining operations. However she grimly admitted, 'Unless the price of gold falls drastically I'm sure that eventually they'll try to level the Black Hills completely.'

She smoothed her hair and crossed her legs in a mildly provocative manner. They were the actions of a very attractive woman, who knew it. I settled back in my chair, enjoying the lecture.

'So far only the legends of the Black Hills meet the test of the Black Elk Rule,' she went on. 'The Book of Genesis, for example, wouldn't stand the test. It talks about God hovering over the water and then from water God made land. That cannot be proved scientifically.'

I remarked that the Government must have been dumbfounded when Charlotte introduced her arguments. 'Yeah, they really were.' She allowed a schoolgirly giggle. 'It's the Lakota warrior in me. It is our tradition to walk right up to the enemy and touch them without them knowing.'

She was fond of meeting the authorities in the court room. The Black Elk Rule had also secured the Sioux's rights to pray in the Black Hills.

Shocking though it may sound, it was not until the Carter administration's 1978 American Freedom of Religion Act that native Americans won full rights to practise their own religions. Until then, so-called pagan ceremonies were liable to prosecution. The legislation outlawing Sioux religion and culture was passed in 1883, although there were no prosecutions after the 1930s.

Thanks to the efforts of missionaries like Father Pierre de Smet most of the Great Plains Indians were converted to Christianity in the last century. Some tribes wanted the option to follow the ancient sacred rituals. But the priests, backed by the authorities, persecuted any of their flock who strayed from the path of Jesus Christ.

'You will meet many people on this reservation who do not speak Lakota,' Charlotte said. 'The reason is that their parents wanted to save them from being beaten by teachers and nuns, who ordered them to speak only English. It was an effort to wipe us out as a people and kill our language. My father spent some time in Europe with the US Army and we used to joke about it. When he came home he said the nuns hadn't taught proper English anyway because no one in England could understand him!'

Even after the 1978 act the persecution continued, albeit in a more subtle and sinister way.

A few years ago Charlotte decided to go on a vision quest – a time of prayer and fasting – in the Black Elk wilderness, part of the Black Hills named after her celebrated grandfather. 'The authorities made it very difficult for me,' she continued. 'For a start, I had to pay a permit of forty-five dollars just to be there – the Government requires you to have a permit for any special use of the Black Hills. For example, hiking is okay, but praying is not. Then they told me where I could camp and where I could fast. And all the time I was there they watched to see if they needed to do an environmental impact statement on me.'

Not being versed in American bureaucratic gobbledygook, I stopped Charlotte. 'What's an environmental impact statement when it's at home?' I asked.

'Oh, they wanted to see if I was going to disrupt the environment. Like they do when they build a road.'

'But that's crazy.'

Charlotte smiled bitterly. 'Well, it's not exactly what you expect from a country that was founded on the principles of religious freedom. Maybe they thought I was being a bit of an old hippy. Trouble is that most Americans come from the Judaeo-Christian culture. If you don't pray in a fixed church, they find it difficult to take your religion seriously.'

Charlotte looked at her watch. She had matters of tribal business to attend to. I thanked her for her time and she showed me out of the building. I pointed the Toyota back through Pine Ridge's dust cloud and took the road for the settlement of Wounded Knee.

I did not stay for long at this sad place. There was little to mark one of the greatest tragedies in Indian history. There was no grand basilica or monument, just a modest chapel surrounded by barren grassland and standing on the hillock where the Hotchkiss guns would have spat their death. There was no one around and the church door was locked. At the foot of the hill was a broken-down concrete platform, which marked the site of the mass grave. It was strewn with depressing plastic flowers. I tried to imagine the rattle of the guns and the crying of the children, but the bleakness of the prairie flattened my senses. A flutter of snowflakes, borne on a freezing east wind, drove me back to the fuggy heat of the car.

The undignified end of the victims of Wounded Knee will be remembered for a long time. 'A people's dream died there,' grieved one Indian poet. 'It was a beautiful dream ... the nation's hoop is broken and scattered. There is no centre any longer, and the sacred tree is dead.'

But Sioux leaders like Michael Jandreau and Charlotte Black Elk believed in the future, that their culture would live again. So, perhaps we should linger instead on the image of the Sioux horseman as the gallant knight of the Great Plains. 'Never was there such rainbow colour brought to combat,' wrote the historian William Brandon in a moving epitaph to the Indian brave. '... the rippling war bonnets, sometimes trailing down to the heels, the jewel-work of beads and porcupine quills, arrow quivers furred with the magic skin of the otter, and hearts made strong by dreams that always came in the form of songs.'

I delayed my return to the Missouri while I checked out Deadwood. I wanted to see this place that, according to the Sioux, summed up the vilest aspects of American opportunism.

It was a relief to leave to monotony of the plains. Seventy miles from Pine Ridge I began to climb into the Black Hills. A fine mist came down as the road cut through dense snow-sprinkled forest skirting deep, dark gorges. There were increasing signs of human habitation, not least the number of roadsigns peppered with bullet holes. Then came the tatty advertising billboards that are as much a part of the American countryside as fir trees. I turned a steep corner and drove into Main Street.

At first sight, Deadwood was a dump. And at second sight it was still a dump: a ghastly, tacky tourist hell-hole that made Las Vegas look posh. There was not even the vaguest attempt at sophistication.

Just a month earlier, gambling had been made legal after a twenty-year ban. The town had woken from its slumbers and every bar along Main Street now featured blackjack tables and banks of jangling slot machines. Tourists from all over South Dakota and the neighbouring states were flocking in to try their luck. They had the glazed, suspicious looks you get from staring into gaming machines all day: pallid faces from too much alcohol and too little fresh air. I hardly saw a person smile once or show any emotion other than greed.

Things hadn't changed much in a hundred years. J. W. Buel in his 1886 volume, *Heroes of the Plains* wrote: 'Deadwood was full of rough characters, cut-throats, gamblers and the devil's agents generally. The arbiter of all disputes was either a knife or pistol, and the graveyard soon started with a steady run of victims... Sodom and Gomorrah were both dull, stupid towns compared with Deadwood, for in a square contest for the honors of moral depravity the Black Hills' capital could give the people of the Dead Sea Cities three points in the game and then skunk them both.'

The 'steady run of victims' included US Marshal turned gunfighter, James Butler 'Wild Bill' Hickok. According to General Custer, Wild Bill was 'the greatest bad man ever in likelihood seen upon the earth'. By the time he arrived in Deadwood he had killed anything between thirty and a hundred men with his legendary ivory-handled pistols, a fact that no doubt impressed another Deadwood resident, Martha 'Calamity Jane' Canary.

Calamity Jane is said to have been the most colourful – and depraved – woman in the Black Hills, a boozed-up hooker and superb shot, who had scouted for Custer. Calamity and Wild Bill furthered their sleazy reputations by embarking on a rumbustious affair. The tryst ended only after Bill was shot in the back of the head while playing poker in Main Street's Number Ten Saloon. Rather than waste his energies on gold panning, Bill chose the less arduous route of gambling by which to make his fortune. He fell to the ground clutching two pairs – aces on eights – which has gone down in history as 'deadman's hand'. Bill's assailant Jack McCall, who had lost his temper after Bill had deprived him of a sizeable amount of cash, was eventually hanged for his murder.

I took a room at the Franklin Hotel. With its classic Greek ceilings

and golden oak panelling, the Franklin had been the smartest place
in town on its opening in 1903. Nearly ninety years later the hotel's
charms were distinctly faded. The once gracious lobby was now
stuffed with slot machines. It shook with the hellish noise of beep-
beeping and clinking coins. Elderly, sharp-eyed women in Crimplene
slacks hovered like vultures by the machines. They clutched plastic
cups containing their change. A nice old lady called Alice gave me
a lesson in winning. What with all the beeps and flashing lights I
hadn't a clue what was going on. In my panic I kept pushing the
wrong 'hold' buttons. Alice lost patience with me and moved on to
another machine. I ended up two dollars down.

After dinner I took a stroll down Main Street. It had begun to
snow and dirty, grey slush covered the pavements. Chipped life-
size figures of pipe-chomping 'old-timers' sat outside souvenir shops
selling an unspeakable array of junk: Calamity Jane tea towels and
plastic buffalo horns for mounting on your car.

I braved one of the bars and ordered a beer. A sign above the bar
read: 'A diplomat is someone who tells you to go to hell in such a
way that you think you might enjoy the trip.'

The place stank of stale cigar smoke. Pot-bellied men in sagging
jeans crowded around well-scuffed blackjack tables. A fat, sweaty
bruiser, was wearing a T-shirt with the slogan Stamp Out AIDS. It
featured a drawing of two stick men engaged in anal sex, with a
large red cross painted over them. Subtlety was not a strong point
in Deadwood.

I got into conversation with a man at the bar. He introduced
himself as Joe. Joe's job was mending the electronic poker machines
in the bars around Deadwood. A bleeper was attached to his belt
and he was taking a few minutes' rest before being called out to fix
the next broken machine.

The machines were Joe's children. 'You've no idea what shit they
get,' he moaned. He talked about unlucky punters who got angry
and head-butted the screens.

'There was a guy last week who must have dropped five hundred
dollars in quarters every night into the same machine. Must've had
callouses on his fingers. Then, regular as clockwork, come 1 am he'd
try to beat the machine to death and it's me who has to come out
and fix it.' I could have sworn there were tears in Joe's eyes. 'These
guys don't understand how sensitive these machines are. They'll tip

'em up, put their fists through 'em. They don't need that shit, poor things.'

I returned to my room at the Franklin and lay awake listening to people running up and down the corridor whooping and shouting. The only thing that was missing from a hundred years ago was the sound of gunshots. A motor somewhere in the hotel kept up an irritating hum. The incessant tinkle of coins came from downstairs.

Before falling asleep I wished that I could be whisked back to the time of Wild Bill and Calamity Jane. It sounded a lot more fun than that of the inhabitants of twentieth-century Deadwood.

Seven

As a small boy I spent many hours looking at the pictures in a biographical children's book called *Cowboy In The Making*. The cowboy bit I understood well enough. But where was this place 'The Making'? It puzzled me for days. Only when I could read properly did I realise the author, Will James, was talking about his life as a fledgling cowboy.

It was a super story about how Will learned to lasso chickens before he 'moseyed on down to the corral' to try his hand on a real, live calf; and how his father died leaving him in the care of an old trapper called Bopy. The nine-year-old Will had a pair of pet wolves and a rifle twice as tall as himself. He roasted rabbits on open fires. And during a particularly exciting episode, when a bear climbed on to the roof of the log cabin he shared with Bopy, I would hold my breath and wonder at the toughness of it all. But more to the point, he never went to school. I envied him dreadfully for his freedom.

Except for the required schoolboy diet of Hollywood Westerns (so dull compared to Will's adventures), I knew little else of cowboys. At least, that was the case until I reached Pierre, picturesque capital of South Dakota.

As I arrived, the town was mourning the biggest rodeo star of them all, Casey Tibbs, who had died that week from cancer aged sixty. With his purple chaps and trademark rocking chair style, Tibbs was one of the most colourful cowboys of the twentieth century. He had grown up on his family's ranch outside Pierre and was on the professional rodeo circuit at the age of fifteen. A six-times world champion bronc rider, he numbered ex-President Gerald Ford amongst his friends. Tibbs had a sharp wit. One night at dinner in the White House, Ford and his family were discussing assassination attempts. Tibbs interrupted. 'Mr President,' he drawled. 'I don' know why anyone'd want to shoot you. You never did anything.'

It was late when I rolled into Pierre after a long drive from the Black Hills. The orange sun was dipping below the prairies as I crossed the Missouri into town.

Poor little Pierre, so lost and forgotten that it was the mid-1980s before McDonald's finally opened a restaurant here. With a population of ten thousand, Pierre is one of the smallest state capitals and, to compound her misery, she is the nation's only capital city that is not situated on an Interstate. And while other US cities celebrate summer with lavish carnivals, her citizens line Main Street with chicken wire, break open the six-packs and enjoy a day of turkey racing.

Pierre stands alone on the prairie, in the middle of the state, with her magnificent, domed Capitol building struggling to prove that she is a seat of government. But were it not for the state legislature, she would be little more than a cow town. She survives on ranching and farming. And it has been said that before the days of central heating, many farmers ran for office not out of political ambition, but simply as a means of escaping their homes in winter. Cowboys are the town's lifeline and divorce settlements are frequently paid in the form of cattle. As one local told me, 'If the farmers are happy then everybody's happy. They come in and spend their money and the businesses do well – and when those guys have money they really splash it around. If farming's bad, then we all suffer.'

Locals describe Pierre as a small town that wants to be a big town, but is too scared to take the leap. They are cautious folk round here, many of German and Scandinavian descent. Change is not welcomed – it took three years of argument before the authorities finally agreed to build the Convention Center. But this conservatism has its advantages. The pretty tree-lined streets and riverside paths are beautifully kept and the town is so free of crime that the theft of a car stereo makes headline news. In short, she's a sleepy old place where the greatest hazard is being bitten by a rattlesnake on a summer picnic.

Across the river is Pierre's smaller sister, Fort Pierre, one of the oldest settlements on the Missouri. An important trading post during the Gold Rush years, prospectors from the south would land here after travelling up river. After stocking up with provisions, they would take ox-drawn freight wagons and stage coaches for all points West.

My return to the Missouri had brought me back on to the trail of Lewis and Clark. Since the tragedy of Sergeant Floyd's death, the journey had been relatively uneventful, although they learned from the Indians that they were now in an area inhabited by a colony of dwarfs. These eighteen-inch high 'deavels . . . in human form with remarkable large heads' were said to live in an ancient mound a few miles from the river where they busied themselves killing stray Indians. The Captains took a party to investigate, but it comes as little surprise that they found no sign of the creatures. The remnants of Madoc's merry band? Probably not. The Welsh may be short, but they're not *that* short.

In late September the expedition plunged deep into Sioux country. Having moored up in the vicinity of what is now Pierre, they prepared to meet the locals.

News of their arrival spread quickly. The Sioux, led by their chief Black Buffalo, swooped down to the river. The Captains handed over a few gifts, including cocked hats and tobacco. The Indians got nasty. Black Buffalo forbad the travellers to proceed unless they left behind one of the boats and all it contained.

Lewis ignored the chief's demands. Instead, he invited Black Buffalo and four of his men onto the keelboat. 'We gave them ¼ a glass of whiskey which they appeared to be very fond of,' Clark wrote. The whisky was not a brilliant idea. The Indians pretended to be drunk and one of them jostled Clark: 'The Chiefs Soldr. Huged the mast, and the 2d Chief was very insolent both in words and justures (pretended Drunkenness and staggered up against me).'

William was outraged and drew his sword. Lewis barked an order. The Indians found thirty rifles aimed at them. The Sioux warriors on the riverbank put arrows to their bows. It was a tense moment. Then the Indians backed down. Having initially brimmed with swaggering arrogance, Black Buffalo hurriedly changed tack. These white men meant business. He mumbled something to the effect that he and his people were very poor. The women and children were almost naked. Surely the rich Americans could spare some of their clothes?

Lewis agreed to talk further, but not on a riverbank swarming with truculent Sioux braves. The chief and two others were taken on board and the party sailed across the river to spend the night in the safety of a small island. Clark named their refuge Bad Humoured Island, because, as he so succinctly put it, 'we were in a bad humer'.

By the next day, the Indians had calmed down enough to throw a splendid banquet in the Americans' honour. The party dined on 'the most Delicate part of the Dog', with a side order of turnips. The pipe of peace was passed round. The festivities ended at midnight after riotous singing and dancing.

The following day the unpredictable Sioux were up to their old tricks again. As the Americans tried to cast off, the Indians made a grab for the ropes and demanded more gifts. Lewis lost his cool and let rip with a barrage of insults. He was about to give the order to shoot point-blank into the crowd when Black Buffalo and his band backed down once again and allowed the boats to leave.

Lewis and Clark's meeting with the Sioux was 'a triumph of foreign policy', according to historian Bernard DeVoto. 'The American no-appeasement policy had taken the starch out of the Sioux . . . the terrors of the Missouri River had been deflated . . . the Missouri was now open and, so far as the Sioux were concerned, would stay open. American authority had been asserted over the Indians . . .' Lewis, however, continued to seethe over the incident. In a note to President Jefferson he raged later that the Sioux were 'the vilest miscreants of the savage race and must ever remain the pirates of the Missouri' until forced to behave themselves. He concluded that the river traders had been letting the Indians off too lightly.

After finding a room in one of Pierre's motels, I checked out the bars. Pierre might be a little hick by world standards, but it was a state capital and therefore should be good for some action. I left the Toyota in the motel car-park and found a taxi.

The cab driver was called Benny. He was keen that I should try the topless bars across the river in Fort Pierre. After my experience in Kansas City, I didn't think this was an awfully good idea. Benny was most insistent. He promised this would be the best place to meet local people. The advantage of the bars across the Missouri was that Fort Pierre was on Mountain Time. Pierre was on Standard

Time. As soon as the bars closed at 2 am in Pierre, you could grab another hour's drinking time merely by driving a few hundred yards across the water.

Benny had a good, earthy sense of humour. 'How would you describe the people in Pierre?' I asked.

'Well, if you don't fish, hunt, make babies or drink you're shit out of line around here.'

We discussed which bar I should try. 'They're pretty much the same,' he said. 'The Bad River has two dancers, the Hopscotch has one.'

The Bad River was a nice name and two dancers seemed better than one. 'Do they both dance at the same time?' I inquired.

'Naw. One dances and the other throws out drunks.'

Benny dropped me at the Bad River and I paid him off. A sign over the door stated: 'No weapons allowed on premises.' It seemed like a good start. Inside, the place was almost empty. A few bearded men sat on stools around a makeshift stage. They grunted amongst themselves and swigged bottles of beer, occasionally turning an eye upwards to the solitary half-naked dancer. A bandage was wrapped around her left leg. She did not present an invigorating sight.

At the bar I fell into conversation with a labourer called Cy, who was in town for a few days on a roofing job. Cy was from Minneapolis and considered himself rather sophisticated. It was his second visit to Pierre and he was unimpressed. 'Full of dumb hicks,' he remarked, adding: 'What's an Englishman doing in a town like this?' I replied that I wasn't really sure, but it had something to do with the Missouri river.

We established that nothing wildly exciting was about to happen at the Bad River. After a couple of drinks we left for the Hopscotch. 'Jesus, will you look at this place?' Cy expostulated as we walked up the street. He gestured at the wooden buildings fronted by warped verandahs. 'Now where the fuck did I leave my horse?'

The Hop, as it was known, was not much better. An uninterested audience watched a blonde who was in the process of a half-hearted striptease. A man lay asleep in one of the cubicles oblivious to the heavy metal blasting from the jukebox. A hat covered his face.

I got talking to an elderly woman with silver-grey hair, who was presiding over the bar. Here at last I had met an example of that character so beloved in Wild West movies, the tough old lady bar-owner.

Her name was Frances. She was quite frail and she walked with a slight limp. She seemed hopelessly out of place in a strip-joint. 'Don't you find it's difficult for a woman of your age keeping order in a place like this?' I asked.

A lovely grandmotherly smile appeared on Frances's face. 'Why, no sir. It's us women who keep the men in control.' She poured the beers. 'Some of 'em can get a little rough, but they don't fool with me. There's nothing like a mother figure to quieten 'em down.'

'What about fights?'

'Oh, we've had a few, but I've learned to sort 'em out. Once in a while we get someone in looking for trouble with a gun and I just go up to him and say you don't need that in here. They usually hand it over.' She paused. ''Course, sometimes they don't. Had a guy in '68, who started shootin'. There was a lady sitting right at the bar and one of the bullets ricocheted right off her belt buckle. My Lord, she was a lucky one.'

The Hop had been in action since the early 1900s when it was a brothel servicing the wagon trains on their way west. It had subsequently been a grocery store and a theatre during Prohibition. Frances and her late husband Russ had bought the place in 1945 soon after he was demobbed. 'Then one day Russ comes home and says he's bought a bar in South Dakota. I just about had a fit. Minneapolis was a nice civilized town. But Fort Pierre? It was like moving to the Wild West. The streets were all dirt in summer, mud in winter. Can't have been too bad though. Been here ever since.'

The strippers arrived during the 1960s. 'That was my husband's idea back in '65. I wasn't too fond of them. but business was slow so we thought we'd give it a try. The other bars were putting on live bands, but the acoustics here were too bad for that.' A searing Judas Priest guitar thrash exploded from the jukebox. The flimsy walls shook like cardboard. I could see what Frances meant. 'But the dancers ain't no trouble. They're nice girls mostly and what they do after hours is their business.' She allowed a sly grin. 'Put it this way: I don't know nothing.'

After a couple more beers I took a cab back into town and dropped Cy back at his motel. It was midnight and I decided to try one more bar before bedtime. At the end of Pierre's Main Street was a place called the Longbranch Saloon. As I walked in I was hit by a blast of yee-haaing country and western.

I'd met the Indians . . . here were the cowboys.

I pushed my way to the bar through a throng of people. Both men and women were dressed strictly Home On The Range: wide-brimmed hats, red bandanas, blue-jeans and boots. The dance floor heaved with sweaty bodies as the band pumped out a frenetic string of polkas and two steps. Other customers sat around plastic-topped tables in front of a frightening array of drinks. Pretty teenaged waitresses charged to and fro with huge trays of glasses.

'Can I have a Budweiser, please?'

'Whaaaatyasay?' The barman bellowed the words. The band stampeded into a Hank Williams number. The noise was deafening.

'A Bud, please,' I yelled. Some of the cowboys at the bar turned round to look at me. I could imagine them thinking: what language is this guy talking? I was beginning to hate my British accent.

'Hey, you're not American.' The barman grinned broadly and stuck his hand across a debris of empty glasses. He had a bushy shock of hair and a smiling face. He introduced himself as Todd. 'Welcome to Pierre. Don't see many Australians around here.'

'Er, I'm English actually.'

'English? Could've sworn . . . shit, never mind.' I held up a dollar. Todd waved it away. 'Nah, this one's on the house.'

According to Todd, foreigners of *any* description were rare in Pierre. I was probably the first Englishman to set foot in the Longbranch. He asked me what I was doing in South Dakota. I dutifully explained my journey up the Missouri. When I had finished, he said: 'So, you've come in here looking for cowboys.'

'That's the gist of it.'

'Well don't be put off by the way some of them look.' He indicated a group of check-shirted gorillas by the pool table. They were bandy-legged from too many years in the saddle. 'There are still a lot of cowboys round here who don't think Saturday night's over 'til they've got in a fight. But usually they're so drunk they can't fight anyway. People are pretty tough and every so often we get a fight round the pool table. But it doesn't take much to break it up.' The house policy was that anyone caught throwing a punch was out for the rest of the night. Hit an employee and you were out for six months. 'Your hired help's gotta be protected.' Todd added. He took a cloth and lazily dried a glass. 'Guess I'm pretty lucky. Nobody's hit me yet. And don't you worry. Can't see any trouble starting tonight.'

I was glad to hear it. One punch from any of these men and I'd be flat on my back for a week.

A woman shouted for more drinks. Todd scuttled away to serve her. The band drifted into a Johnny Cash ballad. Some of the older couples took the floor for a waltz. I leaned back on the bar, took a slug of Bud and proceeded to watch the cowboy at play.

The cowboy is one of the best-loved folk heroes of all time. At least this is what American historians would lead us to believe. Forget about desperadoes like Billy The Kid and Jesse James. They were just a couple of bad apples in an otherwise first-rate basket. The true cowboy was a figure of justice and freedom.

In the freezing cold winters and blistering summers of the Great Plains, he was a symbol of hope in a land where everything contrived to work against him. The work was hard and lonely. He could spend months away from civilization with only his fellow hired hands for company. And he broke the silence of the prairie with his guitar and simple songs.

Ideally, according to Joe. B. Frantz and Julian Ernest Choate in their book *The American Cowboy* he was a superb horseman, a fast draw with a Colt revolver, a dead shot with a Winchester rifle and brave beyond question. He was 'always on the side of justice, even if that justice be a bit stern at times'. He was 'the defender of virtuous women, the implacable foe of the Indian, and a man to whom honor and integrity came naturally'.

But above all, the cowboy maintained a gritty sense of humour when the going got tough. 'I'll loan you my wife and I'll loan you my horse,' went the saying, 'but I won't loan you my gun – my horse and my woman both know their way home.' And the image of the rugged bachelor crept into every aspect of his life. For example, coffee à la cowboy: take one pound of coffee, one cup of water, boil over open fire for thirty minutes. Then drop a horseshoe into it. If the horseshoe sinks, add more coffee.

The twentieth-century cowboy can transfer his foaming steed to a horsebox, drive home in the 4WD, flip open the Marlboro packet (like in the TV commercial), pop a can of beer and recover from a day in the saddle in front of the TV. He *thinks* he's a cowboy, but he wouldn't swear to it. He is suffering from an identity crisis. He does not know if he is the real thing or not.

Ranching conditions of 100-plus years ago were very different. For a start, there were no fences. And when there are no fences to keep your cattle in check, catching a cow is a tough job. How would the modern-day cowboy match up? While the fences remain, he can never know.

The round-up crews would spend all summer on the open range finding their bosses' cattle – up to 15,000 head in a good year – and then branding the calves with the same brand as their mothers. And to ensure there was no foul play, each owner sent along his rep, who saw that the calves were branded the same as the cows. The cowboys moved camp each day, searching for more cows until they had made the whole circuit and all the animals were branded.

The cowboy's life changed for ever in 1875 when a pushy young Illinois salesman called John W. Gates set off for Texas with a supply of his latest product. It was called barbed wire. And although the invention was a couple of years old, no one had yet tried to sell it seriously.

The hard-bitten Texan ranchers took one look at Gates's wares and laughed him off. Don't be ridiculous, they sneered. How could a few strands of wire hold in their feisty longhorns?

Gates ignored their jibes. Using barbed wire, he turned the town square of San Antonio into a huge corral. He filled it with the most bad-tempered cattle he could find, and challenged the ranchers to stampede them through the wire. Despite much shooting and hollering, the beasts stubbornly refused to budge. No, sireee, they weren't going anywhere near this barely visible thing that bit and stung. It was a wild publicity stunt that paid off. The cow's ability to learn fast made Gates a millionaire and changed the face of the Great American Ranch for ever.

Todd stirred me from my daydream. 'Hey, I've got a cowboy you can talk to.' He pointed at a moustached man of about forty who was sitting a few bar stools away from me. The man beckoned me over. I left my place at the bar and joined him.

The man introduced himself. 'Waaaal, pleased to meet you. The name's Keith Briggs, or K for short. But round here they call me the Commander.'

'Oh really? Why's that?'

K pointed at a line of shot glasses on the bar. They were each filled with a brown, sludgy-looking drink. K handed me a glass and I got my first taste of a B-52. 'They call me the Commander,' he drawled, "cos I buy these things in squadrons – ten at a time.'

I tried the sickly concoction, a distinctly un-cowboyish mixture of Irish Cream, Kaluha and Triple Sec. I remarked that you didn't often see cocktails sold in tens. 'Sure,' K said. He put a glass up to the light, inspected it like a chemist, slugged back the contents and wiped his mouth with his sleeve. 'But it saves the bartender a helluva lot of work.'

K spoke with a quick, clipped voice. He was dressed in obligatory jeans and boots. A gold letter K was pinned to his black Stetson. He stuck his hands deep into his pockets and rocked slowly on his heels. With a loud bark he ordered more drinks.

'Yessir!' Todd attacked the bottles behind the bar. 'Another squadron for the Commander. Coming up!'

K had been on the land all his life. He had grown up on his father's farm sixty miles to the west of Pierre on the Cheyenne River. Now he was cattle foreman in charge of six men on a 28,000-acre ranch outside Pierre on the banks of the Missouri. His team were responsible for 1,800 cows.

He was proud to call himself a cowboy. 'But you've got to get it right.' He spoke firmly in between gulps of another B-52. 'Ahm a workin' cowboy, not one of those rodeo cowboys. You'll find they don't know how to fix a fence, how to pull a calf or even change a tyre. All they know is how to sit on their hoss.'

'So you don't have a lot of time for the rodeo cowboys,' I said.

'Got nuttin' agin' 'em. They say they're cowboys and they are in that they use horses. But that's where it ends. They just enter competitions. It's like being a race track driver, football player, basketball star . . .

'The life of a working cowboy is work. When you're calving in spring it means starting early in the morning and finishing late at night seven days a week for sixty days in a row. Then in summer it's hay-making seven days a week for sixty days. And when you're not doing that you're puttin' up barns or makin' silage.' He smiled. 'It's a fun way of life. You're in the open air, you're using your hands and you don't have that city smoke and people. I don't mind coming into Pierre or even Sioux Falls, but Minneapolis drives me nuts. Too big.'

I remarked that he'd go crazy in London. K nodded grimly. 'Crazy as a coyote after a raccoon.'

American agriculture was going through disastrous years. Throughout the 1980s high interest rates had resulted in numerous bankruptcies. 'My boss Mr Sheehan has had his troubles, but he's got over them. He's lucky he had capital to help him through the bad years. We're bigger than most ranches round here. We've spent a lot of bucks on irrigation and it's paying off in soya beans and popcorn. The cattle are making money too.'

After hearing the Indians' complaints about the Missouri dams, I half-expected the cowboys to be in favour of them. But it was the same old story.

'The simple answer is that the dams have not helped farming. Everybody went out and spent a lot of money on irrigation to try and raise more crops. But the commodity prices went down and they couldn't pay their loans. The dams have been nothing but trouble. They should have put in a flood barrier, a dyke, to control the river, like in New Orleans. Flooding never happened in the bottom lands. The grass grew and it was good protection for the trees.' K sighed. 'I gotta say that the Indian reservations probably weren't paid enough for their land. It was probably the market price, but it can never be used again.' He added that the current drought was causing big problems. 'The water's right down and some of the hillsides are sliding down into the lakes. There are places on the west side of the Missouri where whole chunks of land disappear each year.'

'As the Indians say,' I remarked, 'you shouldn't mess with Mother Nature.'

'Yup. Gotta hand it to those Sioux. They know what they're talking about all right.'

I stayed in Pierre much longer than I intended. I felt thoroughly at home in this easy-going town and had made many friends in the Longbranch.

A few nights later I was in the saloon being taught how to dance the two-step. South Dakotans seemed to have a fondness for nicknames. There was Montana Joe and Gene 'The Mean Poker Machine' . . . I was Pete, 'the two-stepper from hell'.

I had become something of a novelty. People couldn't work out where this Englishman had come from and what he was doing here. Word spread quickly that there was a foreigner in the house. I found myself being dragged on to the dance floor by a succession of well-rounded girls evidently brought up on the no-nonsense pioneer diet of meat and potatoes. 'Big' means 'healthy' on the Great Plains and Mom says, 'Eat, it's good for you. How can you haul hay if you're all skinny?' Nor can the South Dakotan farm girl be described as a shy, retiring creature. She is likely to approach your table, grab your arm and growl, 'It's your turn to dance with me, mister.' I had just staggered off the floor after an epic two-stepping session with a tiny girl of about twenty. She had enormous breasts that threatened to knock me down at every turn. Not being the world's greatest dancer, I had trodden on her feet several times. She was remarkably tolerant. My shoe crashed onto her foot again. She gave a little yelp. I apologised profusely. 'No problem,' she laughed. 'I kick hell out of the bottom of my feet all day, so it's fair enough for someone to stand on the top of them at night.'

I was sweating heavily from my exertions. The B-52s were in full flight as I joined K at the bar. He was deep in thought.

'I gotta problem,' he said.

'What's that?'

'We're supposed to be rounding up cattle tomorrow, moving 'em from one pasture to another. But one of the boys has gone sick so I'm a man short.' He looked at me out of the corner of an eye. I waited to hear the worst. 'Guess you'll do.'

'Me? But you've got to be joking. I haven't been on a horse in five years.' The last time I had attempted to ride was in Yorkshire. A brute of a nag had sent me crashing on to a concrete yard within seconds of mounting. 'Absolutely no way. I'm terrified of horses.'

'Nonsense. We'll give you a nice steady one. Won't be no bother.'

I realised there was no chance of getting out of this one. 'Well, I don't think I'll be much help,' I added.

'Sure,' K said ominously. 'Don't you worry. We'll get work out of you. All you gotta do is shout yee-haa.'

'Yee-haa?'

One of the waitresses, a part-Sioux girl called Nicky, was

eavesdropping on our conversation. 'No it's not,' she interrupted. 'It's yippy-yi-a.'

'Shit, no.' K turned to her. 'If you're a real cowboy you go yippy-yappy-yahoooo.' He let out a wolf-like howl. Some of the cowboys near us gave him odd looks. 'Got myself a new hired hand,' he added with gusto. 'Pete's gonna come and punch 'em doggies tomorrow.'

'Punch what?' I asked.

'Punch doggies,' Nicky said. 'It means working cows.'

I had heard the expression before, but I had no idea what it meant. 'Why call cows doggies when doggies are dogs?'

K looked puzzled. 'Lordy, I don't know. Never thought about it. Guess cows have always been doggies.'

K picked me up from my motel at five o'clock the next morning. He was driving a dusty Ford truck towing a trailer containing our horses. A pair of furry dice dangled from the rearview mirror. A long gash ran across the windscreen. I made a remark about how all four-wheel-drive vehicles in this part of the world seemed to have cracked windscreens. K laughed. 'Sometimes I think they make 'em that way.'

With K was another cowboy called Sonny. He was tall and lanky and didn't say much. They were both wrapped up in thick padded jackets and felt hats with brims that tilted down to their eyes. I had not got round to buying a cowboy hat myself – perhaps that was taking things a little too far. I felt absurdly out of place in my acrylic bobble hat bought for ninety-nine cents at Woolworth's in Omaha. But at least I had the Levis and blue denim shirt.

It was cold and dark as we left Pierre. We paused at a gas station to pick up styrofoam cups of coffee before heading west into the prairie. There was little conversation. The three of us attempted to shake the sleep from our heads. The radio crackled quietly with 'beef is good for you' commercials.

K turned off down a minor road that ran near the Bad River, one of the Missouri's many tributaries. This was one of the least populated parts of the state. He broke the silence. 'There's nothing out here,' he said. 'You won't see a house for twenty miles.'

'So what's my horse like?' I asked.

'Real quiet. He's an American Quarter Horse. There's a lot of thoroughbred in him and he'd do well on the race track, but he's too damn lazy.'

'I'm glad to hear it.' The thought of hurtling across the prairie before breakfast on a race horse was too much.

K added, 'A lot of ranches have gone over to three-wheel bikes, but horses are much more efficient. Cows can get spooked real bad by a three-wheeler. They get used to horses.'

The sun cast a lavender glow as it began its climb over the horizon. A deer ran across the road and bald eagles circled the hillocks. A covey of startled grouse took off to the north. K never tired of this vast sea of grass. 'Now you can see why I like being a cowboy. Isn't it the prettiest country?'

The Western wild grasses are wonderfully convenient. Unlike their juicy, cultivated Eastern cousins, they are virtually immune to drought and do not need to be dried and stored like normal hay. Instead they dry right where they grow on the ground. And year after year the grass is replanted by cattle trampling the natural seeds into the soil. The rancher may need up to twenty acres to keep one cow, but it does not cost him a penny. This apparently useless land has created numerous millionaires. As they said back in the Gold Rush days, 'There's gold from the grass roots down . . . but there's more gold from the grass roots up.'

We drove for fifty miles. K turned down a track leading into a shallow valley. As he stopped the truck, the country music on the radio gave way to the 7 am news bulletin. A surfeit of Hollywood high-living had put Elizabeth Taylor in hospital yet again. The actress's misfortunes seemed so pathetically meaningless in this vast, empty place.

Three horsemen were silhouetted on the skyline against the yellow glow of the rising sun. They were the other cowboys we were due to meet up with. We were late and the round-up had started without us. K explained that our job was to move five hundred cows and calves – mostly Limousin-Angus cross-breed – to new grazing land about five miles west across the prairie. The dire shortage of rain in South Dakota meant that the grass was not at its best. Ranchers were continually moving their cattle from one pasture to another.

We unloaded the horses in the early morning chill. My mount snorted loudly through steaming nostrils. K stared the creature in the face. 'Now, don't you cause Peter no trouble,' he whispered. I swung up on to the horse and K adjusted my stirrups. From all around us came the calls of grouse and early morning bird song.

133

Our horses created long shadows as we began a steady canter up the hill towards the other riders.

K instructed me to keep the reins in my right hand and to hang on to the saddle with my left. 'Your left hand's your roping hand.'

'Bugger the roping,' I grumbled. I had no intention of letting go of the saddle for one second. I felt hopelessly out of control. I hung on for grim life as my steed careered across the countryside.

'And forget about English riding,' K bellowed. 'Remember you're on a western saddle, not one of those English horse blankets with stirrups. The only time you stand up in the saddle is to cool your butt.'

'Well, I don't know about you, but all this bouncing around is doing immeasurable harm to my bollocks.'

'Bollocks?' K looked puzzled.

'Oh God, it's English slang for testicles.'

'Ah, you mean nuts.' We had discovered a cultural difference between our nations.

We came alongside the other cowboys. They were called Chris Knox, Rocky Lane and Rocky Tibbs. I was in impressive company. The two Rockys were champion ropers in the South Dakota rodeo association. Later that morning I saw them catch straying calves around the legs. They put on a magnificent display as they swirled the ropes around their heads before throwing them right on target. Even K was impressed. 'I've tried real hard, but I can't do it.' He grinned. 'That's why I leave my rope back in the truck and pretend I've forgotten it.'

I was introduced as Peter from London. 'Huh!' Rocky Tibbs said. He was a huge man with a red, jowly face. He was dressed in traditional leather chaps. 'Well, I'll tell you one thing, K. You're going a long way to git your hired help these days.'

'Don't matter. Cows don't know he's English.'

'Maybe not,' I chipped in. 'But this bloody horse does.' The animal shifted impatiently beneath me. It skittered on its toes and did a little dance. It seemed to know only too well that it had been lumbered with a totally inept rider.

K sensed my anxiety. He explained the intricacies of neck-reining. 'Stop panicking. If you're worried just pull his neck around and he'll go round in a circle and stop.' I tried this. Amazingly enough, it worked. Perhaps it was my imagination, but from that moment the horse seemed to regard me with renewed respect.

We caught up with the cattle over the brow of the hill. The herd kicked up a cloud of dust as it slowly moved west in a pandemonium of mooing. The stale smell of dung mixed with the heat of the animals' bodies. Steam rose from their flanks creating a hazy filter against the early morning sun. Anxious cows jostled their calves. The young ones tottered on splayed legs, their suspicious eyes darting towards the horses.

K gave me orders to round up any stray calves and send them back to the herd. 'They're pretty canny. You have to watch that the little bastards don't take off. Before you know they'll have disappeared over a hill and you won't see where they've gone.' He neck-reined his horse and forced a calf back to its mother. 'The horses get cow sense. You just point the horse in the cow's direction and it will do the rest for you. Guess it's a natural instinct.' He added that cows would only be herded into the wind. 'They like the fresh air cooling their noses. Try and push a bunch of cattle away from the wind and they just won't go.' He galloped away again yelling, 'Yah! Yah!'

What about all this yee-haa business, I wondered? I attempted to mimic K with a discreet 'yah!' I felt rather a prat. Somehow it didn't sound the same in a British accent.

We herded the cows down a hill to a watering hole. Their hooves churned the banks into mud. Dust filled my eyes. I felt a great sense of freedom. Playing cowboys was an exhilarating experience. The clear blue cloudless sky expanded over the range like the cinema-scope of a John Wayne movie.

But the cowboy is not infallible. The trouble started as we tried to move the cattle from the water-hole. In their hurry to drink, some of the cows had become estranged from their calves. The herd panicked. Dozens of bleating calves began to run back in the direction we'd just come from. The cows stampeded towards us. We tried to stop them, but they kept coming.

My horse snorted with fear and pawed the ground. K emerged from the dust cloud. 'Don't worry. Just keep the horse still and they'll move right past you.'

'Er, right.' We made a few more efforts to turn the cattle round.

No luck. Suddenly it was all over and the herd was heading back over the prairie. The morning had ended in disaster.

K got down from his horse and wiped the sweat from his brow. The rest of us joined him. His voice was croaky from shouting. 'The cows are gonna realize their calves aren't with 'em so we might as well let 'em go,' he explained simply. 'We'll leave 'em now and try to move 'em later in the week.' He sighed wearily and looked at me. 'Bet you thought it was gonna be real easy, didn't you?'

'I thought the cowboys always won.'

'Naw. Cows are real stubborn sometimes.'

Herds travelled better without calves, he explained. The older the calf, the better the herd would stay together. But these calves were young and unpredictable. 'A calf will go back to the last place it sucked. And a cow will go back to the last place she nursed the calf. So they'll go back to where they were this morning. It's all down to smell and sound. They say that cattle are colour blind. But I reckon a cow knows the difference between black and white. I can do that and I'm colour blind!'

The work was over. We stood chatting in the sunshine. I said I was surprised that I had not fallen off.

'You gotta crash at least three times before you're a real cowboy,' Chris Knox said. He was older than the rest of them, about fifty.

'Do you have to break a bone as well?' I asked.

'No. Only your pride.'

Rocky Tibbs added, 'Well, if it only takes three times, then I'm gonna be a cowboy for the next forty lives. I'm *always* fallin' off.'

'That may be,' Chris laughed. 'But a real cowboy makes sure no one *sees* him fall off. Then he can say he was only taking a break.'

We returned to the truck and loaded up the horses. On the way back across the prairie we stopped at a collection of derelict wooden shacks. It was the remains of the town of Van Meter: population zero, and one of many ghost towns in western South Dakota.

The main Pierre–Rapid City railroad line ran a few hundred yards away. Sixty years ago, Van Meter would have been a major cattle depot and water halt. But the town died with the introduction of road transport and the collapse of agriculture in the Dirty Thirties. These days the railroad saw only two trains a week. Remote settlements like Van Meter had lost their usefulness long ago.

K and I picked our way over mounds of rubble. Old boxcars, the former homes of the railroad gangs, were scattered either side of what was once the main street. We looked at the old school house before moving on to a long barn-like building in the final stages of collapse. The roof was just about standing, supported precariously by rotting timbers. Flapping in the breeze was a lopsided wooden board that said this had been the dance hall.

K remembered old people talking about Van Meter. 'Back in the early Forties they held dances once a month. Lawrence Welk used to play here. Heard of him?'

'Can't say I have.'

'Yeah, well he was one helluva bandleader.' (I learned later that North Dakota born Welk is probably the best loved US band leader of them all.) We walked inside. A portion of the ornate, pressed-tin ceiling was still intact. Stucco Greek pillars stood at each corner of the room. What had once been a sleek, polished dance floor was covered in dust and plaster chippings that had fallen from the frieze around the ceiling.

'Must have been a pretty fancy building in its day,' K said. He was lost in nostalgia. 'I remember places like this when I was a kid. It was all thrashing crews and barn dances and pretty girls. We'd go 150 miles to a dance. It was the thing to do, it was all we had in the country. There wasn't much of a social life and when we did get together we had a real good time.' He shrugged. 'It's sad that places like this have gone. Nowadays everybody wants to be close to civilization. It's an hour by car to the nearest restaurant, and that's too far in America.'

We returned to Pierre. I was loath to leave the town, but it was time to continue my journey. And after a few more days perfecting my two-step in the Longbranch, I took Highway 83 north.

For the next ninety miles I left the river, or rather what remained of the river in the form of Lake Oahe, well away to the west. There were no decent roads close to the lake and I had been warned of snow. For this next stretch of the journey into North Dakota I had thought of catching a train. A naïve hope. Rivers in America run south to north, major railroads east to west. So I was stuck with the highway, yet another relic of an old wagon trail that had over the years graduated to smooth tarmac.

Of all the members of the Lewis and Clark expedition, the name that arouses the greatest emotion in America is that of Sakakawea.

The party's only woman, Sakakawea first met the expedition in the Missouri wilderness in the winter of 1804. The Indian squaw was to become an invaluable addition to the team. And there are said to be more statues erected to the honour of this extraordinary girl than any other woman in American history.

After leaving Pierre I passed through Mobridge, the last major town in South Dakota. It was the usual forgettable urban sprawl of discount centres and used tractor lots. In 1906 the Milwaukee Railroad built a bridge here across the Missouri. The telegraph operator opted for the contraction 'Mo-bridge' and the name stuck.

I crossed the river and stopped the Toyota on a high windy ridge. Here, overlooking the crystal ice-packed waters of the Missouri, was a monument dedicated to the memory of Sakakawea. Her towering stone obelisk stood a few yards away from a statue of that other Indian legend, Sitting Bull, the man who defeated Custer at Little Big Horn. The empty prairie stretched for miles; it was a lonely place to be remembered.

Sakakawea was born a member of the Hidatsa tribe. She was raised in the western Rocky Mountains. At the age of eleven, she travelled east with her parents to find new hunting country. But while camped near the Missouri headwaters in what is now southeast Montana, the party fell victim to one of the frequent tribal conflicts within the Hidatsa Indians. Sakakawea was captured and her parents were believed killed. She stayed with her captors until she was fourteen when she became the wife of a roguish Canadian-French adventurer called Toussaint Charbonneau. It is thought that the wild 'n' woolly Charbonneau, an interpreter for traders and Indians in the upper Missouri, either bought or won his bride from the Hidatsa chief.

Charbonneau turned up at Fort Mandan, the expedition's winter refuge, in November 1804. With him were his three wives, including Sakakawea. And on 11 February the next year, Sakakawea gave birth to her first child. Captain Lewis helped out as midwife and gave Sakakawea some rattlesnake rattle, which was supposed to help speed the birth. Whether the remedy worked is uncertain. But in any event she produced a fine baby boy called Jean Baptiste.

Lewis was impressed by Sakakawea's hardy nature and mild,

gentle disposition. So when he hired Charbonneau as interpreter for the next leg of the journey, he insisted that the 'Indian woman', as he called her, come too. With her came baby Baptiste, strapped in a cradle to his mother's back.

Sakakawea's role in the expedition has long been debated. On one hand she is a beautiful, trailblazing scout, the stuff of romantic fiction. On the other, she is a resilient Indian squaw, who came in darned handy, but whose usefulness has been exaggerated. 'If she has enough to eat and a few trinkets to wear,' Lewis wrote, 'I believe she would be perfectly content anywhere.' It is a revealing remark.

There is no doubt that Sakakawea was highly competent in the field. She stitched moccasins and collected edible roots, which became a welcome addition to the expedition's meaty diet. Her delicacies did not always agree with the men. After one ghastly night of thunderous belching and farting, Clark complained: 'Capt Lewis and my selfe eate a supper of roots boiled, which filled us so full of wind that we were scercely able to Breathe . . .' The dependable Sakakawea came to the rescue with a herbal concoction that prevented flatulence.

Her moment of triumph arrived in late 1805 when the expedition reached the Rockies. At last Sakakawea was amongst her own people, the Shoshones. She was elevated to the position of interpreter and public relations lady. Through her the expedition was able to find the much-needed horses to take them through the mountains. Without the Shoshone horses it is unlikely that the expedition would have succeeded in its goal of reaching the Pacific Ocean.

The historian Bernard DeVoto provides the best character study: 'She is better known than any other Indian woman and she has an unusual resourcefulness, staunchness, and loyalty, a warmth that can be felt through the rugged prose of men writing with their minds on a stern job, and a gaiety that is childlike and yet not the childishness we have associated with primitives . . . she has become a popular heroine and something of a myth, a Shoshone Deirdre created out of desire. And from Bismarck to the sea many antiquaries and most trail markers have believed that Lewis, Clark, and their command were privileged to assist in the Sakakawea Expedition, which is not quite true.'

According to the inscription on the monument, Sakakawea ended up at Fort Manuel, thirty miles north of Mo-bridge, where she died of a 'putrid fever' on 20 December 1812. This has since proved to be nonsense and it is likely that she was muddled up with another of Charbonneau's wives. Historians believe that she lived to be an old lady of ninety-five, ending her days on Wind River reservation in western Wyoming. Her son reported that she was buried in a white man's graveyard 'because she was a friend of the white people'.

Thirty miles north of Mobridge I crossed into North Dakota. The landscape remained the same gently undulating prairie, although there were more patches of snow on the ground.

The division of North and South Dakotas has long been the subject of controversy. Farmers say that the Dakota territory should have been split into West and East Dakota with the Missouri as the natural boundary because it is on either side of the Missouri that you get the great changes in land.

To the east is the sandy loam soil that suits arable farming; the properties are smaller and the population is more dense. West of the river are the great grasslands that are good only for ranching; some spreads cover 200,000 acres. True, some of the land to the west has been ploughed up for farms. But that should never have happened. The soil blows away creating the horrendous dust storms of the kind that blighted the 1930s. There is a story told in North Dakota about an anonymous Indian, who watched an early pioneer plough up grassland for wheat. The Indian grunted simply, 'Wrong side up!'

To a casual onlooker the states are fairly similar. But there are differences. North Dakota folk are even more reserved and conservative than their southern neighbours. The state is run by an older generation, who almost shy away from tourism. South Dakota proudly shows off its tourist attractions like the Badlands and Mount Rushmore. In North Dakota there are the Great Plains and the Missouri, but not a whole lot more.

North Dakota is even more agricultural than its neighbour. Farms cover ninety per cent of the land and the state boasts the nation's highest pick-up sales. Only Kansas produces more wheat. And, of course, it's damned cold. They say that in winter in Florida you can easily spot the North Dakotans: while the locals are huddled up in coats, they're wearing T-shirts in sixty degrees.

I continued north under a wide blue sky on Highway 1806, along the west bank of the Missouri. The name commemorated the year that Lewis and Clark made their return journey. The roadside was dotted with morbid signs bearing the warning: 'Drive Safely! X Marks The Spot.' They indicated where motorists had died in accidents.

I stopped briefly at the remains of Fort Yates, another of the Dakota Territory cavalry outposts. A series of signs informed visitors where the buildings would have been. They were interposed with the usual picnic tables that make the tourist comfortable. Not even a lunatic would use the tables today. Ice covered the ground like marble mortuary slabs. A bitter wind blew from the river. I walked around for a few minutes, but the arctic gusts ripped through my thermal underwear. I stumbled back to the Toyota pursued by balls of tumbleweed. When you're sitting in a heated car and the sun is shining brightly through the windows, you are lulled into a false sense of security. You have no idea how cold it is outside. As I sat in the snug warmth smoking a cigarette, I reflected that the US Army certainly knew how to choose the most miserable and desolate places for their forts.

Next stop was Bismarck, state capital of North Dakota. I did not hold high hopes for this city of 45,000 people. Founded in 1883, it was named after the Iron Chancellor by an overseas steamship agent keen to attract German-speaking settlers to the area.

Months earlier, in the first stages of planning the trip, I had discussed my itinerary with a friend in New York.

Gill was a sophisticated advertising lady of twenty-six, a Manhattan career girl with back-combed ebony hair that she tossed like a mane. She had travelled all over the world, including Australia. But her own country? I should think Boston was the limit. In common with many East Coasters, US geography was not Gill's strong point.

'So where does the Missouri go exactly,' she had asked me over a glass or five in an Upper West Side wine bar.

'Well, Bismarck for a start,' I replied.

'Bismarck!' She almost screamed in horror. 'Jesus Christ! But what the hell happens in Bismarck?'

'Er, I don't know.'

She thought for a moment. Then she replied damningly, 'I guess they must be nice people there. They can't have much else to do than be nice to each other. Jeez, all I've ever heard about Bismarck is in the newspaper weather reports and it's always either boiling hot or freezing cold. Are you sure it actually exists?' I assured her that it did.

The point is that Bismarck, indeed North Dakota as a whole, is not on the way to anywhere by car. You might sometimes fly over it, but that's about all. Gill was not alone in having preconceptions about this forgotten part of America. I later heard about a social scientist in New Jersey, who made a study of North Dakota. He declared that the population was dropping so rapidly that the remaining people might as well leave too. Then you could turn the entire state over to recreation and create a huge buffalo park.

The North Dakotans were unamused. In that case, they replied with their wonderfully down-to-earth sense of humour, why don't we turn New Jersey into one big airport?

As I got closer to the city I switched on the radio. All I could find was one of those God stations. A hellfire preacher was conducting a 'phone-in on the subject of sarcasm. One of his listeners had rung to complain how her father had tried to sleep with her. I couldn't quite work out what point she was trying to make. Apparently this incest had started as a result of 'sarcastic remarks'. Fascinating stuff, just the thing to relieve the boredom of the prairie. Rather incongruously, the programme was sponsored by a fast-food chain.

The long drive had tired me. As I reached Bismarck I narrowly avoided shooting a red traffic light. I stopped at the last minute, forcing a farm boy in a battered red Dodge truck to slam on his brakes. He waved his fist at me. I thought he was about to leave his car and teach me a lesson. Thankfully he drove off with nothing but a barrage of abuse. All good tough stuff. But then I was to learn that snarling machismo was what Bismarck was all about.

Eight

At Bismarck I checked into the Sheraton Hotel on a cheap weekend package. I justified the expense on the grounds that the Lewis and Clark state tourist trail ran right outside the door. The place was crawling with Canadians taking advantage of America's cheap liquor taxes. The city was only 160 miles from the Canadian border and some local hotels catered exclusively for Canadian shoppers.

That evening I enjoyed a drink in the Sheraton bar with a motel designer called Al, who had flown down from Minneapolis on a consulting job. Since I had seen a good many motels in the past weeks, I asked him what his ideal room would look like.

'Forget the looks,' he said sharply. 'These days Americans want security, nothing else.' Al was about fifty and shabbily dressed in a tatty tweed overcoat. He was the vague, arty type with that lost look as if he had been separated from a tour. I suspected he would be happier painting portraits in an artist's garret. A wife and four children forced him to direct his talents to a more lucrative occupation.

'Double locks,' he said grimly. 'You want a feeling of security and warmth.' Al set about his third Martini. He spoke in a rasping whisper. A hint of paranoia had crept into his voice. 'You need special key systems, a telephone that puts you straight through to security so you can say "I'm in trouble". I'm telling the truth. Americans walk into hotel rooms and the first thing they do is check the locks. I certainly do.'

'Is this place safe?' I asked.

'Hmmm. Yeah. At least in Bismarck you don't get the crazies like you get in New York or Chicago.' Though the bar was stifling Al tightened his coat with jumpy, furtive movements like a cold-war spy. 'Let me tell you, there are a lot of crazy people out there breaking into motel rooms. I've never been attacked in a hotel room, but I've known many who have. It takes years to get over it; you'll lose your job, you'll go crazy.'

I left Al picking gloomily at the free peanuts. Back in my room I inspected the doors. They seemed safe enough. I had seen a magazine advertisement for a portable executive fire escape that fitted into your brief case. It could support 2,230 lb and let you down slowly on a strap from up to twelve storeys. Ideal for fooling the rapist that has managed to beat Al's security locks: just climb out of the window and wave bye-bye to your neighbourhood psychopath.

The telephone woke me early next morning. It was my girlfriend calling from London. She dispensed with the gossip. We got down to the nitty-gritty. 'I was wondering,' she said sweetly, 'if you'd mind getting me some . . .' Static crackled over the transatlantic line.

'What was that?' I shouted.

'. . . some Calvin Klein knickers.'

'What? Is that all you were ringing about?'

'You can post them to me. You can't get them in England and they must have them in one of the big stores there.'

Having seen Bismarck, I wasn't so sure. 'Why can't you buy Marks and Spencer's underwear like everybody else?' I grumbled.

She said something about Calvin Klein producing a superior kind of knicker. I grudgingly agreed to see how I got on.

I found the things in a store in Bismarck's Kirkwood Mall. Eight pairs, to be precise. The assistant was a lady of about sixty with bouffant hair and long, red fingernails. She gave me a peculiar look, but seemed to accept that they were not for Sir.

It turned out that Calvin Klein did four kinds of knickers: the regular bikini, the string bikini, the high-rise string and the high-rise brief. Good grief, I thought, surely knickers are knickers. I settled for the regular bikini. 'Regular' sounded a nice, safe word.

'What size, sir?'

'Oh I don't know. She's about five feet seven inches.'

This was not going to help regarding the purchase of underwear. 'Shall we say a medium then, sir?' The assistant rapped her nails on the counter.

'Yes,' I said, not really caring by now and prepared to do anything to get out of there. 'I suppose a medium will do. I think she's fairly medium.'

I left the store and walked through the mall. It was snowing hard outside and the place was crowded with shoppers. In weather like this the mall was the most social place in town. Young people with nothing better to do slouched in fast-food restaurants.

I reached a large glass-covered square in the centre of the complex. A stage was set up in the middle. Across it was draped a large sign proclaiming: 'North Dakota Arm-Wrestling Championships.'

A crowd of youths had surrounded a short, podgy man who stood by the stage. He appeared to be the organizer, and was writing down the details of would-be contestants. As I approached the stage I tucked my parcel tightly under my arm. I did not want anyone to see what I had bought. They might get the wrong idea. I had a feeling that the men of North Dakota would be deeply distrustful of an Englishman with a silly accent in possession of a large quantity of ladies' knickers.

The organizer spotted me. He waved a clipboard. 'Wanna take part, do you? Just put your name down right here.'

I took one look at the crowd. They seemed to be mostly farm boys. And they looked mean. 'Actually, no,' I said. 'I was only passing by.'

The men studied my puny biceps closely. 'Hmm. Guess you're right.' Well, I thought huffily, there was no need to be so obvious about it.

I explained that I was looking for things to write about in Bismarck. The man introduced himself. He was a Californian called Steve Simons and he owned the largest shopping mall promotions company in America. The company's major event was arm-wrestling. Steve had flown up from Los Angeles to run the North Dakota heats of the World Professional Arm-Wrestling Championships.

With his Beverly Hills Country Club tennis shirt and deep suntan, Steve was horribly out of place in provincial Bismarck. 'I have guys who usually run this thing for me,' he said. 'It was eighty degrees in LA and I should have been playing golf. But what the hell! Back home I'm known as Hollywood Steve. I'm typical LA, playing tennis, permanent tan. My friends can't understand when I come up to some place like North Dakota. But I like it, really do. There are real people up here and they know how to have a good time. I thought I'd give the guys a break and come up here and do it myself.'

Steve was like an enthusiastic little, brown bear. Girls would have called him cuddly. He was about forty with beady eyes that poked out from under a mop of black hair. He walked with a wobble and he enjoyed Jewish American Princess jokes: 'How does a JAP make love doggy-style? Her husband sits up and begs while she rolls over and plays dead.'

He never stopped talking. He had recently married a much younger woman called Ruth. She was the girl of his dreams. 'When we started dating she said to me: "I know you've been out with a lot of girls, but here's what I'll do. I'll go to Frederick's of Hollywood and I'll buy three different wigs: blonde, brunette and black. Then I'll go out to a bar. You can come in and pick me up and go home with a different woman." ' Steve rocked with laughter at the memory. 'I liked her attitude. We've been together ever since.'

He was a great Europhile. Earlier this year he had toured Italy with his two children from his first marriage. 'God, you should've heard me at the Leaning Tower of Pisa.' He grimaced. 'Talk about the unsophisticated American abroad! We're walking down the street and all of a sudden we get to the tower. I said, "My God, it's really leaning, isn't it?" My son – he's ten – said, "Oh Jeeze, Dad, you're so uncool." '

He paused for breath. 'And England! You people are *sooo* polite. But you have the strangest expressions. Like when your girl's playing tennis and a guy comes up and says, "Would you care to knock up?" What's he trying to say? That he wants to screw your girlfriend? You gotta be kidding!'

More contestants came up to register as the morning progressed. On the stage was a tubular steel frame with leather elbow pads over which the contestants would wrestle. Plastic trophies were lined up on a table. Next to it were a pair of boots that Gary Glitter would die for. They boasted six inch platforms. Steve explained that they helped you get more leverage if you were short and needed to build up your height.

A teenager with long, blond hair swaggered up to the stage. He was a professional iron-pumper. Steve dutifully took down his details. 'That guy's a wimpo,' Steve confided as soon as the youth's back was turned. 'Thinks he's Schwarzenegger. But you'll find it's the small ones, not the big surfer types, that make good arm-wrestlers.'

Steve had been organizing arm-wrestling competitions for fifteen years. What was the secret of winning? 'Speed and strength. The most important thing is getting your body as close to your arm as possible so you can get the leverage. After that, it's sheer guts. We aim at the guy who drinks beer, watches Monday night football and wants to be an athlete with minimum effort.' The rugged farmers of North Dakota made excellent arm-wrestlers. 'They pride themselves on how tough they can be. And when they get a chance to do it in public in front of lots of girls . . . well, wow! It's a case of who's the toughest kid on the prairie.'

'Do you arm-wrestle?' I inquired.

'Shit, no. Too much for me.'

After lunch in a hamburger joint, I returned to watch the action. A crowd of about three hundred had formed around the stage. Steve had been joined by Derby, a fresh-faced young man in a dark suit and Clark Kent spectacles. He was the shopping mall manager.

Derby was polite and keen. He was only just out of college and had recently married his school sweetheart. He had been brought up in Bismarck, but, in common with many local young people, he dreamed of moving to Minneapolis. Bismarck didn't really suit him.

'Why are North Dakotans so good at arm-wrestling?' I inquired.

'I suppose,' he sniffed, brushing a fleck of dust from his immaculately tailored sleeve, 'it comes from humping pigs all day on the farm.'

'It's interesting you should mention pigs,' I said as an attempt at further conversation. 'I suppose the English answer to arm-wrestling is bowling-for-a-pig contests at our summer church fêtes. That's very popular amongst farming folk.' Derby looked nonplussed. Why anyone wanted to win a pig was beyond him.

Steve took the microphone. He read the rules: elbows must not leave the table . . . one foot on the floor at all times . . . you must not use your body to bring your opponent down, ie no head-butting.

The contest began. The tension mounted as each pair of competitors took the stage. Most were bar-room arm-wrestling veterans. They clenched their teeth as they attempted to keep their arms vertical. Some matches were over in seconds; others lasted more than a minute.

The crowd bayed for blood. 'Rip 'is arm off, Terry!' . . . 'Don't let the bastard pull you down!'

Steve bellowed encouragement. 'You gotta good opening pull . . . we've got a barn burner here . . . Good pull!' Yet another tattooed farmboy threatened to burst all his blood vessels in one go. 'Look at the agony on his face – this is a great match!'

Many of the men were products of North Dakota's German heritage: blond Aryan looks and names like Richter and Schweitzer. Haystack hauling was a popular profession.

Some of them displayed serious psychopathic tendencies. This was a perfect US Marines recruitment ground. Bearded gorillas uttered bear-like growls and stared madly into their opponents' faces. They spat on the floor. Eyes popped and veins stood out on necks; they screwed up their faces like pugs. T-shirts advertising brands of fertilizer became drenched with sweat.

Derby nudged me. He raised his eyebrows. 'Once they get on that stage they turn into animals.'

Arm-wrestling seemed out of place in a shopping mall. It should have been in a clearing in a forest or in a Western saloon with everybody wearing guns. A shopping mall filled with suburban housewives and toddlers in push-chairs was far too clean and tidy for such a messy sport. But on the Great Plains, Rambo rules.

Steve inflamed the mob. 'Come on, you sound like a Beverly Hills crowd. Make some *noise*.'

They screamed like coyotes. 'Kill 'im, you fat hog!' Two men of epic proportions were in a duel to the death. One of them wore a T-shirt with the slogan: 'I love my wife.' Oh yes, they were good family boys in North Dakota.

The afternoon grunted on. We reached the finals. The featherweight section was won by a part-Indian farmhand called Terry. He was a popular winner. None of his matches had lasted less than a minute.

Then it was the turn of the women. They seemed so slight and fragile as they walked up to the stage. But all that changed when the 'powerlock' was on. If anything, they were more frightening than the men.

'Animals,' Derby repeated.

There was Sharon, a legal secretary, and Jenny, a student. Sharon won all her bouts. She was twenty-one and wore tight jeans, boots and a delicate lacy bodice that you did not expect to see at an arm-wrestling contest. She faced her opponents like a wildcat. 'Boy, she may be a sexy little thing,' Steve remarked, 'but she's got one hell of a grip.'

Steve, Derby and I adjourned later to a cocktail bar called Peacock Alley. It was all olde-worlde and fake art deco. Steve and Derby stayed for a couple of drinks and then left. Steve had to fly back to LA and Derby's wife was expecting him home.

I began talking to an extraordinary looking man sitting on his own. He wore a lurid green paisley shirt with long, early-1970s lapels, brown Crimplene flared trousers and glasses. He had buck teeth and ears the size of Mr Spock's. He looked the typical nerd, but he turned out to be absolutely charming.

Spock-Ears was in town visiting friends. He worked for a company that specialized in fibreglass. Fibreglass water tanks, fibreglass hot tubs and . . . fibreglass coffins.

We embarked on a bizarre conversation.

'I've never heard of fibreglass coffins before,' I said.

Spock-Ears missed the point. 'No, they're pretty thin. They're nothing fancy. You have a mould and you spray fibreglass on it mixed with resin. Then you roll the air bubbles off. Or else it leaks.'

'Do a lot of people around here ask for them.'

'We do maybe twenty-four a year. There's no big demand or anything. I suppose it takes a certain type of person who wants to be buried in a fibreglass coffin.'

'Exactly. Is this a cheap alternative to wood?'

'Sure. But I'll never be buried in one now that I've made them.'

'Why's that?'

''Cos they stink.' Spock-Ears became quite agitated. He shifted on his bar stool and clamped his fingers on his nose. 'Boy, you should smell those bastards. I come home from work and I smell like a glue factory. Fibreglass stinks real bad.'

'Are fibreglass coffins common all over America?'

'I don't know. The great thing about fibreglass is that it won't rot. That coffin's going to be there a long time.'

'Fascinating,' I said. I wondered what archaeologists would think when they stumbled upon those monstrosities in a few thousand years' time.

Spock-Ears finished his drink and got up to go. 'Oh yeah, forgot

to tell you,' he added as we parted company, 'the coffins are orange.
Like a speedboat.' Not only would you be buried with an appalling
smell, but you would also be dazzled until eternity.

The next day was Sunday. And I can say only this: Bismarck on
a Sunday must be one of the most depressing places on God's earth.
The snow had gone, but a gloomy overcast pall now covered the
city. Thanks to North Dakota's strict laws of the sabbath, everything
was shut – shops and bars.

I pottered around the museum and strolled in the grounds of
the Capitol building, a 1930s skyscraper that dwarfed every other
building in town. It looked smug and ridiculous. The upper storeys
loomed clumsily over the prairie. It seemed to have been a desperate
attempt at grandness by small-time local politicians with over-
inflated ambitions.

'Spacious' is the polite word North Dakotans use to describe their
capital. I found it a badly-planned, urban sprawl with no centre; a
wild mess of neon-lit fast-food shacks, gas stations and concrete
parking lots. I could see why young people like Derby wanted to
move to Minneapolis. As far as I was concerned Bismarck could go
the way of its battleship namesake.

I finally cracked after eating the filthiest meal of my life at one of
the city's Chinese restaurants. I ordered something called Buddha's
Feast. It was a putrid, slimy swamp of vegetables with a smell that
would be hard to find in Calcutta. When I left, the waiter handed
me a fortune cookie. It read, 'You will soon have an opportunity to
make a change to your advantage.'

A change? Too right. I left Bismarck the next morning.

I gunned the Toyota's engine and continued north. Perhaps that is
not the right word; the car was hopelessly underpowered, not the
sort of vehicle to be 'gunned'.

It was also filthy, crying out for a wash, the white paintwork
streaked with gritty grime. I have never been good at looking after
cars. The floor was a chaos of Coke tins, empty cigarette packets,
and beef jerky wrappers. Half a dozen stray McDonald's French
fries lurked festering under the seats. Somewhere north of Omaha I
had bought a bag of peanut butter biscuit snacks. The bag had burst
– south of Pierre, I recall. The carpet was a sticky, peanut-buttery
mess. Budget were going to love me. But much, much worse was

the bleeping. The throttle-you-slowly seat belts were slowly driving me mad.

Fifty miles north of Bismarck I turned down a dirt road through a forest to the site of Fort Mandan where Lewis and Clark spent the winter of 1804–5. The original structure would have rotted away years ago. A replica now sat in its place surrounded by clumps of ragweed and wild liquorice. It lay a hundred yards from the Missouri riverbank in a campsite scarred with tatty picnic tables and barbeque pits. The natural, woodland setting was emphasized by two wooden privies marked Bucks and Does.

The fort was like a glorified barn. Triangular in shape and made of cottonwood logs, it was surprisingly small: barely 75 feet long on each side with an 18-foot barricade; ten rooms led off a small earthen yard. The walls were chinked with mud.

The expedition took three weeks to build the original fort. They moved in on 27 November 1805, just as the first snow fell. It was a miserable winter, but the team kept up high spirits.

After the troublesome Sioux, the Mandan Indians, who lived in a village of earth-covered lodges nearby, were easy-going, and polite. The Mandan girls were more than eager to entertain their white visitors, although their free and easy approach caused problems. Clark wrote of 'Venerials Complaints, which is verry Common amongst the natives'.

The men kept themselves busy by collecting wood and with hunting expeditions. Food was plentiful. '34 deer, 10 elk, five buffalo' was the result of just one day's kill. There was also plenty of corn and beans. The fort was kept warm with huge log fires and in the evenings the men enjoyed parties where they danced to fiddle and tambourine. Lewis's hulking black servant York was a big hit with the Indians: 'I ordered my black Servent to Dance which amused the crowd Verry much, and Somewhat astonished them, that So large a man should be active ...'

But their cruel enemy, winter, was always lurking in the background. Snow-blindness and frostbite were common. Lewis was amazed at how the Indians managed to survive in only G-strings and buffalo robes.

The Mandans were different to other tribes in the area. They were much fairer-skinned, and it was their light complexions and alleged language similarities that had prompted Welsh-watchers to declare that the Mandans were the descendants of Prince Madoc's people.

They also used boats made from buffalo hide stretched over a frame of willow branches and light enough to carry – just like the Welsh coracle. And, as if that wasn't enough proof, the wanton Mandan women never stopped talking in bed – as Welsh girls were said to do!

While at the fort, Lewis and Clark came into contact with Indians who had known the intrepid Welsh clergyman John Evans, the man sent to investigate the Welsh connection nine years earlier. And in late 1804 the story reared its stubborn head once again.

It was all typically muddly. A Mr Henry Toulmin had taken down a statement from a Mr Childs, who had known a Welshman called Morris Griffiths. Mr Griffiths claimed that he had encountered the nation of Welsh Indians while on a trip up the Missouri in the 1760s. They had not taken kindly to his presence and had discussed whether to kill him. Mr Griffith's captors only spared his life after he spoke to them in Welsh.

The story spread in the American and British newspapers. Before long there were said to be 50,000 pure white Welsh Indians living in the Missouri wilderness.

Evans had concluded that there was no such tribe. But Welsh fanatics refused to believe him, claiming that he was concealing the real truth. They alleged that when Evans had returned to civilization he had got drunk and boasted that the Welsh Indians existed, but anti-Welsh factions had paid him to keep his mouth shut. Like Evans, Lewis and Clark's brief included an order to investigate the Madoc link. Like Evans, they returned with a resounding negative. There were no Welsh Indians on the Missouri.

A hellishly cold wind whistled through the trees around the fort. I was now on my way to Fort Berthold reservation, sixty miles to the north and present-day home of the Mandans.

The countryside was as desolate as I'd seen anywhere. There were few signs of civilization and only the occasional car on the road – usually a battered pick-up with hunting rifle hanging in the back window. I passed boarded-up cafés and tumbled-down barns. It was blowing a gale as I crossed Garrison Dam, another of the Missouri's hydro-electric plants. The ice lay thick on the river. Beyond the dam the car plunged into the fine brown haze of a dust storm. The view became grainy like an oil painting. More and more tumbleweed scattered across the road. The plains looked angrier than ever. I thought about the original settlers to this godforsaken land – 'I reckon it was like going into the unknown like in *Star Trek*,' commented one North Dakotan. They must have had a terrible time. For unlike its television namesake, the Little House on the Prairie was a hideous place to live.

Lured by free land offered by the 1862 Homestead Act, immigrants flocked into Dakota Territory. Among them were many Scandinavians, who found it difficult to acquire farmland back home because of the law of primogeniture inheritance of property. Likewise, Russo-Germans came here to escape persecution in Russia and to avoid military service in the Russian army.

Homesteads on the Dakota Frontier varied in comfort from a simple cave hollowed out of the bank of a stream to houses with earth walls and wooden boards for the roof. If settlers stopped by a wooded river, they built log cabins. The Germans made large sun-dried mud bricks and built thickly-walled houses.

Life was unbelievably tough. Summer brought droughts, prairie fires, dust storms, mosquitos and intense heat. Spring saw heavy floods. The winters were the worst: numbingly cold and a wind that never ceased. Sudden blizzards would kill people and animals without warning. Whole families eventually succumbed to frostbite. The homes were drab with cramped living spaces. Diseases like typhoid, diphtheria and smallpox flourished and parents watched their children die one by one. It could be a hundred miles to the nearest doctor and childbirth was a dangerous business.

The isolation of prairie living led to homesickness. People could stand it no longer. 'It is very different from back East,' wrote a settler, Mary Woodward, in 1888. 'Nobody keeps track of his neighbours here. People come and go, families move in and out and nobody asks from whence they came nor wither they go.'

Back in Omaha, Father Peter had talked about these great pioneers. He spread his arms wide and declared, 'Can you imagine that a hundred years ago out on this prairie there wasn't a soul for as far as you could see. It was the Jeffersonian view that America would be destroyed if it ever became so populated that you could hear your neighbour's dog bark at night. You could go for days without seeing anything on the horizon, not even the mountains. It made you sensitive to the needs of your brothers and sisters. There were times when if you didn't get help, you simply perished.'

The homesteader was a person shaped by the land. He could be immensely practical. An old-timer I met in North Dakota told me a story about a man who was eking out a living on one of the most remote farmsteads in the state. One day he travelled a hundred miles into town to marry his sweetheart. But she had got the wedding day wrong and was out of town. Her sister opened the door instead, 'Shucks,' he said. 'Can't waste no more time, will *you* marry me?' The sister agreed. They went to the justice of the peace, got married, jumped on his wagon and drove back to his farm. And that was that. You married out of necessity. You needed someone for companionship and to help with the cows and the crops. Love on the prairie meant working together.

The love on this prairie came in the form of a church that appeared out of the dust haze on the outskirts of Fort Berthold reservation. On the church roof a neon sign announced 'Jesus Saves' topped off by an enormous, pink fluorescent cross. It was big enough to attract all the angels in heaven.

According to the eighteenth-century Scottish historian William Robertson, the only connection between Welsh and any Indian languages spoken either in North or South America, was the word 'penguin.'

'The affinity of the Welsh language with some dialects spoken in America,' Dr Robertson wrote, 'has been mentioned as a circumstance which confirms the truth of Madoc's voyage.

'There is a bird, which, as far is yet known, is found only on the coasts of South America, from Port Desire to the Straits of Magellan. It is distinguished by the name of Penguin. This word in the Welsh language signifies White-head. Almost all the authors who favour the pretensions of the Welsh to the discovery of America, mention this as an irrefragable proof of the affinity of the Welsh language with that spoken in this region of America.'

I had a feeling that this was not going to help much in my search for the descendants of Madoc. For apart from the fact that penguins have black heads, it must be said that you don't find many on the Great Plains. In fact, you don't find any penguins at all.

Fifty years after Dr Robertson, the anthropologist and painter

George Catlin was compiling his magnum opus *North American Indians*. Catlin spent eight years from 1832 among the Great Plains tribes and he was convinced that the Mandans were of Welsh extraction. He even collected a list of Mandan words that sounded similar to Welsh. For example, the Mandan for 'head' was *pan*; the Welsh was *pen*. Similarly great spirit, or soverign – Mandan: *maho peneta*; Welsh: *mawr penaethir*.

'I believe it has been pretty clearly proved,' Catlin wrote, 'that they [Madoc and his crew] landed either on the coast of Florida, or about the mouth of the Mississippi and . . . settled somewhere in the interior of North America, where they are yet remaining, intermixed with some of the savage tribes.'

Madocians took these words as concrete proof. After all, Catlin, a native of Wyoming, had no vested interest in promoting the Welsh cause. Why should he say these things if they weren't true? However, conveniently for Catlin, the Mandan tribe was all but wiped out in the smallpox epidemic that swept the Great Plains in 1837. Thus he was able to add in the appendix to his weighty work that the Welsh Indians were now extinct.[1]

Following the ravages of smallpox, the Mandans could no longer exist as an independent unit; neither could the Hidatsa, who also suffered great losses. They were joined by another dwindling tribe, the Arikara. Today, these three nations are known as the Affiliated Tribes. Their home is Fort Berthold reservation, which encompasses 450,000 acres around the shores of the Missouri in north-west North Dakota.

It was early afternoon by the time I arrived at the Fort Berthold tribal offices, a large, modern building sitting alone on the prairie at the northern edge of the reservation. The lobby was the usual higgledy-piggledy jumble of broken furniture and scuffed linoleum. Pasty-faced Indians in thick coats hung around chatting and keeping out of the cold: the outside temperature had fallen to well below zero with a vicious wind-chill. I explained to the girl on the reception desk that I was researching a book about the area. Who did she suggest I speak to?

---

[1] Catlin was a wacky anthropologist. His other theory was that the American Indians were of Jewish blood and descended from the ten lost tribes of Israel.

She pointed down a corridor. 'Gerard Baker is the person you need. You'll find him down there.'

Gerard was sitting in an office with another man, whom he introduced as his cousin, Hugh. They were both dressed as if they were about to go out: bulky padded jackets and sturdy work boots. You betcha, they'd be delighted to talk to me, but they were about to leave for an inspection of the reservation's buffalo herd. Would I like to come along? I remembered Michael Jandreau's words: 'The buffalo are never there when you need them.' I expected to spend three or four hours trundling around the plains with not a hope of seeing one animal. But I had nothing better to do. I agreed to go with them. I made no mention of my Welsh quest. That would come later.

With his long plaited braids that stuck out from under a knitted bobble hat, Gerard resembled a Dutch doll. He was a huge man with a wry smile and a lurking sense of humour. He was a National Parks ranger with a degree in wildlife management and his job was to look after the buffalo herd. He was also the reservation's historian.

Hugh Baker was more dour. An ex-US Marine, he was a member of the Fort Berthold tribal council. His tribal name was Bad Buffalo. 'Hell, I don't know why. Guess my parents thought I was rowdy or something. Buffalo bulls are always in trouble, raising hell.'

A fierce wind greeted us as we stepped outside the offices. I remarked how the cold must have terrified the early settlers. 'And you lot can't have been much help to them either,' I added.

Gerard and Hugh laughed. 'It must have been dreadful,' Gerard said. He pulled his bobble hat hard down over his braids. 'At this time of year you never get warm. I'll say one thing, those white settlers were a hell of a lot tougher than us Indians are now.'

We stopped by a car containing two non-Indian men. They were bankers from the nearby town of Watford City, who had an appointment to see the buffalo. The reservation was trying to secure a loan to pay for additional fencing so they could expand the herd – a profitable business with hides worth up to $3,000. Hunters spent big money on licences to shoot the beasts. At present, Fort Berthold kept eighty buffalo on 1,000 fenced-in acres. If the bank agreed, the reservation planned to increase the herd to 1,000 animals.

The bankers were enthusiastic young men in trilby hats and herringbone tweed overcoats. They were dressed more for a saunter down Fifth Avenue than a bumpy drive across the prairie. Their car followed behind as we set off in Hugh's dusty Chevvy truck.

We talked about the Missouri. Like all the other reservations on the river, Fort Berthold had lost a large chunk of land to the dams. Before the Corps of Engineers moved in, the reservation had enjoyed a strong agricultural base. But the tribes had lost some of their most productive acres when the river bottoms were flooded. They were scornful of the land that was left. They nicknamed it coyote land because coyotes were about the only animals that would live there. Now, with little to support the people, unemployment was running at forty per cent. More than half the population had left the reservation.

But the last straw had been the fate of their ancestors' burial mounds. Before the bottoms were flooded the authorities had removed the remains to museums for scientific testing. The tribes were fighting to get them back. 'Can you imagine the outcry if someone dug up a white man's cemetery and took away the bones?' Hugh said. 'You'd have thought that after all these years the Government had learned something. But no, they still have no respect for Indian dead. Our dead forefathers are nothing more than a source of archaeological interest for them.'

Hugh reiterated the views I had heard further down the river. 'The tribes should take over the management of the Missouri. It is our river. We understand it. The white man does not.' He had a theory that states like Arizona would eventually run dry thanks to lack of rain and population increase. Supplies would have to be piped down from the Missouri basin. 'The tribes are trying to stake a claim on the Missouri water so that we can sell it. In ten years' time that could be a real possibility. We've got good lawyers and we're getting cleverer at understanding how the Government's mind works. This time we won't take empty promises. We'll be ready and waiting for 'em.'

We found the buffalo on a ridge overlooking an area called Skunk Bay. The animals were on a hillside sheltering from the bitter wind. Gerard and Hugh pointed excitedly. From the look on their faces you'd have thought they had never seen a buffalo before. But that is the effect these creatures have on the Plains Indians.

The buffalo was life. It housed you, clothed you and fed you. And you can't ask for much more of a package.

His hide became everything from boats and teepees to moccasins, drums and shields – after it had been tanned by his brain. His mane became rope, belts and ornaments and you used his blood, gall and bile for paint. You got glue from his hooves and bow-strings from his sinews. His stomach was a water bag. The skull was for ceremonial purposes and his tail became a fly swat.

The buffalo had an average life span of twenty-five years and a high reproductive rate. Herds thrived in astonishing multitudes. Until the 1830s an estimated thirty million animals roamed the Great Plains.

But then the white man arrived.

Buffalo fur meant money. Hunters flocked in with their breech-loading rifles. The lumbering beasts did not stand a chance. They were slaughtered in their millions by men like Vic Smith, one of the most famous Plains hunters, who killed 107 animals in a single stand in the winter of 1881–2.

With the near-extermination of this species came the destruction of the Plains cultures. The Indian was confused. Why did the white man cause such waste? Why did he leave all those carcasses rotting on the prairie? And when the Indian heard the answer, that the white man wanted only the hide because it fetched many dollars in St Louis, he still not understand. But then the Indian saw his food supply diminishing. His confusion turned to anger. And when he tried to stop the buffalo slaughter, the white man's army came and slaughtered him instead.

Gerard stopped the Chevvy. He sounded the horn. The herd began to amble slowly towards us. Hugh laughed, 'This is how you dom-esticate them. They know if you hoot the horn they'll get fed. It's like federal government and the Indians – they domesticated us with their beads and their subsidized canned food programmes.'

The bankers drew alongside us. They grinned at us through the car window. They were thoroughly enjoying their day out in the country.

The buffalo came closer, their thick coats ruffled by the wind. Soon they were around the cars, their bright, startled eyes staring at the intruders. They sniffed, snorted and pawed the ground. They seemed dangerously unhappy when they realized we had no food for them.

Gerard was one of the greatest buffalo experts on the Plains. But even he didn't trust these nervy creatures.

'You want to look out for their tails,' he explained. 'If the tail goes up it means one of two things: either they're going to the bathroom or they're about to charge. When their eyes get real big and the outsides go all white, that's the time to watch them. They're much more intelligent than ordinary cattle, who are stupid damned things. When a storm comes the ordinary cows will gather up in a corner by a fence and they'll stand there until they're covered in snow and they die. A buffalo will scratch away underneath the snow and find food. He's very resilient.'

Buffalo were not easy to keep. Fences would hold them for a time, but as soon as the grass got short, the young bulls would bust out taking the rest of the herd with them. 'You can keep them in by regularly feeding them. They can be domesticated, but only to their satisfaction. Let me tell you, these beasts are stubborn.'

The bankers snapped away with a Polaroid camera. A young animal tried to poke its nose through their car window. They looked nervous.

Hugh and Gerard laughed. It was sod's law that one of the buffalo would ram the bankers' car and that would be the end of the loan. We waited for a few more minutes. Then Gerard said it was time to go. 'Once they've worked out that we've got no food they could get funny.'

We began the journey back to the tribal office. Now was the time to hit Gerard and Hugh with Madoc. I took a deep breath. 'I suppose you know about the Welsh theory, that a twelfth-century Welsh prince and his followers are supposed to have sailed to America and ended up living with the Mandans?'

'No way,' Hugh replied, quick as a flash. 'The outer migration occurred here.'

'Sorry?' I faltered. 'Are you trying to say that the Mandans went to Wales?'

'Sure.'

'And that the Welsh are actually descended from the Mandan Indians?'

'Right in one.'

I suppose it was some sort of start, but it was not quite what I was after. I muttered something about how I was not sure that this theory would go down a storm in the Valleys. Hugh looked at me dead seriously. For a moment I could not tell if he was pulling my leg. Then he began to laugh, slowly and sinisterly. Gerard joined him. Oh God, I had landed myself with a pair of nutters.

'You're joking, of course,' I said.

'That's right, Peter. We're joking.'

I played them at their own game. I mentioned that there had indeed been such a story doing the rounds a couple of centuries ago. The historian William Robertson mentions a party of American Indians, tribe unknown, who are alleged to have landed near Hamburg, Germany, in the tenth century. Had Gerard and Hugh heard of that one? No, they had not.

'But I like it a lot,' Gerard said. He had learned German in High School. 'And do you know what? The language structure is exactly the same as Hidatsa. We put verbs at the end of sentences just like the Germans do.'

'How absolutely fascinating.' This was no good at all. I had come to discuss Welsh, not German.

I pressed on. 'But people must have asked you before about this Madoc business.'

'Sure,' Gerard said just a little wearily. 'George Catlin had this big thing about the link-up with skin colour. Like the Mandans were supposed to have got their blond hair from Madoc. Well, I've had white hair since I was five so maybe that came from Wales.'

There were no full-blooded Mandans left – they had all integrated with the Hidatsa. Only fourteen people were still able to speak pure Mandan. 'It's a very complicated language,' Gerard added. 'The problem is that the male and female speak differently. If I learned Mandan from a woman I wouldn't speak right – I'd be speaking the woman's language. For example, if a man is greeting somebody he says *dashka anja*, with a 'D'. That's hard, masculine-sounding. The woman says *mashka anja*, which is softer. The way you answer also means two different responses. None of the other native American languages are like that. Mandan is the only one that separates the sexes.'

Gerard lifted a hand and flicked his braids. He added: 'George Catlin said Welsh and Mandan were similar. I don't know what

Welsh sounds like, but it would have to be pretty unusual to sound anything like Mandan.'

The great moment had arrived. I revealed my secret weapon.

'Guess what,' I said, 'I've brought a Welsh tape with me.' And I dug into my camera bag and brought out a 'Say It In Welsh' cassette, described by its creator Degwel Owen as 'a guide to simple Welsh phrases and pronunciation'. I had bought the thing a few months earlier at the Welsh tourist shop in London. It had been in my luggage ever since.

Gerard and Hugh looked at me suspiciously.

'You want us to listen to *that*?' Hugh said.

'I thought this would be the best way of seeing if Welsh sounds anything like Mandan. You don't mind, do you?' Hugh sighed impatiently as if he was dealing with an over inquisitive small child.

'Go right ahead if you want to.'

I snapped the tape into my portable cassette player. The sing-song tones of Dewgal Owen filled the car.

I had not listened to the tape before. It was only now that I realised that Mr Owen had compiled an eccentric selection of phrases.

'*Mae Abertawe yn y bedwaredd* – Swansea are in the fourth division.'

Gerard cocked his head on one side. Hugh looked equally puzzled. This did not mean much to a pair of Mandan-Hidatsa Indians living in the middle of North Dakota. 'Er, that's fourth division as in football,' I explained. 'You know, soccer. We play it a lot in Britain.'

Not a glimmer of a smile appeared on either face. We continued.

'*Mae Cymru'n chwarae Lloegr ddydd* – Wales play England on Saturday.'

I shifted uncomfortably in my seat. After giving us the translation of 'Glamorgan County Cricket Club', Mr Owen launched into the glories of seaside holidays at Rhyl.

'*Allwyn ni farchogaeth yr asynnod?* – Can we ride the donkeys?'

'*Croeso i garafannau teithiol* – Touring caravans welcome . . .'

'. . . *cor meibion* – Male voice choir . . .'

I could bear it no longer. As we reached 'Which is the way to Harlech?' I switched off the tape player.

There was a ghastly silence.

'So,' I said nervously, 'does that sound anything like Mandan?'

Gerard and Hugh exchanged glances.

'Nope,' Hugh said.

'Nope,' Gerard said.

'It sounds like English to me,' Hugh added brightly.

'Yeah.' Gerard joined him. 'Sounds like English to me too.'

'And it doesn't sound just a teeny-weeny bit like Mandan?'

'Nope,' they chorused again.

'Are you trying to tell me,' I stuttered, 'that, as far as you're concerned, Welsh is the same as English? Have you any idea how nationalist the Welsh are? Do you realise that if you said that in a Pwllheli pub you'd be lucky to escape with your life?'

'Don't know what they're so proud about,' Hugh said. 'It sounds horrible.'

'It's nothing like Mandan,' Gerard said.

'Nothing at all,' Hugh said. 'Our language is much smoother, much more beautiful. That's a guttural language. Ugh!'

So that was that. The world's oldest living language had been torn to shreds in minutes. Any hope of finding a Welsh-American connection had been irrefutably shattered. My Madoc quest was a failure.

It was early evening when we parted company at the tribal offices. The sun cast a crimson glow over the prairie. I must have looked rather depressed. 'Never mind,' Gerard said. 'I still say Mandan is closer to German. Sure, your Prince Madoc existed. But the chances are he was a kraut.'

I arrived in Williston fearing the worst. Of all the Missouri river-towns, this was the one that attracted the most flak. Okay, Bismarck was an idea of hell to outsiders, but at least it had capital status. But Williston? Someone back in Omaha had remarked: 'It's not the end of the earth . . . but you can see it from there.'

Williston, population 13,000, skulks in a dust bowl sixty miles from the Canadian border. After beginning life as a tented colony of fur traders, the town exploded into life in 1887 as homesteaders arrived courtesy of the newly-opened Great Northern Railway. The railroad baron, James J. Hill, dreamed of boosting his profits by turning the Great North West into a prosperous farming community. Alas, he did not account for the lack of rain on this arid part of the prairie. Thirteen inches a year was the norm and harvests were notoriously dependent on the weather.

In the 1950s oil was struck in the Williston basin. Since then the town has ridden on the precarious crests of booms that have come and gone. The early 1980s saw a huge influx of wealth: new motels, bars and condominiums sprung up along the gaudy main strip. Everybody had cash to spend.

When I arrived, the city was going through a rough phase thanks to the Arabs cutting the price of their oil. Only twenty-two rigs were operating out of an original 180. Several Canadian drilling companies had deserted the town because of high local taxes.

Local people were fiercely loyal to their town, if only because it boasted one of the lowest crime rates in the United States. Nobody bothered to lock their doors and neighbours were always looking out for you. In winter there was virtually no crime at all. You don't find many thieves on the streets when it's thirty below. 'All you'll get stolen is your electric blanket,' one Willistonian told me. 'The great thing about North Dakota is that it scares away the freaks like murderers and rapists. How can you go out and be freaky when it's so fuggin' cold?'

The worst crime I read about in Williston concerned youths busted for under-age drinking. But then the local press was not noted for great exclusives: the police are fondly remembered for issuing a front-page appeal for help in tracing the owner of a set of false teeth found in the park.[1]

This part of North Dakota became home to thousands of Norwegian and Swedish homesteaders. And the Scandinavian influence lives on. Apart from the countless Olaf and Lene jokes, you will find many second-generation Norwegians, who can still speak their language. Visitors are encouraged to learn the expression *uff-da*, the Norwegian equivalent of 'aw, shit'.

It was dusk by the time I left Gerard and Hugh. The seventy-mile drive from Fort Berthold was the loneliest I had experienced. I was heading due west for the first time since arriving in Kansas City nine hundred miles away. The temperature had plunged and I dreaded the thought of breaking down. There was not a soul on the road and I was too far from civilization even to pick up a radio station, a horrible feeling for a European who is accustomed to seeing habitation at every mile. At least it wasn't snowing – a bad North Dakota winter means 25-foot-high drifts.

Suddenly I was over the ancient Indian burial mound of Medicine Lodge Hill and Williston was spread out on the plain below. The streets glowed yellow like a vast electronic circuit board. I fiddled with the radio. A country station burst into life with a song entitled 'You Can Eat Crackers In My Bed Anytime.' Ah, the flippancy of

---

[1] Newspapers in North Dakota have a reputation for their dry journalism. One of them once printed a story headlined 'Horse Jumps On Auto': 'Frightened by a bus, Dave Sanders' workhorse made a lunge. He landed on top of an automobile in one bound and, had it not been for the fact that he had a clumsy old wagon behind him, he would have set a hurdle record . . .'

America! Who needs thirty million buffalo when you can eat crackers in bed?

The El Rancho was like every other motel on the Great Plains: a central lobby, restaurant and bar, with the rooms in a couple of long blocks across the car park. A neon sign announced: 'Salesmen and Travellers Welcome.'

I retreated to my room. It was distinguished by a fluffy brown nylon carpet that created lightening flashes of static electricity. Whenever I touched the light switch my fingers lit up like a Christmas tree.

After wearily dumping my bags I had a shower and relaxed in centrally-heated comfort. The temperature outside had dropped to minus fifty degrees. I could almost smell the cold. It seeped into my skull and around my eyes. I was reluctant to go out again. Life on the road was beginning to depress me. Somehow I couldn't face the effort of meeting new people.

I tried the television: the usual drivel. Five minutes of *The Cosby Show* convinced me what to do. I got dressed and plunged through the icy blast across the car park to see what entertainment the El Rancho had to offer.

The lounge was decorated with vomitous, squirly wallpaper. In one corner a blackjack croupier with a beer-gut that obscured his knees supervised a table of cowboy card-players. Above the table hung a sign warning: 'Please No Profanity.'

I sat at the bar. The moment I opened my mouth to order a beer, I heard the usual cry of: 'Hey, you ain't from around here.' A little guy in his forties with long sideburns and Mexican moustache was seated on the stool next to me. I had just met my guide to Williston.

Pat Falcon was the first off-reservation Indian I had encountered. The antithesis of the likes of Charlotte Black Elk, he was a non-intellectual joker with an unbelievable gift of the gab. One of his friends told me later that he was known as Walking Eagle ''cos he's so full of shit he can't fly'.

I never learned Pat's real tribal name. But he agreed that some of his family had colourful nomenclatures: 'Like, I got a cousin called Karen White Owl and she married Tom Yellow Wolf so now she's called Karen White Owl-Yellow Wolf. It's a good thing she didn't marry my other cousin Danny Crows Fly High, otherwise she'd sound like a fucking aviary.'

He enjoyed Indian jokes. Q: Which general killed more Indians than any other general? A: General Motors. Or the one about the Indian, who drank 120 cups of tea and was found drowned in his tee-pee. 'A lot of people tell Indian jokes round here,' he said. 'You can usually tell if they're being mean or not.'

Pat was a motor man on a Canadian-owned oil rig outside Williston. He earned good money, but the work was hard: 'Hey, the Indian women did all the cooking and cleaning while the men hunted and fished. Then these Europeans arrived and said they would make our lives better? Who were they kidding?'

He was a bizarre mix: his father was a full-blooded Chippewa Indian and his mother had left her native Liechtenstein when she was four years old. He was so fair that I would have not guessed he was Indian. 'Wintertime I kinda bleach out,' he explained. His wife, Mary, was of Norwegian descent. 'A big blonde Viking' is how he described her.

Pat's Liechtenstein side of his ancestry didn't interest him – and who can blame him? But he was proud of his Chippewa roots. He could speak his native language. 'Our greeting for "how are you?" – *ton chay tu gas?* – translates as "how are your balls?" meaning "how are you as a man?" Then your reply translates as, "Sure, they're fine, they're still danglin' and draggin' on the ground as usual." '

He was a bouncy man, always unshaven. He never stopped smiling. He was the backbone of America, not especially well-off, but utterly committed to the American way of life. He admitted that a reservation would have little to offer him.

He had a cynical view of how liberal white people were now trying to be nice to the Indians. 'Ten years ago we were a lump of whale shit at the bottom of the ocean. Now everybody wants to be an environmentalist. These liberals say we'd better look after these Indians 'cos there are so few pure ones left. What pisses me off is that it's kinda glamorous to say you're an Indian. Everybody's trying to say their Grandma was a Cherokee princess.'

Like thousands of other Native Americans Pat had served in Vietnam. 'I wasn't keen on going, but it was what your family expected of you if you were an Indian. You weren't a man if you didn't fight. It was like I was fighting for my tribe.

'Vietnam was a joke. Everybody called you "chief" and out in the bush the officers put you on point duty because they figured if you were an Indian you were a good tracker. They didn't remember that we'd been herded into a small square of land and that we'd lost all that stuff.'

The Indians claim that they suffered more casualties per capita than any other race in Vietnam. They were often placed in the most exposed areas of fighting. 'The officers figured you'd make a good scout, that you were supposed to be light-footed through the woods. I mean, Jesus Christ, how much jungle do we have on the Plains? Then they had the cheek to talk about "Indian Country" when you were in Vietcong territory. I guess those white generals thought there was some mystique about going into Indian country. We thought they were real crass.'

We both laughed at the stupidity of it all. Pat was firing on all cylinders. 'And then you'd say you're from North Dakota and they'd look at you like where on hell's earth is that? And you'd say, "Shit no mail today – the stage coach got held up again." And I'm not kidding, these guys from New York actually believed you. I even had a black guy from New Jersey who refused to sleep near me because he thought I was gonna lift his curly little nubbin of a head and go running around the camp with his scalp.'

I said that back home in England we knew very little about native Americans except for what we'd seen in cowboy movies. 'That's nothing new,' Pat grinned. 'There are people in Washington who don't know nothing about native Americans neither and they live here.' He drummed his fists on the bar and roared with laughter.

He ordered more drinks. I told him what I was doing in the United States and that I had just driven from Fort Berthold. I explained the Welsh theory. Pat didn't think much of it, but he had his own theory about Madoc.

'It would have been pretty tough for those Welsh guys to go all the way up the river. What puzzles me is that the Mandan were not a warlike people. Everyone else like the Sioux was beating up on them. I thought the Welsh were supposed to like a fight. There can't have been much Welsh in the Mandan.'

He thought about this for a moment. Then he added, 'Maybe Madoc ended up at Trenton.' This was Pat's birthplace, a town with a large Indian population ten miles up the Missouri from Williston. 'Oh, Jesus! Saturday night at Trenton. The fights were great. Everybody wanted to come out and beat up the Indians. Shit, they didn't stand a chance.'

Twenty years ago. white people studiously avoided Trenton. Even in the early 1980s it was dubbed Williston's backyard ghetto. 'There were twenty-seven of us in the house when I was a kid. We were real poor. We never had nothing, but we never thought about it. We used to run in a pack and go hunting with slingshots. That was pretty good fun.'

New Year's Day was the best. You could walk into any house and eat. You had no foes that day. Even your greatest enemy welcomed you like a brother. 'The oldest man in the house would sit by the door with a pot of whisky and dip you a drink as you walked in. And the children would sit up all New Year's Eve night and the women would cook and bake while the men would be in the next room partyin' and singin' and fightin'.'

His grandmother still lived in Trenton. She raised thirty-three children, fourteen of her own and sixteen of her brother's. The other three were orphans. 'That was the Indian way. You always had a place to go as a kid. If your parents died, someone would take you in.'

But the whites wanted nothing to do with the Indians. Discrimination was rife. In the 1950s, all liquor sales to Indians were banned. The shops displayed signs telling dogs and Indians to keep out. 'My dad couldn't even buy a beer. He'd have to stand outside a bar and get a white man to go in and buy it for him.'

I mused that we could have been talking about South Africa, a country that today's so-called liberal US politicians spend so much time condemning. 'Yep,' Pat said. 'Ain't it a funny old world?'

He talked about his Chippewa great-grandfather who had gone on the warpath in the 1890s. This had been a rare occasion when the cowboys had lost. 'One day this white woman homesteader arrives and claims the land Great-Grandpa's been farming all his life. One day she goes into Williston to get supplies and while she's out he burns her house down. She comes back and I guess she really likes the neighbourhood because she builds another house. She doesn't want to leave, but she has to because she runs out of food. And Great-Grandpa goes and burns it down again. He has to burn it down three times before she decides the neighbourhood's kinda rough after all. Then he went and filed a homestead claim himself and that's how he ended up with the little land he had.'

Pat laughed again. There was no bitterness in his voice. 'But you know what? After all this shit that the Indians have had to suffer, I think that some of our values rubbed off on the white people. Like, don't steal from your neighbour . . .'cos he'll end up stealing from you.'

It was getting late. The El Rancho bar was almost deserted. We arranged to meet each other the next day when Pat said he would take me driving on the Missouri. '*On* the river?' I queried.

'Sure, it's all iced up. Real thick and real safe.'

Next morning I drove round to Pat's trailer home a few blocks from the El Rancho. It was warm inside and furnished with an incredible array of souvenir nick-nacks. A Swiss cuckoo clock hung on one wall. 'The big blonde Viking' had her feet up on the couch watching TV gameshows. 'Wheel of Fortune' was her favourite. On her lap was the family Siamese cat. It was cross-eyed and regarded me nervously. Mary was embarrassed to see me. 'She doesn't like receiving visitors until she's done her hair,' Pat confided.

He grabbed his baseball hat. We drove over the brown patchwork of the prairie towards the river. The sun shone in a cloudless sky. Yesterday's wind had gone, although it was still freezing. It was hard to believe that in summer Williston suffered from one of the worst mosquito infestations in America. Even Lewis and Clark had noted that the 'musquetors' in this area were dreadful.

The previous year the city authorities had been deluged with complaints. They had tried aerial and ground spraying with little effect. A group of six women had formed a group called Bug-Busters to study ways to control the pests. They had come to the conclusion that the answer lay in bats: apparently one bat can eat up to seven thousand mosquitos a night.

Pat said that the Indians kept the insects away by rubbing themselves with bear grease. I pointed out that bear grease was neither practical nor ecologically sound these days.

Pat was as talkative as ever. As we crossed the hills, he told me his dream was to buy a plot on the prairie and move his trailer. But Mary was having none of it. She did not want to leave town; she would miss her friends. 'I love it out here. I guess this is what they call wide open spaces. You can walk these hills and be alone.' He had worked in the oil business down in New Orleans, but nothing compared to Williston. 'I made a lot of money there, but who wants the hassle? Like there have been only two murders here in the last five years.

'There's no one out here. Just a lot of abandoned farms. Right up to the 1930s people used to take only their clothes and leave. I remember finding an old place where the table was still set with dishes. The people had gone bust and moved out without thinking.'

There was an area near here named Poker Jim's after a cowboy who died there. It was one of Pat's favourite stories. 'Happened back in the 1880s when some cowboys were out in winter patrolling the herd. One of them, Jim, froze to death. The ground was so hard that they couldn't bury him. So they decided to wait until spring and they took him back to their shack and stuck him up in the rafters, stiff as a board.

'Well, one night they're playing poker and they've got the stove on. Jim thaws out and falls out of the ceiling and right on to the card table scaring the hell out of 'em. That's why it's called Poker Jim's.'

We reached the river. I turned down a track through sand dunes to the water's edge. When we got to the ice I stopped the car.

'What are you stopping for?' Pat sounded surprised. 'Go right ahead. Won't hurt you. It's seven foot thick.' The frozen Missouri glistened bluey-white, calm and silent in the sunshine. After the rushing torrents I had seen earlier in my journey, the river was now at peace.

The ice was dotted with little fishing shacks stretching into the distance. As soon as winter came, fishermen towed the buildings out on trailers. They cut a hole in the ice inside the house, put a line down and then played cards and drank until the salmon or wall-eye bit. The shacks were warmed by little wood-burning stoves and you could stay overnight. 'You should see the place at weekends. Covered in cars. It's like a village with everyone partying and having a good time. And there's no shortage of ice for your drinks.'

Very gingerly, I left dry land and steered the Toyota onto the ice. It seemed to be firm enough and Pat claimed to know what he was doing. But I didn't like the look of it.

'Look, Pat, I'm not sure this is such a good idea.'

'Sure, people do it all the time round here.'

I patted the Toyota's steering wheel. 'Ah, yes, but I bet they don't do it in a hired car.' Nice though the people at Budget were, I did not think they would appreciate it if I sank their vehicle.

'Well, you've got your accident damage waiver, haven't you?'

'Yes, but I'm not sure that it will cover a Toyota at the bottom of the Missouri.'

Pat wasn't listening. He was jabbering on about contests that the fishermen held before the big spring thaw. They'd take a wrecked car onto the ice and place bets on which day it fell through. There was a big pool of dollars for the winner.

Pat's face had a schoolboyish look. 'Tell you what: you go fifty miles an hour and then slam on the brakes and turn the steering wheel. Boy, that's a blast. You go zoom, zoom round in circles.'

I had absolutely no intention of going zoom, zoom. I drove sedately across the glassy surface. The Toyota's tyres skidded and crunched over a layer of sparkling, powdery snow. We bumped over rough ridges that threatened to tear off the sump.

The reflection of the sun on the icy crystals was dazzling. I leaned forward over the steering wheel and squinted through the windscreen in an attempt to see where we were going. We drove around the ice houses. Outside one of them sat a snowman next to a tatty fir tree left over from Christmas. A piece of tinsel was stuck in its branches. I had never expected to see the Missouri like this. It was a strange feeling, utterly unnatural.

Pat laughed at my discomfort. 'In spring when the ice ain't too good cars fall through all the time.'

'Thanks for telling me,' I said.

'Nah, we got a few days to go before that starts happening.' As an afterthought he added, 'And not many people drown.'

'What, you just scramble out?'

He guffawed. 'When you're going through the ice you ain't hanging around to see how deep you're going. You get out quick. Best thing is to watch someone else drive over first and see if they make it. It's the same as in life: there's always someone who'll try it first.'

I did not have much confidence in this simple philosophy. A loud booming sound came from somewhere outside the car. 'What the hell's that,' I asked.

'Gunshot.'

'Oh yeah?'

'Yep. Someone out hunting.'

'Not unless he's using a howitzer. It sounded like the ice moving to me.'

Pat went quiet. 'Know what? You could be right.'

'Told you so.'

Pat put his hands up in surrender. 'Okay – shoot low Sherrif, I'm riding a Shetland.' Another big smile. 'Yep, it's bits of ice banging against each other. Shifting, contracting. Often happens when the sun's out.'

'Charming.'

'But it's nothing to worry about. No, when the ice really cracks there's a helluva bang. You'll see the river rise up three or four feet like a whale. That's the time to move your ass. Now take that bit of ice over there . . .' He pointed at a ridge about two hundred yards away. 'That's where the pressure builds up and it gets really weak. Boy, no, don't want to go there.' There were also underground springs and water courses that could weaken the surface. And just to make things really exciting, they had a habit of changing position from year to year.

This was all too much for me.

Barrrooooom! Another of Pat's 'gunshots'.

'Right, that's enough.' I adopted a schoolmasterly tone.

Pat looked disappointed. 'We could drive right over to the other side.' This was about a mile away.

'No way.'

'Okay, on reflection maybe it needs someone with a bit more balls than us to do that.'

All right, no need to rub it in, but this Englishman wasn't going any further. I wasn't so much worried about my own safety as that of the Toyota. Although, on second thoughts, it would be a neat way of disposing of the bleeping seat belts.

I left the ice with immense relief. It was several weeks later before I realised that, in fact, we had behaved quite rashly. A letter from Pat was waiting for me when I returned home to England. 'Well, you missed the excitement,' he wrote, and I could imagine his chirpy voice. 'Three days after we were out on the river a Ford Bronco fell through the ice near where we had been. Guess we were lucky.' It had cost $5,000 in diver's fees to recover the vehicle from the riverbed. Pat didn't mention the driver. I presumed that the unfortunate man had 'moved his ass'.

Driving on the frozen Missouri had been unnerving. But I was about to undergo the scariest moment of the journey.

Through Pat I met a woman called Beth Witt. A lively lady in her fifties, Mrs Witt was home economics teacher at Williston High School. When she realized that an Englishman was in town, and an English journalist at that, she insisted that I give a talk to her fifteen-year-old pupils.

'Oh God, what on earth shall I tell them?'

'How about the cultural differences between Britain and America?' And so I turned up at the school one afternoon to address her 'family living' class.

I felt like Lewis and Clark among the Sioux. Thirty-five pairs of unsmiling eyes stared at me across the long classroom: a mixed class of fifteen-year-olds, the boys in heavy metal T-shirts and the girls in the tightest jeans imaginable. Such a tricky age, when children seethe with adolescent trauma. Okay, dickhead, tell us something that we don't know. I had invaded their territory. It was my job to amuse them.

Once we got over the sniggers about my accent, I attempted to find some of Mrs Witt's 'cultural differences'. A girl in the third row loudly popped her bubble gum – there was one for a start. Mrs Witt stood at the back of the room smiling encouragement.

I said that the big difference between England and America was the great distances between towns, particularly in the Dakotas. Did they realize how much space they had out here? No. Or at least I could not work out if they did or they didn't such was the blankness of their expressions. This was getting sticky.

Prices next. Gas – or petrol as we call it – was ridiculously cheap compared with Europe. In fact, everything in America was cheap. And wasn't it amazing how you could eat 24-hours-a-day in this country? No, they didn't seem to think it was that amazing.

And what about drive-in McDonald's hamburger restaurants? It is customary in American drive-in fast-food joints to place your order through a microphone first. A tinny voice tells you how much it will be and you crawl forward to the pick-up counter. By the time you have reached the front of the queue of cars your Big Mac is waiting. The first time I had tried this I failed to order first at the microphone. Instead, I drove straight to the pick-up point. The counter girl gave me an 'aren't you one of those Martians?' looks. A traffic jam built up behind while she rushed to prepare my burger. I felt a complete prat.

'And that's a little bit of American culture that we don't encounter back home,' I concluded. A few laughs. The girls and boys of Williston High found my embarrassment quite amusing. But I was still struggling.

'What about the Royal Family?' one of the girls asked. 'Have you ever met them?'

The inevitable question. After all, hasn't *everybody* in England met the Royal Family? It was time for the cheap thrills.

'Funny you should ask that,' I said, 'but I was in a restaurant in London the other day and Fergie was at the next table.'

The class perked up. This was more like it.

'And I'll tell you one thing,' I continued, 'Fergie's got the biggest bottom you've ever seen.'

Cheap thrills, as I said. But it worked a treat. The class disintegrated into raucous giggles.

I had chosen the right subject. While I was in the States the Duchess of York was receiving a lot of stick in the newspapers. I had read an article by a columnist who said that, judging by her hairstyle, she could easily find employment as a hay-raker. (Although he had conceded that Fergie should 'get come credit for writing a book [*Budgie The Helicopter*] that her sister-in-law can actually read.')

Mrs Witt looked a touch horrified at the reference to Fergie's bottom. That was enough of the Royals.

I think that by the time I had finished, the class was on my side. They ended up asking my views on America's liquor laws. I replied that it seemed crazy that you could fight for your country and elect a president at eighteen but in most states, including North Dakota, you were not allowed an alcoholic drink until you were twenty-one. I had reached deep into the teenage heart. Williston High broke into wild applause.

A couple of days later I was on the road again. The weather was warmer and considerably better than back home. My friends in Williston had been horrified to hear that fifty people were dead after hurricane-force gales had lashed the British Isles. Little ole England was not supposed to have weather like that. We put it down to global warming.

Fifteen miles out of Williston I stopped at Fort Union, the most important of the western frontier's trading posts. Established in 1828 at the confluence of the Missouri and Yellowstone rivers, Fort Union was for nearly forty years the major depot for trappers returning from the wilderness with beaver pelts and buffalo robes.

The Fort was reigned over by Kenneth McKenzie, one of the great characters of the Wild West. The ablest trader in the American Fur Company and a rampant *bon viveur*, McKenzie held court in such style that he was dubbed King of the Upper Missouri.

Visitors to the fort found it an oasis of luxury in this barren land. They dined off a table set with china and silverware. 'Mr McKenzie is a kind-hearted and high-minded Scotchman,' George Catlin enthused. 'His table groans under the luxuries of the country: with buffalo meat and tongues, with beavers' tails and marrow-fat; but *sans* coffee, *sans* bread and butter. Good cheer and good living we get at it however, and good wine also; for a bottle of Madeira and one of the excellent Port are set in a pail of ice every day, and exhausted at dinner.'

McKenzie's high-life was cut short after he installed an illegal whisky still to circumvent the strict liquor laws. His embarrassed employers were forced to retire him. In 1858 he settled in St Louis with a 50,000-dollar fortune. Three years later he was dead, having blown most of it on rip-roaring parties that were the talk of the town.

The original Fort Union was dismantled in the last century, but it has since been reconstructed to provide the area's major tourist attraction. I strolled around the white painted wooden palisade, inside of which lay a replica of McKenzie's palatial dwelling.

Judging by the dinky little turrets and pillared verandahs, I mused that perhaps Hollywood did get it right after all. The warden in the visitors' centre assured me that the complex had been built according to strict historical guidelines. But as far as I was concerned, it resembled a movie set; an absurdity plonked on a grassy plain in the middle of nowhere. The original edifice must have looked extremely strange to the Indians.

Before taking the road into Montana I paused at nearby Fort

Buford, a cavalry outpost that held great strategic importance for steamboat traffic to the West. Little remained except for a cemetery and a stone powder magazine.

The deadpan North Dakotan sense of humour was much in evidence here. They joke that there are so few trees in North Dakota that the state tree is a telephone pole. A lone fir stood near the old parade square. Someone had nailed a sign on it: 'Fort Buford National Forest.'

Ten

Captains Meriwether Lewis and William Clark left Fort Mandan in high spirits. They were advancing into the unknown – the Great North West where no white men had been before. 'I could but esteem this moment of my departure as among the most happy of my life,' wrote Lewis. 'The party are in excellent health and spirits . . . not a whisper or murmur of discontent to be heard among them.'[1]

I wish I could have agreed. But had there been anyone to murmur discontent to, I would have murmured. Loudly.

I was suffering from prairie sickness – boredom on a grand scale. As I crossed into Montana the scenery looked as sickeningly familiar as ever. A mesmerizingly straight ribbon of tarmac cut through an ocean of flat, parched grassland under a murky sky. Rows of

---

[1] There are so many good quotes in the journals that it is impossible to list them all. But one of my favourites concerns Lewis's thoughts on leaving Fort Mandan. He is just a little pompous as usual: 'Our vessels consisted of six small canoes, and two large perogues. This little fleet altho' not quite so respectable as those of Columbus or Capt. Cook, were still viewed by us with as much pleasure as those deservedly famed adventurers ever beheld theirs; and I dare say with quite as much anxiety for their safety and preservation. We were now about to penetrate a country at least two thousand miles in width, on which the foot of civilized man had never trodden; the good or evil it had in store for us was for experiment yet to determine, and these little vessels contained every article by which we were to expect to subsist or defend ourselves.'

electricity pylons stretched into the distance. The most exciting sight was the occasional yellow sign warning of bumps in the road. Local motorists talked of 'tunnel vision'. So hypnotic was the highway that if your eyes left it for a moment you were likely to veer into a ditch.

I glanced at the map. Eastern Montana went on for ever. The Indians call this state 'the land of shining mountains', but there were more than three hundred miles of plains left before I caught my first glimpse of the Rockies. I gritted my teeth and pressed on through sporadic snow flurries.

Montana is vast and empty with more deer per square mile than people. Her land mass is greater than Japan and she is America's fourth largest state after Alaska, Texas and California.

She has known perilous times. The collapse of agriculture in the 1920s led to numerous bankruptcies and the place is littered with abandoned homesteads. During the 1930s depression twenty-five per cent of the population was said to be on welfare. But Montanans are cautiously optimistic these days. She is more progressive than the Dakotas, which are sleepy and resistant to change. Montana encourages change. If the population cannot exactly be described as exploding, not so many people are in a rush to leave.

I made an overnight stop at Glasgow for no reason other than the name intrigued me. Would the bars be full of kilted caber-tossers yelling, 'See you, Jimmy' and head-butting the Indians? No, they were not, although I did see a saloon called the Clansman, next door to an amusement arcade called the Funny Farm. Otherwise it was the usual grain elevators, railroad sidings and John Deere tractor sprawl.

And taxidermists. Stuffing furry animals seemed to be a favourite occupation in these parts. But fur-trapping on a professional scale was on the decline. The anti-fur brigade were making hell and at seven or eight dollars a mink it was hardly worth the long trudge through the snowy wilderness. A beaver pelt might fetch fifteen dollars if you were lucky – a puny sum when you consider that as far back as 1810 a prime pelt fetched six dollars.

Back in Williston, Pat had advised me on the drawbacks of trapping. 'The thing I hate is the fleas. You pick up a dead fox and the fleas crawl all over you. Best to let it lay for a day until they go.'

The barmaid at my motel did not think that Glasgow's settlers had been particularly Scottish. 'I've always heard that someone spun a globe and stuck a pin into it,' she drawled. 'I guess they hit Glasgow, Scotland.'

The only other people in the bar were the resident guitar duo, who, with the lack of an audience, were making the most of the beer. One of them was called Lee. Upon hearing I was English he told me his funniest joke: 'Know what? Prince Charles should have called his first son Up. Then he could have sent out Christmas Cards "with love from Up, Chuck and Di." ' That was the trouble with being an Englishman in America. All people wanted to talk about was the Royal Family . . . or Benny Hill. It was disturbing that Americans – cab drivers were the worst offenders – regarded this overweight buffoon as a great British humourist.

Next morning I began the big trek across Montana to Great Falls, the last major town before the Missouri headwaters. It had snowed hard in the night. The road was treacherous and bright from frost. A vicious wind whipped around the car.

Twenty miles south of Glasgow I came down the hill to Fort Peck Dam. It was a beautiful sight. There was hardly a ripple on the lake below the dam walls; the bleak serenity reminded me of a Scottish loch.

I stopped at the powerhouse, a massive art deco pile that housed Fort Peck's hydro-electric plant. I thought I should speak to someone from the Corps of Engineers. After all, this was the Missouri's major dam. And, according to the Corps' detractors, this was where the trouble started. It was time for the Corps to defend themselves.

I knocked on the powerhouse main door. No one answered. Judging by the size of the place, the employees were down miles of corridor well out of earshot. Icicles hung like spun glass from the roof. The wind was appalling. My nose was dead from cold. I jumped up and down to keep warm.

Still no one came. I tried a telephone that was on a wall by another door. I got through to the dam's superintendent, Sam Richardson. I blurted out my business. 'Please let me in,' I pleaded. I felt like a Captain Oates who has just changed his mind.

Sam arrived two minutes later. He opened the door. I barged past him. 'Terribly sorry about this,' I mumbled. I wrenched the Woolworth's acrylic bobble hat from my head. My hair crackled with static. I frantically blew on my hands and rubbed the warmth back into my ears.

'A little cold for you?'

'Huh?' Great sense of humour, these Americans.

The dam had been Sam's life ever since his father had quit farming in 1934 to become a construction worker on the project. Sam had joined the Corps of Engineers in 1969. 'Guess the dam's a family business,' he laughed. 'Quite a few of us are second generation dam workers.'

Sam was in his fifties with thinning, reddish hair and glasses. We talked in his office high up in the powerhouse.

Fort Peck was the first of the Missouri's dams, built during the Roosevelt administration as a $110-million public works project. Work began in 1933. On completion seven years later the walls stood 250 feet high with a base 3,500 feet thick. They backed up a reservoir with a shoreline equal to the coast of California – 1,500 miles long. For many years it was the largest earth-filled dam in the world. Now it ranks fourth. The nearby town of Fort Peck was built specially to house the workforce – more than 10,000 at the peak of construction in 1936.

'I'll tell you something,' Sam said. 'This ole dam's been good to families. It's certainly provided me with a good livelihood.'

So what about the criticism? How did he feel when people accused the Corps of Engineers of doing more harm than good?

Sam looked cross. 'There's always gonna be folk who complain. Nothing's ever right for some people.' he sighed. He'd heard all this many times before. 'I'll bet they're just plain ignorant. Bet they weren't around before the dams. Bet they don't know what it was like. What you've got to remember is that this was the first time anyone had attempted to control the Missouri. It was a dreadful river. You had ferocious floods in spring and after that it would dry up and was no good for irrigation. It was one thing or the other, no balance. If the water wasn't held back it rushed down the Mississippi into the ocean and was gone.'

The lake provided excellent boating and swimming. The hydroelectric plants kept the region in electricity. 'Bet you think of 1940s America as a modern country,' Sam went on. 'But do you realize we had no electricity in some of the rural communities round here until 1949? We were still using kerosene lamps. I can tell you, the dam's made a big change in farm life.' He paused and held my gaze. 'Oh yes, you can forget what they say about the Big Muddy. 'Cos it's a darned sight better than it used to be.'

Big Sam Richardson was not a man to be argued with. And certainly not when it came to his beloved dam. I thanked him for his time and returned to the car. I brushed a jigsaw of frost from the windscreen and continued on my way.

By midday, the clouds began to clear. A puffy blue sky with a hint of sunshine hung over Canada to the north. According to a series of blue markers bearing a cow's face, I was on the Old West Trail. A lone coyote loped across the road fifty yards in front of me. The slinky grey cur gave me a surreptitious look and disappeared into the wilderness.

At the railroad town of Malta — another pin stuck in a globe? — I was faced with a decision. Should I continue west and then swerve south via Fort Benton, another American Fur Company stronghold? Or should I turn south down Highway 191, cross the Missouri and head west for the Rockies? I chose the latter route. Looking at the map, south seemed to be the quickest way to the mountains. I had been on the plains too long.

I paused at a sign informing me that this was once important buffalo country. Some tribes killed the beasts by stampeding them over a cliff. They then collected what they could from the bloody heap of bones and fur at the bottom. I mused that this was little less sporting than shooting buffalo from a prone position with a high-powered rifle, as hunters do today. I'd discussed this with Pat. He couldn't see the point of shooting the animals either. 'A bow and arrow on a trained buffalo horse is the only decent way,' he declared.

The landscape brightened up as I approached the river. An eagle circled overhead. I descended into the polar glow of a tree-lined gorge. This was a national wildlife refuge named after Charles M. Russell, the cowboy-turned-artist, whose gung-ho cowboy paintings are legendary reminders of those range-roaming days.

The sun burst through the fir trees as I crossed a short snow-covered bridge spanning the Missouri. The river was much narrower — somewhere between here and Fort Peck it had shrunk. But it was delightfully picturesque and a good place to take photographs. I made the rash mistake of driving down a steep, icy track to the

's edge. I took my pictures and then tried to return to the
way. The wheels spun furiously. I was stuck. I spent a freezing
ten minutes collecting brushwood to stick under the wheels. Eventually they bit. After several run-ups I was back on the main road.

I realized how foolish I had been. There was no other traffic on
the road and not a sign of a farm. I was lucky to have escaped so
easily. Memo: do not even attempt to be adventurous in snowbound
Montana.

Out of the gorge, it was the dreary old prairie again. There were
momentary bouts of excitement when I reached what appeared to
be rolling hills. But they soon fizzled out. The flat emptiness droned
on as monotonously as the Toyota's engine. The only signs that
anyone had been here before me were the tarmac and telegraph
poles. Barbed wire fences marked the boundaries of huge ranches. I
drove on, munching on a strip of beef jerky and listening to a
Canadian radio station. Canadian radio was quite fun, with chat
shows and soap operas, a welcome change from the incessant diet
of American country music. When the reception faded I amused
myself with counting what percentage of male 4WD drivers on the
road wore baseball hats and moustaches. A boring game. After thirty
miles I had scored a hundred per cent.

I passed through Roy. According to my notes it was 'flat as it's
ever been, like being out to sea, a few broken-down shacks, bugger
all else, what lunatic decided to settle here in the first place?' The
next town – if you could call it a town – was Hilger. It wasn't much
better than Roy. I bought a packet of cigarettes in a rickety shack
called the Pioneer Bar. The glum-faced bartender made no comment
on my accent. Perhaps he thought I was Canadian.

I stopped again at a roadhouse outside Lewistown – named not
after Meriwether, but for a Major Lewis, who established a fort
there. Eddie's Corner was an old fashioned pit-stop. Huge trucks
filled the parking lot. Their drivers had left the motors running to
keep them warm. Clouds of exhaust fumes rose into the cold air.
Inside the restaurant a row of greasy hulks was lined up on low
vinyl stools at the food counter. They were hunched over platefuls
of roast beef and gravy, eating silently and with great determination.

I eavesdropped on the waitresses as I sipped a coffee. They were
typical corn-fed girls with large apron-clad midriffs. They were gossiping about diets, and the amount of sodium in food. Sodium was

the latest American health fad, yet another ingredient that was said to be bad for you. The newspapers were full of it. Looking at the waitresses' chunky figures and the food they were serving, I wondered why they worried. What harm is a little sodium when you're clogging up your arteries with a 10-ounce burger and a bowl of fries?

Two hours later I arrived in Great Falls. I found a room in the Rainbow, which upon its 1911 launch was the most elaborate, well-furnished hotel in town. A grand blockhouse of a building, the Rainbow was a little scuffed these days, and the chandeliers had been sold years ago. But it oozed atmosphere: who knows what land and mining deals were clinched here? How many fortunes were won and lost?

Strictly speaking, I was still on the Great Plains, but I did not care. For, from my bedroom window, I could at last see the sparkling, snowy caps of those elusive Rocky Mountains.

The portage around the Great Falls of the Missouri was one of the most arduous tasks undertaken by the Lewis and Clark expedition.

On 13 June 1805, Lewis caught his first glimpse of this mighty series of waterfalls. He saw a 'perfect white foam which assumes a thousand forms in a moment sometimes flying up in jets of sparkling foam to the hight of fifteen or twenty feet . . . from the reflection of the sun on the sprey or mist which arrises from these falls is a beautifull rainbow produced which adds not a little to the beauty of this majestically grand scenery.'

The Captain was a happy man. And that night the team celebrated with a splendid meal. 'My fare is really sumptuous this evening,' Lewis noted, 'buffaloes humps, tongues and marrowbones . . . and a good appetite; the last is not considered the least of the luxuries.'

A month later, after they had carried the equipment eighteen hard miles across land around the falls, their spirit was severely dampened. The weather was hot, the mosquitos 'extreely troublesome' and their buffalo rawhide moccasins were no match for the cactuses that carpeted the ground. Everyone complained of sore feet. They had to put up with sudden hail storms of such frightening velocity that their heads bled, and, to add a little spice to the adventure, there was the constant threat of grizzly bears.

Lewis was in awe of these 'furious and formidable' creatures. 'It is asstonishing to see the wounds they will bear before they can be put to death.' On 14 June, a bear surprised him as he reconnoitred the five waterfalls. The bear pursued him for eighty yards until Lewis dived into the river. He turned to face the animal. With his customary reserve, Lewis makes no hint of the danger in his journal. 'The moment I put myself in this attitude of defence he sudonly wheeled about as if frightened.' Our gung-ho Captain described the bear's decision to leave him alone as a 'novil occurence . . . I felt myself not a little gratifyed that he had declined the combat.'

Thanks to a hydro-electric power plant the Great Falls of today look nothing like the magnificent sight that would have greeted the expedition. As Bernard DeVoto so succinctly put it, 'Nowhere in the entire length of the river has industrial civilization, if the noun be permitted, more hideously defaced the scene . . .'

I spent an afternoon exploring the falls. Despite the powerhouses and dams, they retained some degree of impressiveness. The Missouri was frozen over with a layer of emerald green ice. At Black Eagle dam, named after an eagle's nest found there by Lewis, a fine Arctic mist rose up from a hotch-potch of jagged glacial formations. The visitors' centre was closed for winter. A sign at the door requested summertime hunters and trappers to 'please leave animal parts outside'.

On 18 June 1805, Clark reported the discovery of Giant Springs: 'the largest fountain or spring I ever saw.' The springs continue to discharge 388 million gallons of water each day.

The short distance from where Giant Springs begin and end in the Missouri is known as the Roe, acknowledged as the world's shortest river. A couple of geese eyed me as I clamped the Woolworth's bobble hat firmly over my ears. The warm water from the ground mixed with the cold air to create a thick vapour, like dry ice at a rock concert. A thick frost hung in the surrounding cottonwood trees.

I set out with determined strides. It took me less than a minute to walk the Roe's 201 feet. I was rather pleased with myself. Holt may not be the world's most hearty explorer, but he could at least report that he had walked *one* river during his travels.

Thanks to a dreadful cold (caused, I suspected with disgust, by the rigours of the Roe) I spent the next two days in bed. Eventually I felt well enough to struggle across the road to a bar called the Club Cigar. Here I was to meet the locals.

The Club Cigar was a Great Falls institution, the type of saloon you expected to find in the Wild West. The massive mahogany and cherry wood back-bar, with ornate, carved pillars, was made in Chicago. Wood panelling rose up the walls to meet the ceiling fans. You could imagine it fifty years ago: the horses tethered outside and the cowboys jostling loudly for drinks.

The Club Cigar's clientele included everyone from lawyers to ranch hands. There were few niceties here. The staff were likely to approach customers with a 'whadja want?' But then Montana bar staff are known for their blunt speaking. I heard a story about a barman in the mining town of Butte who was asked for a glass of milk by a non-drinking visitor. 'What?' the barman exploded, gesturing at the crowded saloon. 'Do you see any room in here for a fucking cow?'

It was early evening and the only other customer was a black man. He was leaning on the bar slowly sipping a beer. I was surprised to see him. I had seen virtually no black people since leaving Omaha. And there did not appear to be *any* in the Dakotas.

Racialism in the western states tended to be confined to the Indians. Blacks were seldom mentioned. Bob, the lawyer I had met back in Sioux City, recalled that when he first arrived there from Cleveland twenty years ago he had been horrified to hear people referring to 'niggers'.

'I thought that these prairie folk were the most prejudiced people in the world,' he said. 'But once I got talking with them, I realised what they meant was Omaha niggers, Des Moines niggers, Chicago niggers . . . local blacks didn't worry them at all.

'First day I arrived I saw a black man walking along the street with a tall, beautiful Scandinavian blonde. Nobody turned around, I couldn't believe it. This was 1970. And you've got to remember that in Cleveland people would have been scandalized. Here on the plains no one could give a damn.'

I got into conversation with the man. His name was Billy Miller. Originally from the Deep South, he had moved north three years ago. He proudly informed me that he was the first and only black lawyer in the entire state of Montana.

'No, there's not a lot of us in the North-West,' he agreed. With a deep chuckle he added, 'Put it this way, man: we stick out in the snow.'

Billy was a smiling man of fifty-two with a grey beard. He wore a flat tweed cap and bomber jacket. He had spent his life on the move. Raised in South Carolina, he had joined the Navy in his twenties before moving to California to study law. After a spell as an English teacher in Japan, he returned to San Francisco to practise as a criminal attorney.

'Then Ah say to myself, "Billy, you gotta find yourself another adventurous situation." So Ah moved to Montana. Hey hey, hey. Best decision Ah ever made.'

He admitted that he was a big fish in a little pond. 'I wanted to practise law where I could be guaranteed work, simple as that. There are a few thousand other black people in this state and they like to have a black lawyer. I get their business.'

There was little prejudice in Montana. 'They don't see colour. I tell you, they are colour blind in Montana.' He pronounced the word 'blahhnd'. 'They are unspoiled, they don't feel they have to be prejudiced towards anyone. It's your character that matters. Nothing else. Now, I like that because I think I have a tremendous amount of character.'

Billy lived outside Great Falls in a house overlooking the Missouri. From his picture window he could see the spot where Lewis and Clark celebrated Thanksgiving in 1805. 'I arrived here with 1,200 dollars and I didn't know one person. I got myself an office, set myself up as an attorney and in one year I had a 150,000-dollar house.'

'So is this what they call the black American dream?' I asked.

'Right. At first people were surprised. I mean, you gotta remember, I was born in semi-slavery, segregation. South Carolina was not a good place to grow up. You couldn't go certain places, you had to do certain things and, man, you had to be subservient. Things have changed down there, but it hasn't changed to the point that it's progressive, they're not making any history.' A contented smile spread across his face. 'But the first day I arrived in Montana? I can tell you, I was impressed. Everybody treated me real nice. And that was a unique feeling. I'm proud to be a part of this country.

'If I've learned anything from those days down south, it's to mould your own destiny. Don't let anyone say how you should be, how you're going to lead your life. That is up to you an' nobody else. I am the one who determines my destiny. Live free, or die. There are people getting ready to retire at my age. Hell, I haven't started yet. Maybe I'll try Australia next. Or even Spain. Yeah, Spain sounds like a cool place.'

Rod Stewart blasted on to the jukebox. Billy ordered more beers. I remarked that he had shown great courage by arriving out of the blue in somewhere like Montana.

'Courage? Shit, no. First thing I did was buy all the gear and go to those cowboy bars. I love country music.'

'God, you must have got some strange looks.'

'Right. Those cowboys thought it a little weird at first. Only black cowboy they'd ever seen was the dude with the Gucci saddle bag in *Blazing Saddles*. But they got used to it. Man, I have a good time, dancin' and everythin'. I wear my long, snakeskin boots and I walk tall, man, I walk *tall*.' Billy bellowed the words. The beers were flowing and nothing could stop him now. 'Shit, I'm a military man; I was in the Navy. When these kid cowboys see me they step aside. You gotta have attitude. Treat people decent and they'll treat you decent. But when they wanna kick ass, you be ready to kick ass.'

I said that I had found some of the West's cowboy bars quite unnerving. And I was white. If anyone tried kicking my ass, I'd leave quick – before the glasses started flying.

'No, man, you kick ass! I was a Navy man, I was trained to kick ass.'

'Well, I wasn't, and I'm not going to start now.'

By the end of our conversation Billy was sounding like Martin Luther King meets John Wayne. 'I appreciate the Big Sky! . . . Oh, man, I have seen it! . . . I like the Western style! . . . all those rodeos . . .'

These Wild West hallelujahs were suddenly interrupted by a loud growl from across the bar.

'Rodeos? Rodeos are shit!'

I looked up. The voice belonged to the barmaid. She was an oriental-looking girl of about thirty with a mane of lush, black hair that hung to her waist.

'Hang on a moment,' I said. 'But this is rodeo country. I thought Montana was where the rodeo practically began.'

'I won't go to a goddam rodeo. The cowboys treat the horses real

bad. They get these baby cows and twist their necks and all that
shit and I can't watch it. They're no better than muggers in New
York.'

I did not think it was possible for anyone in Montana to dislike
rodeos. But then, Carol Riley was not just anyone.

Carol was the sweetest girl and an incredible character. Her
mother was Japanese and her father Irish. 'I may look Japanese, but
I consider myself Irish and damned proud of it.' Her nickname was
Riley-san – or Samu-Riley when she was angry.

She had left school at sixteen with a minimal education and had
worked in saloons ever since. She was a professional bartender. But
in the quiet moments, you would see her perched on a beer crate
behind the bar reading a book. 'Maybe school didn't teach me much,
but I've learned a lot since. You know, Shakespeare, that sort of
stuff.'

Customers did not mess with Carol. She was a lady of few social
niceties and greeted you with 'wadjawannadrink?' She had a wealth
of insults for dealing with troublemakers: 'Did your ma have any
kids that lived?'; 'If assholes played music, you could be the whole
band.' With a cry of 'Have you heard the Riley mating call?' she
would grunt like a pig, and she could play 'Mary Had A Little
Lamb' (and, for my benefit, 'Rule Britannia') by slapping her blown-
out cheeks with her hands – 'I can do "Waltzing Matilda" on my
armpits, but I guess that's anti-social.' She was a true eccentric and,
in common with other Americans who could not understand my
English pronunciation of Peter, she called me Pizza.

Through Carol I learned the history of the Club Cigar. She had
worked here for eleven years and knew the place well. Her Irish
ancestry had blessed her with a gift for story-telling.

The bar dated from 1914, but its heyday came in the 1930s with
the arrival of a new owner, Lena Ford.

The upstairs rooms became a brothel. Lena was a madame of the
old school. She was famous for introducing an informal banking
system for her customers. Sheep herders and cowboys arriving in
town for a 'big drunk' would hand her their paychecks. It was up
to Lena to decide how much they could spend on booze and girls.
When it was time for the men to return to their ranches, Lena made
sure they were properly fed and had new clothes and travelling

money. Her morals might not have been of the highest standard, but she was a good woman at heart.

But woe betide any of her boys who did their drinking in another bar and then returned to the Club Cigar to fall asleep in one of the booths. She would crack a wine bottle over the offender's head, yelling, 'Get the hell outa here, I'm not having my boys drinking some place else.' Amazingly, she never killed anyone.

'Back in those days you didn't have bouncers in a bar,' Carol said. 'Lena did her own bouncing. If you missed the spittoon, she'd kick your ass right out the door.' Carol smiled grimly. 'I can think of plenty of customers I'd like to hit over the head for spitting on the floor. Trouble is, these days I'd get sued.'

Spittoons had vanished from Western bars. 'But they should bring 'em back,' Carol declared. 'These days they spit into a plastic cup with a napkin in it. It's disgusting. I don't know why, but they call it a Murphy Cup round here. First time a guy ever asked me for one I thought he wanted a jug of Irish whiskey.'

'No shit, man.' Billy was enjoying the story of Lena as much as I was. 'Well, I've never heard of a Murphy Cup neither. Hey, I learn new things off you every day, Riley-san.'

I mentioned that during the 1970s the Chinese authorities tried to ban people from spitting in the street. They encouraged children to circle an offender's spittle with a ring of chalk and write his name on it.

'Oh my God, how humiliating.' Carol thought this was a great idea. 'That's what I'm going to do in this bar. I'll get my chalk and write those ranchers' names all over the floor.'

She returned to Lena. A tiny, fragile woman with a ton of hair, she would stride around Great Falls, her white miniature poodle at her heels. She had remained a character until the day she died aged ninety-four in 1980.

Carol had worked as a waitress in a supper club where Lena regularly ate. 'She must have been a millionairess, but she was the cheapest person. She'd bring this big carpet bag to the restaurant and she'd take out these plastic cups and pour the salad dressings into them. Then she'd take all the breadsticks and put them in her bag. Yeah, goddam cheap 'n' tacky, she was. I suppose that's how you get rich. I mean, look at Donald Trump. Can't get much tackier than him.'

Carol moved on to the most celebrated of Lena's hookers, who had gone by the name of Big Tits Lou.

Lou had died five years ago, but even in her seventies she was wearing the low-cut dresses of a twenty-year-old. She had become a hooker aged fifteen. 'Now that girl was amazing. She had so much cash that the Government never knew about. She stuffed it everywhere, in her socks, pants, jacket, down her bra.'

Carol smiled at the memory of Lou's phenomenal physique. 'I don't mean this to sound dirty, but she was a *big* lady. She was real petite and short, but she had so much on top she could rest her bazoobas on the bar. I always used to serve her in here, and until the day she died she never bad-mouthed me, always asked politely for drinks. Used to come in for a shot and a beer back and she'd sip on it and tell you stories about her old customers.'

Carol looked at her watch. Midnight. There were no other customers in the house, so she could close for the night. She suggested we have a drink a few blocks away at another revered Great Falls establishment, the Minneapolis.

The Mini-Bar was still crowded. A jukebox blared country music. This was the oldest saloon in Great Falls, dating from 1886. Like the Club Cigar, it featured a vast mahogany back-bar with Greco-Roman pillars and an ornate, tin ceiling.

The clientele had reached the stage where they were staggering rather than standing. Columns of stacked-up, empty shot glasses littered the bar. A poker game was in progress in the back room. A mean-looking crew sat around a table covered in greasy, green baize. They included two elderly women and a man with not a tooth in his head. A Chinese woman with a thin, anxious face was dealing cards.

'This looks fun,' I announced. 'I've always wanted to play poker in a place like this.'

The toothless man looked up. 'Sure, come and join us.'

Billy grabbed my arm. 'No way, man.'

'What do you mean?'

'What I mean is that they're just looking for a sucker like you. Y'know, English guy sits down and thinks he knows how to play and next moment they've taken every cent off him.' He steered me back to the bar. 'They might look friendly, but they'll skin you alive.'

We sat on ripped vinyl stools next to Carol. Billy may have deprived me of my first Wild West poker game, but compensation soon arrived in the form of a Wild West brawl.

It happened as Carol was telling North Dakotan jokes: Why do North Dakotans get buried with their butts sticking out of the ground? So the kids can have somewhere to park their bicycles.

Our hilarity was interrupted by a 'Well, screw you, asshole!' A wave of beer splashed over our heads.

I looked over at a man and woman sitting a few stools away. The man's shirt dripped with beer. 'A lover's tiff,' Carol whispered. And, with a right hook that would have impressed Calamity Jane, the woman took a slug at her boyfriend.

Her fist connected with his face with a terrifying *thwack*. He would have a prize black eye in the morning. The bar went silent. Everyone turned round. The man looked as if he was about to hit back. Then he thought better of it and contented himself with an avalanche of abuse. The pair growled at each other for a few minutes before the man slunk away.

'Does this sort of thing happen often in Great Falls?' I asked.

'*Correcto mundo*,' Carol said. What else could you expect in a state with the highest number of alcoholics per capita in the United States? Montana also boasts one of the nation's highest rates of divorce – or 'splitting the blanket', as the Indians so quaintly call it. 'Alcohol talks too much around here. It's a noisy neighbour.'

She pursed her lips. 'Know what, Pizza? I'm glad it's 1990. If a woman had hit a man like that fifty years ago, he'd have shot her.'

Eleven

Enough of this bar-room gossip. I felt that Montana must have more to offer than bottle-wielding madames and tax-evading hookers. The saloons were beginning to bore me. It was time to seek out some godliness in this abyss of brawling and booze.

Which is how I found myself with the Hutterites, one of the most curious religious sects in the United States. If black Billy Miller was a novelty in Montana, then the Hutterites were as out of line with America as a Kalahari bushman on the Champs-Elysées.

The Hutterites are part of the Anabaptist movement, the most radical religious group of the Reformation era. The Anabaptists emerged in Switzerland in 1525. They believed that Christians should be baptised upon their faith, not as children. They argued that baptism of children was never intended; there was nothing to suggest it in the New Testament. Their claims were greeted with derision. The Catholic authorities denounced them as arrogant revolutionaries and persecuted them mercilessly. Many were executed.

The Anabaptists' beliefs became more extreme as the movement grew. They decreed that there was more to Christianity than merely accepting doctrines and going to church. To be a good Christian meant a daily walk with God. The Bible must be followed to the letter. 'No one can truly know Christ except he follow Him in life,' one Anabaptist said.

The Anabaptists established self-sufficient farming communities so as not to be tainted by the outside world. One of their branches, the Hutterites, named after their leader Jakob Hutter, settled in the

192

Tyrol. When the Tyrolean church authorities began to hound them down, they moved to the more religiously tolerant Moravia in what is now Czechoslovakia.

The persecution continued. And in 1874 they joined the legions of prospective homesteaders in the mass emigration from Europe to the United States. With them came another Anabaptist group, the Mennonites. The Hutterites settled in Colorado and South Dakota where they remained until the First World War when their refusal to fight landed them in trouble with the Government. They moved to Canada where they remained until 1949, when they returned south to Montana.

There are now twenty-seven Hutterite colonies in Montana with an estimated three thousand members. Their mother tongue is still Tyrolisch, the German dialect that their forefathers spoke 450 years ago. Their church services are conducted in *hoch Deutsch* and English remains a second language.

Their philosophy is one of simplicity in all things. The men continue to dress in nineteenth-century black tunics and Russian-style pillarbox hats; the women wear shawls and headscarves. Everyone wears the same clothes because God does not expect you to express yourself in any other way. Jewellery is banned and no one wears wedding rings – you are married in the eyes of God, and that is enough.

Locals told me that if I wanted to visit the Hutterites I should try a colony just 'up the road' to the north-west of Great Falls. I should speak to a man called John Wipf, who could answer my questions. But nowhere is quite 'up the road' in Montana, and after a seventy-mile drive I found the colony outside the tiny farming town of Dutton.

I turned off the main road up a rough track. The colony lay in front of me, three rows of gleaming white cottages next to a collection of Dutch barns. The wintry sun glinted off the roof of a steel grain bin. A combine harvester sat next to a haystack.

The Toyota crunched into a gravel yard. There was not a soul around. Then I spotted two little boys of about eleven walking across the yard. In their black hats and tunics They resembled a combination of the Artful Dodger and Tom Brown. I wound down the Toyota's window. 'Can you tell me where I can find John Wipf?' I shouted.

The boys peered at me suspiciously. They broke into beaming smiles, turned on their heels and scampered away in a fit of giggles. This was a great start. I parked the car outside the cottages and got out into a sharp wind. I walked up a path. A pair of long johns fluttered on a washing line.

I knocked on a door. A woman clutching a duster opened it cautiously. In her nineteenth-century garb of ankle-length skirt and peasant headscarf, she resembled a character from a Jane Austen novel. She had an unhealthy pallor with red-rimmed eyes and a pale face that did not seem to have seen the sun for years. Did she know where I could find John Wipf? She was supremely unchatty. She pointed at the second row of houses.

I found John Wipf's cottage. His wife answered the door. She was holding a broom. I seemed to be making a habit of interrupting the colony's housework. With a cross 'tut-tut' she fetched her husband.

I introduced myself. 'Zo, you are from Enkland?' he said. With his heavy Tyrolean accent, he could have just stepped off an Austrian alp.

'That's right,' I replied brightly. 'I was hoping you might show me around and tell me something about the Hutterites.'

'Pah! I am busy. You have come on the wrong day. We are unloading cattle trucks. All day.'

'I'm sorry to be a nuisance, but I've driven all the way from Great Falls.'

'*Ach.*' John Wipf reluctantly grabbed his hat from a peg in the hallway and threw on his black coat. 'Come with me. I will try to find someone who can show you things.'

He took me over to the colony's communal dining hall, a spotlessly clean cafeteria with a tile floor and long wooden refectory tables. Half a dozen women in knitted shawls fussed around with scrubbing brushes and mops. In the kitchen chickens bubbled away in vast vats of boiling water. From the ovens came the welcoming aroma of freshly-baked bread.

'This is where we all eat together,' John Wipf explained simply. 'You are free to look.' And with that he left me. I felt rather spare. Who was I going to talk to? The women seemed quite friendly, but they had no intention of abandoning their chores to chat to this stranger.

Just as I was about to leave, another man came in from the cold.

He eyed me suspiciously. I explained what I was doing there. He looked quite interested and said, yes, he could tell me something about the colony. 'But you must talk slowly.'

He was called George. We sat on a bench in the cafeteria. After five minutes it became obvious that we were getting absolutely nowhere. It's one thing for a German-speaking Hutterite understanding English spoken with an American accent. But *English* English? Not a hope.

I attempted some bad German. Still no good. A bastardised Tyrolean accent was not my strong point. 'I am sorry,' George sighed. 'I am not the man to talk to. You must try Mr Wipf.'

'But I've already been with Mr Wipf and he's unloading cattle.'

'*Nein*, not John Wipf. You need Jacob Wipf.'

'And where will I find Jacob Wipf?'

'There.' He pointed an arm in the general direction of the prairie.

'How far there?'

'Not far there. Next colony. Miller Colony. Jacob Wipf is head minister at Miller Colony.'

I was becoming impatient. 'Marvellous,' I said. 'And can you give me a clue as to which direction I should be going?'

'Back up track and turn left at oil.'

'Oil?'

'*Ja, ja.*' Enthusiastic nods. 'Oil.'

I looked at him helplessly. What was the man talking about? This was turning into a tough day. 'Oil,' he repeated. 'Pavement!'

'Oh, you mean oil as in tarred road?'

'*Ja.* You betcha.' The Americanism sounded absurdly out of place. With a wave and a '*veilen Dank, mein Herr*', I returned to the car and set off again.

'Not far there' turned out to be another twenty miles. I drove down endless gravel roads towards the slopes of the Rockies above that boundless cloak of blue known as Montana's 'Big Sky'. At the town of Choteau I stopped at a gas station to ask the way. The attendant directed me north. I eventually found Miller Colony ten miles out of town perched on a hillock in the shadow of the Rockies near the headwaters of the Teton river.

I left the main road and drove up a rutted drive. Miller Colony was the same tidy cluster of bungalows and farm buildings. Patches of snow lay on the grass by a criss-cross of neat, concrete pathways.

A man trotted by with a basket of eggs. I asked him where I could find Jacob Wipf.

'Vot are you selling?' he asked.

'No, I am not a travelling salesman.' I explained my reasons for being there. He directed me to one of the houses.

Jacob Wipf was not thrilled to see me. Like everyone else, he was busy. He could spare me only ten minutes. We did not have much in common, but perhaps we got on well. I don't know. Whatever the case, we were still chatting two hours later.

Jacob was a tubby man in his fifties with the traditional Hutterite goatee beard, Abraham Lincoln-style with no moustache. Penetrating sapphire eyes sparkled from a weather-beaten, suntanned face; the tan ended in a white line on his forehead suggesting that he never left the house without his hat.

We talked in a bare, whitewashed room that doubled up as the Wipfs' sitting room and bedroom. It was furnished with a bed, a couple of simple wooden chairs and Jacob's desk that overflowed with papers. Gleaming, immaculately scrubbed blue linoleum covered the floor. Jacob was married with seven boys aged from eighteen to twenty-nine. His wife was in the small kitchen next door violently scrubbing a table.

The spiritual leader of the colony's 100 inhabitants Jacob bore the official title, Minister of the Word. He was noisy and enthusiastic, and a little bombastic. I could see him waving his arms and lashing his congregation with blazing sermons. He was a fascinating man to spend time with, although I found the Biblical references a little bamboozling.

Jacob offered me one of the chairs. He sat down opposite me. 'So what do you want to know about us?'

'Everything, I suppose.'

'Then I will tell you.' He sat back in his chair, a firm look in his eye. 'Our religion is based on the New Testament and nothing but the New Testament. We believe that to live this way is the ultimate will of God. It is a religious communalism – I won't call it communism because that word gives a bad impression. Nothing is owned individually, everything is shared.' His voice took on a low growl. 'But we do have individual family life. We don't go to the extremes which we are reputed to at times. Some people slander us and say that our women are shared. That is not true, but then some people will always go to the bottom line.'

Abortion was not even considered. Divorce was virtually unheard of. Jacob claimed there had been only one case of divorce in the sect's 460-year history. 'That person happened to be my uncle,' he said sadly. 'He left the colony, left his wife and married again outside. Outsiders can be a big source of the problems. We strongly recommend' – he did not quite use the word 'order' – 'that people marry within the colony.

'*Ach*, outsiders. They simply could not adapt to our ways. Take you, for example.' He looked out of the window and nodded in the direction of the Toyota. 'You can sit in your car and go where you want to go. But here, if somebody wants to take a truck somewhere they have to ask me for permission. I take their request to church in the evening and our seven elected elders give their final permission.' An outsider could join the colony, but it was very rare. 'There would be no chance of him ever becoming one of the elders. But if he proved good and lived up to the standards of the colony, then his children would have no problem.'

During the First World War, the sect's refusal to take up arms led to dreadful persecution by the authorities. Many members escaped to Canada where they remained until the 1940s. The Hutterites describe themselves as non-resistant, rather than pacifists. 'Pacifists go out and demonstrate against war,' Jacob said. 'We do not believe in demonstrating. That is a form of war in itself.'

When America entered the war the colony's young men were called up. 'They explained that God would not let them fight. "You shall not kill," they said. We do not believe in war or anything that aids war like working in factories making guns and bullets. Well, you can imagine, the Government got tough on us.'

Three of Jacob's uncles were incarcerated in Alcatraz. The guards tortured them. Jacob spoke quietly. 'They set 'em in the shower and made 'em stand all day under cold water. Then they tied 'em up so their feet were off the floor. They had to stay like that for weeks. They still refused to fight so the military shipped 'em to Fort Leavenworth, Kansas. It was winter. When they got there they had to stand outside the prison gates in nothing but their underwear in very cold temperatures. They caught pneumonia. They got 'em in the hospital, but it was too late. Two of my uncles were dead.' Jacob's eyes were watery. The memory of what happened three-quarters of a century ago still saddened him.

The Hutterites' philosophy might be three hundred years behind the times, but they are not against mechanization. Without tractors and combine harvesters they could not hope to compete in today's agricultural markets. Much of Miller Colony's 17,000 acres was poor-quality grazing land. They grew wheat and barley and raised hogs and cattle. But farming was a constant struggle.

I mentioned the Amish, the strongly puritan sect in Pennsylvania, who shun all forms of modernization.

Jacob did not have much time for the Amish. 'We don't think that way. We use any modern inventions as long as they don't hurt us. For example, telephones were a no-no when they first came along. But it didn't take us long to agree to them. You need telephones for doctors. They're not a luxury, they're an allowable necessity.'

Radio and television were banned – it was a relief to find a corner of America free of *Teenage Mutant Ninja Turtles*. 'We believe TV and radio will hurt us. But books are okay. The mobile library comes every two weeks and the kids can choose anything they want. But the library doesn't keep this pornographic stuff, they screen that. Whatever they let their children read ours can read. The world is losing its standards, but so far we haven't had any complaints. And of course the kids can read the two volumes of our history.'

Two volumes of Hutterite history did not sound like desperately exciting reading for a thirteen-year-old. How were the younger members influenced by the outside world?

Jacob sighed. 'Everything rubs off on us. It's like colds. If they're around, we get 'em.' All sports were banned. 'We discourage sport strongly, both watching and playing. Take my kids. They grab the newspaper and the first thing they look at is the sports page. I'm not going to choke or anything, but I'm going to tell them: "Here boys, that's something you'll never get anything out of. Not a thing, it won't help your life, it won't help the colony." We try to encourage our children to do things that build their characters. Like doing things for the colony. Like learning about electricity or carpentry. Or: "Read the Testament, something that will be beneficial to you. Learn something!" '

I found it difficult to believe I was hearing this in a sports-mad society like America. He went on, 'This ball game business, all it does is encourage idol worship. Okay, I admit it, when I was young I was into sport myself. When I went to church I was thinking about the ball game, how was the pitcher gonna make out? I've been there. And I can tell them ball games didn't help me one hair.'

'But don't you think you're taking things a bit seriously?' I interrupted. 'After all, sport is only entertainment.'

'Why do you need to be entertained when you can do something useful?' he answered. A note of severity crept into his voice. 'Can you read me?'

'Sure, as clear as a bell. Actually, I couldn't agree with you more. I hate sport. Can't stand football.' Jacob looked puzzled. It wasn't quite the point he was trying to make. 'There,' I added, 'we're not all sports fans on the outside.'

'Glad to hear it.'

So was this Utopian lifestyle free of crime? Jacob's smile returned. 'Ha! The question I always hear. We have virtually no crime here, but we're still human. Okay, occasionally, there is petty crime.'

'Like burglary, that sort of thing?'

'There are bad apples in every basket and we are no exception. We don't pretend to live angels' lives. We'd be fooling ourselves if we did.'

He continued mournfully: 'More and more we have to guard against evil. The difference between our life and the life outside is getting greater and greater. The outside world is going by leaps and bounds against the boundaries of morality. Take birth control and abortion. There's no way we could ever say that was right. And charging your neighbour interest. We could never do that.'

'Do you use banks?' I asked.

'Of course. We have to. Don't get me wrong. When we have our money in the bank it is earning interest.'

'So how can you justify using a banking system that gives you interest?'

He spread his hands in a gesture of resignation. 'I don't think there is a bank in the world where you could put your money without taking interest. And anyway the IRS would tax you on it if you took it or not. Up to five years ago, any colony could loan money to another colony for nothing. But the IRS stepped in and said we had to pay income tax on it. We were pushed into a corner. We decided we might as well use the outside banks.'

Jacob's wife interrupted us. She marched into the room wielding a screw-driver. She was with another woman. Together they began noisily removing the doors from Jacob's desk.

'They're gonna scrape everything off and revarnish them,' Jacob explained. He turned to the women. 'Hey, watch you don't untidy that mess in there.' He said something in Tyrolisch to his wife. She ignored him and continued chattering to her friend. 'Huh!' He rocked back in his chair and laughed in mock irritation. 'Spring-cleaning. Just like the 'flu. Starts one end of the colony and it spreads and spreads.'

The chattering continued. One of the desk doors crashed to the ground. Jack stood up. 'Oh, I can't stand all this.' We adjourned to the kitchen. 'I've learned one thing, let the women have their way with spring-cleaning: it's over that much quicker. I think us men would rather go on vacation when it comes to cleaning.' This was meant as a man-to-man remark. But I suspected that feminists would not go down a storm in a Hutterite colony.

'Perhaps we are male chauvinists,' Jacob agreed, 'but it is religiously based. The women accept it – it has always been that way. When our girls leave school we like them to read cookbooks or books on home-making or study the Bible. The role of the woman is home-making. We do not allow women to vote in the colony, but that is not to say that the women don't have the vote at the end of the day.' A guttural chortle. 'They probably tell their husbands how to vote. Remember, we're human like anyone else.'

I looked around the kitchen. On the shelves were tins of hot-dogs and a packet of biscuits.

I nodded at the tins. 'Hot-dogs don't seem very self-sufficient,' I said.

Jacob smiled as if he knew I had caught him out. 'Things are changing, I admit. We buy food with the money we make from selling hogs. And at Christmas we hand out candy. We have a better standard of living than thirty years ago, but I honestly don't know if that's good for the colony. But obviously we want the colony to be comfortable so that people will stay. Simple as that. There are not many of us left and we can't afford to lose anyone.'

'In that case, I'm surprised you still wear those old-fashioned clothes. Surely your younger members would rather be in T-shirts and trainers like any other American kid?'

T-shirts and trainers? Jacob was startled. The very mention of T-shirts and trainers was enough to invite a thunderbolt from God. 'Our clothes are traditional and we are very strict about them,' he insisted. Although the sect's founder Jakob Hutter was a hatter by trade, his followers have since lost that profession. An outside company now supplies their headwear. 'The hat is symbolic. We are so strict that even I, the head minister, am not allowed outside the house without a hat. And the women can't go out without their shawls. These are all things that have to be done. When you let people start doing as they please then pretty soon the system breaks down.' With a mischievous twinkle in his eye, he added, 'But we don't say that a guy dressed like you will go to hell for it.'

'I'm jolly glad to hear it.' We both laughed. 'Anyway,' I added, 'it doesn't seem so odd to me.' I explained that at Eton our school uniform had been tail-coats. 'We looked pretty bizarre to outsiders too.'

'In England? At school?' Jacob was impressed. 'So you understand, then. That was what was expected of your conduct and it's the same here.'

'Frankly,' I said, 'I'm surprised your young people put up with this. Surely one whiff of the outside world and they're off?'

Jacob conceded that more members were leaving the colony. 'But ninety per cent come back. It makes me sad when people leave. We don't like it and we try to get 'em back if we can. We try to show 'em that it's not better outside. A few leave and marry outsiders, but from what we've heard they usually wish they hadn't. A boy who is brought up in our system and then marries a girl who has lived in a liberal system is going to find life very difficult.'

'So what are you giving the world?'

'We hope that we are setting a good example. We hope that outsiders will take notice of our code, our lifestyle. For example, divorce. In America they say "till death us do part." They don't mean a word of it. Over half the outsiders I've known have been divorced. We believe divorce is wrong: the scriptures do not record it. We want to show that you can marry for life and that it can work out very well.'

The only time that Jacob faltered was when I asked about drinking. I had heard that the Hutterite colonies were famed for their lethal rhubarb wine. 'So alcohol is allowed,' I said.

'Oh yes, within moderation.'

'Come on, I bet you tie one on from time to time.'

Jacob laughed. He wasn't giving anything away. 'But we're not allowed to smoke,' he added hastily. 'At least, we're not *supposed* to smoke. If someone is caught smoking he gets punished.'

Which brought us to the colony's legal system. This is where outsiders will not stand a chance. The Hutterites deal with offenders by using public humiliation that is hardly better than the village stocks.

'For a minor offence you have to stand up in church for the whole service.'

Jacob's wife had come into the kitchen. She overheard our conversation. 'An' everybody's looking at 'em,' she added with a harsh cackle.

'It's the shame of it,' Jacob continued. 'I stand up in church, but I am the minister and that is an honourable position. It is dishonourable for a member to stand.'

If a member persisted in doing wrong there was a punishment called the *Unfrieden* – the un-peace. In Britain, it is known as being sent to Coventry. 'It means you are not at peace with the community. For a week no one will acknowledge you or talk to you. You are shunned until you repent. And if you come back time and time again for the same offence, like fighting, you are put on probation. If you do something small, like taking a vehicle without permission, you have to stand up in church and beg forgiveness.'

For severe offences like adultery or sex out of marriage the penalty was excommunication. 'That's not very often, but it does happen. And when they repent they are allowed back into the colony again.'

'I should think you have to repent pretty hard for adultery,' I remarked.

'Hmm, yes. It can take time.'

With his gnome-like smiling face, Jacob did not look like a particularly strict man. 'Can you be pretty frightening when you want to be?' I asked.

He slapped his knees and laughed. 'You have to be. You put your foot down and you don't put it back up until a person repents.' He was serious again. 'But I prefer the gentle way. I think that's the way Christ did it, that's the way the Apostles taught us. I have a motto: "Punishment is for correction not for ego satisfaction." So I punish in order that a person changes his ways. I have the authority to say this and that, and a person will have to do it. If I'm just trying to show who's boss, that is the wrong approach.'

There was a moment's silence. I didn't really know what to say. Eventually I offered: 'Well, it all makes for a more interesting world. If everyone was the same it would be very boring.'

'Unfortunately, not everyone thinks like that,' Jacob grumbled. Small town Montana reacted viciously when the colony arrived in the 1940s. Meetings were held in an attempt to ban the Hutterites. 'The animosity was so great you could feel it. People shouted abuse and shopkeepers charged us double. But they were only hurting themselves. We went to Great Falls instead. There was always a shop somewhere who would sell to us.

'But people here are rural conservatives and they probably reckoned we were pretty weird. We understood their feelings. We had come into their area and we didn't associate with them. We didn't go to their dances, we didn't marry their girls. I got to know the local education superintendent. One day she said, "What's wrong with the American way of life, why can't you live like we do?" I told her that I can come home and be sure that my wife is still here; that my kids aren't running off causing trouble. Do you know what? She never asked me anything else.'

Jacob glanced at the clock on the kitchen wall. He mumbled something about reading scriptures. But he had time to show me the colony. He put on his hat and we went outside into the sunshine. A youth walked past the house. I pointed out that he was not wearing one of the traditional hats, but a wide-brimmed cowboy fedora. 'They are just about acceptable,' Jacob sniffed. 'A lot of 'em wear 'em and I don't like it.'

Miller Colony was older than most. The houses had outside privies and communal washing facilities. A refurbishment programme was in progress and eventually all the houses would have bathrooms and running water.

Jacob did not approve. 'The modern colonies have got too fancy,' he declared. 'Don't like it when things are too shiny. That's when the outside world rubs off on you.'

He took me round the dining hall and kitchens. He showed me the cooking range that had been made in the blacksmith's shop.

Noodles lay drying on tables. We moved on to the bakery and then the school.

At two-and-a-half-years-old, children were removed from their parents' home and placed in the kindergarten where three unmarried women looked after them. They lived there until the age of six. This seemed unnecessarily hard on the parents. 'No,' Jacob protested, 'it makes it easier for them to work properly if someone else is bringing up their children.'

The school doubled as a church. 'It doesn't work too good.' A perplexed shake of the head. 'Our church should be completely bare, but there's all these posters and maps stuck on the walls for the children.'

'Dear me, things really are going to the dogs.'

'Yep. Posters, maps. That's another thing that's rubbed off on us.'

Members were expected to attend church every evening. Only the cooks and people working in the fields were excused. There was no cross, no altar. A school desk doubled as a pulpit. Jacob spoke in a hushed tone. 'We think *we* should bear the cross, not the church. We do not need a graven image.'

It was time to leave. Would Jacob mind if I took his photograph?

He politely refused. 'No, thank you. Visitors do take photographs, but it is against our philosophy.'

'Don't tell me,' I said, ' "Thou shalt not make a graven image . . ." ' I struggled to remember the second Commandment.

Jacob came to the rescue. 'Ecclesiastes: a man had a son and the son died and the man loved him and they made an image out of him and pretty quickly they bowed on their knees toward him.' He took a deep breath. 'So just to avoid those things we say no pictures. It is like having a shield on a machine – even when there is no danger, the shield has its purpose. We mean no offence.'

I left Jacob complaining about the rising cost of doctor's fees. The Montana Hutterites had clubbed together in their own health plan, but they were finding it increasingly difficult paying the premiums.

'Up to now we've survived all kinds of persecution, but I'm wondering about this one. Our economy doesn't generate the money needed to pay these high doctor's bills. In Britain there is socialized medicine, but here a person will get sick worrying how he's going to pay for being sick! You don't know how lucky you are in Britain.'

A short burst of anger: 'Take a premature baby. It'll cost eighty thousand bucks. The doctors saved the baby of one of our girls and she thought they were wonderful. But it was so premature it was congenitally deformed. I told her, "What is wrong with God's will? This baby probably won't have a healthy moment in its life. Why should the medical profession save a premature baby from death when it should really go to heaven? And why at the same time are they ripping out millions of healthy babies from their mothers' wombs? What's so wonderful about that?" The girl shut up and hung her head.'

We shook hands and I got back into the Toyota. Jacob stood by the car while I turned the ignition. He looked up at the sky. He smiled again. Setbacks like medical fees were tiresome, but God would come to the rescue. 'The medical profession in America is such that they won't let a person die until they have emptied his pockets.' And with a dry laugh he concluded: 'I hope they leave me alone. For when my time comes I will see death staring in my face and I will know it. And then it will be my time to go.'

Back in Great Falls I spent the evening at the Club Cigar. Carol called out as I walked in. 'Hey, Pizza, didya have a good day?'

'Not bad. I've been on one of the Hutterite colonies.'

'Ah, the Huts. Did you ask them about the studs?'

'Studs?'

One of Carol's customers, a lawyer, chipped in. 'Yeah, we hear that the in-breeding's got real bad because there's so few of them. They're supposed to have brought in blond-haired, blue-eyed, six-foot men to service their women.'

'No,' I said flatly, 'I did not ask them that.'

'Why not?' Carol asked loudly.

'Because I didn't think of it. Anyway, it sounds like vicious propaganda.'

'Yeah, you're probably right. It's sad that people are so nasty about them.'

But maybe the Day of the Hutterites was not far away. On the way back from Miller Colony I had turned on the radio. A cowboy love song filled the car. It was followed by a Government AIDS warning with the slogan: 'It won't kill you to wear a condom, but not wearing one might.' Now here was something unlikely to affect the clean-living Hutterites. If AIDS did its worst, they had a good chance of being among the last people left alive in America. They might even hold Government office. A Hutterite in the White House? The idea was irresistible.

My journey was nearly over. Billy had deprived me of my chance to play poker, so for the remainder of my stay in Great Falls I settled for second best by playing dice with Carol for a quarter a point.

Carol said I had a lot to learn about the etiquette of dice throwing. For the tenth time I placed the dice back in the thrower and handed it to her. 'I've told you before, Pizza,' she said crossly, 'first rule of the West: never, ever, load another person's dice.'

'Why on earth not? It seems the polite thing to do.'

'That's the trouble with you English, Pizza, too damned polite.' She shook her head in exasperation. 'Don't ask me why, but it's bad ju-ju. Loading someone else's dice is the sort of thing that gets you shot around here.'

There was a hint of spring in the air as I left Great Falls for the Missouri's final stretch. The sky was as grand and blue as I had yet seen. Cotton wool clouds hung lazily above the prairie like puffs of smoke from an ack-ack gun.

At last the grasslands ended and the Interstate wound into the deep pine-studded gorge known as the Missouri River Canyon.

I sighed with relief as the road began to climb. I had the distinct feeling that I had seen enough prairie to last me a lifetime. The canyon was a welcome gash in a hitherto pristine landscape. Scattered banks of snow lay in the crevices of enormous boulders that rose up from either side of the Interstate. The trees up either side of the valley pointed in all directions, blown into position by the unpredictable winds that buffeted and blew everywhere. After the roughness of the prairie, the roadside life was all rather twee. 'Homestead-style' holiday homes, with miniature garden windmills and absurdly neat stacks of firewood at the back doors, perched at the foot of steep crags.

I did not stop until I reached the Missouri headwaters 140 miles later. I was eager to see where the Big Muddy began its ferocious drive. There were no major towns between here and Great Falls and I was losing my enthusiasm for meeting new people – in two months on the road I had done more than enough talking. I put my foot down on the Toyota's accelerator and sped south.

It was early afternoon when I arrived at the town of Three Forks, named after the trio of rivers that flow into the Missouri. It resembled so many other towns I had been through: clapboard houses, the peeling wooden fences of the rodeo ground and a dusty, deserted main street. I would not be sorry to see the last of places like this.

I drove through Three Forks and looked in vain for the way to the headwaters. Until now, signposting in America had been the height of efficiency. It was ironic, that in these last two miles of my journey, there were no signs anywhere. I was lost. I did left turns, right turns and U-turns, but the headwaters were nowhere to be seen. It took me half an hour before I found the right road.

Lewis and Clark arrived at the headwaters on 27 July 1805. Lewis declared this was 'an essential point in the geography of this western part of the Continent.' And he gushed, 'The country opens suddonly to extensive and beatifull plains and meadows which appear to be surrounded in every direction with distant and lofty mountains.'

The Captains named the most important north fork of the Missouri after their patron Thomas Jefferson. They named the two other rivers the Madison and the Gallatin after the President's Secretaries of State and the Treasury. Of course, the expedition did not end here. Led by Sakakawea, the team continued across the Rockies and down the Columbia river. They eventually reached Pacific tidal waters on 'a cool wet raney morning' on 8 November 1805: a momentous occasion that prompted Clark to exclaim, 'Ocian in view; O, the joy!' Even after all this time his spelling showed no signs of improvement.

Armed with their valuable information about the West, the expedition returned to civilization a year later. They may not have found the fabled North-West Passage, but their researches were to open up great tracts of land for trade and settlement. With the expedition's return Americans suddenly realized what a vast country they had. America the 'big' was born.

At high noon on 23 September 1806, the Captains and their men, still dressed in their ragged home-stitched buckskins, made their grand entrance into St Louis.

Meriwether Lewis and William Clark became national heroes. Balls were held in their honour and a grateful President Jefferson persuaded Congress to grant each officer a 1,600-acre farm. Each enlisted man received 320 acres and there was double pay for all.

Clark enjoyed happy post-Missouri years. In 1808, he married his longtime love Judy Hancock. After a spell as brigadier-general commanding the Louisiana Militia, he was appointed Governor of Missouri Territory in 1813. He died in 1838 aged sixty-seven while still in his position as the greatly-respected Superintendent of Indian Affairs.

After his years in the wilderness lonely Lewis never properly readjusted to civilized life. He was appointed Governor of Louisiana Territory, but politics stifled him. Nor could he find a woman prepared to put up with his solitary ways. He wooed the ladies without success. On one occasion, when the current love of his life turned out to be engaged to someone else, he confessed bitterly to a friend that he was 'a perfect widower with respects to love'.

He became moody and depressed. He was found shot dead on 11 October 1809, at a remote farm at Hohenwald, Tennessee where he had been breaking a journey to Washington. He was thirty-four. Suicide was suspected – Lewis's behaviour had become increasingly irrational and he was said to be suffering from mental illness brought on by a fever. Then came the rumours that he had been robbed – his body was found with only twenty-five cents in his pockets. But his murderer was never found. His death remains a mystery to this day.

The Missouri headwaters lie a few hundred yards from the ghost town of Gallatin City. Once a substantial community, it had sat astride the main stage route to the gold camps of Bannock, Virginia City and Helena. The town died quickly when the railroad by-passed it in the 1880s.

There was nothing left except for three wooden shacks, and a beaten-up barn that had been part of the Gallatin City Hotel. I left the car and strolled around the remains. With no warning, two large, snarling dogs appeared from a battered farmhouse across the field. I did not intend to be savaged in these last few minutes of the journey. I turned tail and ran back to the Toyota. The dogs followed me with wolfish howls. I leapt into the car and slammed the door. The dogs circled the vehicle for ten minutes before they got bored and lolloped back to their farm.

Eventually I found the courage to leave the car. I took a snowy path down to the riverbank. I walked slowly, savouring every final moment. There was no one else around. Thick wedges of ice covered the river. A flight of geese, surprised by my presence, took off from a patch of grey-green water.

The US Geological Survey had erected a small sign: 'This point marks the beginning of the Missouri-Mississippi river drainage, the longest river system in North America.' I was exactly 2,546 miles from the mouth.

I sat on the bank and finished off a sliver of beef jerky washed down with a can of Coke. Well, c'mon, let's be American about this.

I reflected on how everyone I had met on my journey had been so incredibly kind to me; so patient with my incessant questions. Before leaving England I had suffered many fears about a lone English writer turning up unannounced in small, remote prairie towns and being treated with the utmost suspicion. My apprehension had been proved totally unfounded. From cowboys to Indians, from millionaires to arm-wrestlers, I had received nothing but good old-fashioned hospitality, the sort of friendliness that has become a hallmark of the West ever since the first trappers took to the Missouri in their flimsy craft. For as Father Peter had said back in Omaha: 'You have to show compassion to strangers in this sort of country. It can be a dangerous land and there will come a time when you yourself may need compassion from the stranger. If we do not work together, we die.'

I gazed at the river. A soft wind ruffled the reeds that sprouted from the ice. A sentimental urge overtook me. I would take home a souvenir of the Big Muddy's famous mud. I fumbled in my pocket. I took out an empty film container in which to put my treasure. With a nimble leap, I jumped from the bank down to the water's edge.

A mistake. From up on the bank the mud had appeared to be firm and frozen. Far from it. The shoreline was soft and gooey – the Missouri was playing her old tricks again.

I put my foot in the mud. Suddenly I was sliding at horrifying speed. I landed heavily on my behind. Mud covered my jeans. My glasses flew off. I groped wildly for them.

I remained sitting there on the mud feeling foolish, peering at the river through smeared spectacles. Out in the middle of the water, the ice moved with a powerful rumbling crack. The Big Muddy was speaking. It was if she was trying to say: 'They may have tried to tame me with their dams. But remember. I must never be trusted.'

EPILOGUE

The English barbarians can sneer all they like, but the story of Madoc, or Madog as his countrymen call him, lives on in Wales. Of the fact that Prince Madoc, son of King Owen Gwyneth actually lived, there is no doubt. But even the most capricious Welshman will admit that the founding of a twelfth-century Welsh-American colony is dubious to say the least. However, Welsh schoolchildren, primed on a diet of romantic verse, will tell you there is no argument about it: Madoc discovered America three hundred years before Columbus had learned even to tie his first reef knot.

A few months after returning from the States, I spent a weekend in North Wales looking into Madoc's roots. The trail took me to the Caernarfonshire seaside haven of Porthmadog.

It was October, and the town was only just beginning to cool down after an uncharacteristically hot summer. The slate-grey houses were bathed in warm sunshine. Hanging baskets dangled from wrought-iron balconies. A rag-taggle of day-trippers, ice lollies in hands, shuffled along the High Street past sweetshops where gobstoppers are still sold from glass jars. The doorways were cluttered with chaotic jumbles of seaside essentials: buckets and spades, rubber rings and Welsh dragon flags, to stick in sandcastles. Visitors who had hitherto believed that the Welsh national food was the leek could think again. The seaweedy air mingled with the cloying smell of fish and chips.

In the little harbour seagulls picked delicately at worms in the black mud that oozed around little sailing boats with names like *Poppin* and *Squiffy*. Their halyards clattered in the light breeze.

There was no sign of life at the ramshackle yacht club. The wharf, lined by old slate warehouses, was deserted except for a posse of children speeding up and down on bicycles.

Porthmadog was founded in the early 1800s by the Denbighshire MP William Madocks. Madocks was an idealist born with the spirit of the great eighteenth-century improvers. With money left by his father he bought a marshy estuary on the wild north-western Snowdonian coast and set about reclaiming the land. His creation, Porthmadog, grew into an important port, handling 50,000 tons of Welsh slate a year.

People who know no better believe that Madocks named Porthmadog after himself. Nonsense, say locals. The good William was so fascinated by the Madoc myth that he named the town in honour of the prince, who is said to have sailed from the island of Fadog, a mile to the west. Thanks to Madocks's land reclamation, Ynys Fadog now lies inland. The steep cliffs jut abruptly out of the countryside and from the summit is a fine view of Tremadog Bay.

So is the similarity of the names of Porthmadog's founder and our intrepid prince no more than coincidence? I like to think that Cymric magic was at work when Madocks settled on this area to build his showpiece.

The legend is strongly maintained at Porthmadog's tourist information office where I chatted to a charming lady called Iona Williams. Iona was born and bred in the town and, like most of the inhabitants, she was fluent in her native language.

Visitors often asked her questions about Prince Madoc. Americans were especially curious.

'An American lady was in only last week. She wanted to know everything about Madoc. Some of these Americans can be quite obsessive about him.'

'Do you believe the story?' I asked.

'Like everyone else, I learned about Madoc in primary school. He definitely lived – no question about that. But America?' Iona smiled. 'It's nice to think that it's true.'

I mentioned my visit to Fort Berthold reservation, and how Gerard and Hugh said they didn't think much of the Welsh language, that it sounded guttural to them. This was not the wisest remark to make in the heartlands of Welsh nationalism. Iona's smile vanished. She hurrumphed. When in Wales you do not even dream of criticizing the language.

'But have you heard the poem?' she asked.

'Poem?'

'The poem about Madoc's ships. Every child in Wales knows it.' I did not know the poem. I apologized for the shortcomings of the English schools syllabus. Iona shook her head as if to say 'no matter'. And in a soft, lilting voice she began to recite the words of the turn of the century Porthmadog bard Eifion Wyn:

> *Wele'n cychwyn dair ar ddeg,*
> *O longau bach ar fore teg,*
> *Wele Madog ddewr ei fron,*
> *Yn gapten ar y llynges hon.*
> *Mynd y mae i roi ei droed,*
> *Ar le na welodd dyn erioed*
> *Antur enbyd ydyw hon,*
> *Ond Dew a'i deil o don i don.*

These beautiful words lose everything in translation: 'See them setting sail/Thirteen small ships on a beautiful morning, There is Madoc standing there bravely/As captain of this fleet./He is going to set foot/In a place no one's ever seen before,/This is a dangerous adventure/But God will sustain him from wave to wave.'

So here's a thought. When next in Wales, take yourself to Porthmadog and climb Ynys Fadog. And while you sit on the dewy grass, gazing out to sea towards that vast continent three thousand miles away, try murmuring Eifion Wyn's verses out loud. The language may mean nothing to you. You may feel foolish as you attempt to wind your tongue around the unfamiliar sounds. But who knows? Perhaps even you will begin to believe that thirteen ships set sail . . .

Selected Bibliography

Boorstin, Daniel J., *The Americans: The Democratic Experience*, Cardinal, London, 1988

Boorstin, Daniel J., *The Americans: The National Experience*, Cardinal, London, 1988

Boye, Alan, *The Complete Roadside Guide to Nebraska*, Saltillo Press, St Johnsbury, 1989

Brandon, William, *Indians, American Heritage*, New York, 1961

Brown, Dee, *Bury My Heart at Wounded Knee*, Arena, London, 1987

Burchell, R. A., *Westward Expansion*, Harrap, London, 1974

Catlin, George, *Letters and Notes on the Manners, Customs, and Conditions of North American Indians, Volumes I and II*, Dover Publications, New York, 1973

Chittenden, Hiram Martin, *The American Fur Trade of the Far West, Volumes I and II*, Press of the Pioneers, New York, 1935

Clark, Ella E. and Edmonds, Margot, *Sakakawea of the Lewis and Clark Expedition*, University of California Press, Berkeley, 1979

DeVoto, Bernard, *The Course of Empire*, Houghton Mifflin Co., Boston, 1952

Dillon, Richard, *Meriwether Lewis*, Western Tanager Press, Santa Cruz, 1965

Dunbar, S., *History of Travel in America*, Tudor Publishing Co., New York, 1937

Furnas, J. C., *The Americans: A Social History of the United States*, Putnam, New York, 1969

Gunther, John, *Inside USA*, Harper, New York, 1947

Hanson, James A., *The Buckskinners' Cook Book*, The Fur Press, Chadron, 1979

―――― *History of Public Works in the United States*, ed. Ellis L. Armstrong, American Public Works Association, Chicago, 1976

James, Will, *Cowboy in the Making*, Charles Scribner and Sons, New York, 1937

Jefferis, Prof. B. G. and Nichols, J. L., *Safe Counsel*, J. L. Nichols, Naperville, 1895

―――― *King's Handbook of the United States*, ed. Moses King, Moses King Corp., Buffalo

―――― *Let's Go: USA*, ed. Mallay B. Charters, St. Martin's Press, New York, 1990

―――― *Living Ideas in America*, ed. Henry Steele Commager, Harper, New York, 1951

McHugh, Tom, *The Time of the Buffalo*, University of Nebraska Press, Lincoln, 1972

Malone, Michael P. and Roeder, Richard B., *Montana: A History of Two Centuries*, University of Washington Press, Seattle, 1976

―――― *Mobil Travel Guide: Northwest and Great Plains*, 1990

Morison, Samuel Eliot, *The European Discovery of America*, Oxford University Press, New York, 1971

Milton, John R., *South Dakota: A History*, W. W. Norton, New York, 1988

Neihardt, John G., *The River and I*, University of Nebraska Press, Lincoln, 1910

Peirce, Neal R., *The Great Plains States of America*, W. W. Norton and Co., New York, 1973

Rogers, Alan, *Lewis and Clark in Missouri*, Meredco, St. Louis, 1981

Russell, Osborne, *Journal of a Trapper*, ed. Aubrey L. Haines, University of Nebraska Press, Lincoln, 1965

―――― *The American Guide*, ed. H. G. Alsberg, Hastings House, New York, 1949

―――― *The History of the Lewis and Clark Expedition*, Volumes I, II and III, ed. Elliott Coues, Francis P. Harper, 1893

―――― *The Journals of Lewis and Clark*, ed. Bernard DeVoto, Houghton Mifflin Co., New York, 1953

―――― *The Journals of Lewis and Clark*, ed. John Bakeless, Nal Penguin Inc., New York, 1964

Turtle, Walking, *Indian America: A Traveler's Companion*, John Muir Publications, Santa Fe, 1989

Van West, Carroll, *A Traveler's Companion to Montana History*, Montana Historical Society Press, Helena, 1986

Williams, Gwyn A., *Madoc: The Making of a Myth*, Eyre Methuen, London, 1979

Zurhorst, Charles, *The First Cowboy*, Cassell, London, 1974

INDEX

216

Index